Concepts, Issues and Practice

Information Systems Series

Series Editor: Professor Ian O. Angell

Developing Information Systems

Concepts, Issues and Practice

Chrisanthi Avgerou
Tony Cornford

Department of Information Systems
London School of Economics

Second Edition

First edition 1993
Second edition 1998

Published by
MACMILLAN PRESS LTD
Houndmills, Basingstoke, Hampshire RG21 6XS
and London
Companies and representatives
throughout the world

ISBN 0–333–73231–6

A catalogue record for this book is available
from the British Library.

This book is printed on paper suitable for recycling and
made from fully managed and sustained forest sources.

10 9 8 7 6 5 4 3 2 1
07 06 05 04 03 02 01 00 99 98

Printed and bound in Great Briatin by
Creative Print and Design (Wales), Ebbw Vale

In addition to his reading and his work on the estate, which required special attention in springtime, Levin had that winter begun writing a book on agriculture, the idea of which was that the temperament of the agricultural labourer was to be treated as a definite factor, like climate and soil, and therefore the conclusions of agronomic science should be deduced not from data supplied by soil and climate only, but from data of soil, climate, and the immutable character of the labourer.

Anna Karenina, Leo Tolstoy

Contents

Preface

This book is based on our experience of teaching information systems development and management over a number of years to students of various backgrounds and career aspirations. The process of information systems development and management is presented here in its full richness and as an undertaking which requires the contributions of many different intellectual disciplines and skills. The book describes the backdrop against which many different tasks are performed by many different types of specialist: programmers, systems analysts, knowledge engineers, project managers, software engineers, information systems managers, and of course 'users'.

Our objective is to introduce students to information systems as early as possible in their degree studies, and certainly not only after they have specialized in particular aspects of computer science or information technology. The subject of information systems is usually taught as an advanced course, often at a postgraduate level, after students have acquired a background in computing or other special topics of information technology. As a result, both teachers of such courses and books on information systems expend a great deal of effort in overcoming biases and misconceptions that have been formed from prior specialist technical training. Most teachers of information systems have a difficult task to explain that information systems development involves more than the design, coding and testing of computer programs, and that it is not equivalent to software engineering.

Information systems is also a topic taught to management and business studies students. It is, however, usually assumed that managers do not need to understand in great depth the technicalities of information systems development and evolution. Students on business courses are often provided with some level of knowledge of the various technologies applied in information systems today, and they are usually introduced to the options and the dilemmas faced in exploiting information as a business resource, and to a lesser degree managing information technology resources. However, books for management students do not usually treat the *process* of information systems development in any depth.

The result of these distinct focuses is that most professionals contributing to the development of information systems today, whether computer specialists or managers, have never studied the full process of information systems development and management. It is our contention that it is possible, indeed necessary, to teach information systems to students of computer technologies and those on business courses alike, and to do so in parallel with their other studies. Technical experts need to develop a clear sense of where their special skills fit into the overall effort that an organization makes when it sets out to change an information system, while managers need to appreciate fully the effort and particular expertise that is involved in information systems development.

Our intention is that this book can be used as a textbook for both types of student on both undergraduate and postgraduate information systems courses. It is also suitable for business studies and management courses, complementing texts which elaborate on information technology topics. The presentation is such that it can be used alongside textbooks with detailed descriptions of the more technical aspects of information systems development and the methodologies that support it. Each chapter introduces material, structures a debate, and concludes with points for further discussion, possible activities and exercises for students. The concluding section of each chapter provides openings for follow-up study, not in general in the form of simple 'exercises' but of open questions that are suitable for research outside the classroom and group discussion. Each chapter has its own set of references together with suggestions for further reading.

The book proceeds from a simple description of fundamental information systems development tasks to a deeper presentation of current practices and their theoretical underpinning. It examines and clarifies key concepts relevant to information systems development and describes models used to view and organize the information systems development process. The book considers alternative approaches to information systems development, ranging from the engineering of a complex technical artefact to interventions leading to substantial organizational change. The book also considers the methodologies used to prescribe and promote professional practice and discusses the issues involved in managing information systems resources and in exploiting the potential of information technology.

The organization of the book is in three parts, together with an introductory chapter. Part 1 sets out a basic description of the tasks required to take an information systems project from its conception through its construction and to its actual operation. Chapter 2 considers the question of determining which system to develop, while chapter 3 considers how to set about launching a systems development project. Chapter 4 considers the essential tasks that are required to proceed to the delivery of an actual system, while chapter 5 considers the problem of installing and using a new information system. These four chapters are intended to provide a solid background of practical understanding against which the rest of the book is set.

Part 2 of the book goes on to examine the theoretical foundations that exist for the study of information systems and identifies and discusses themes which have influenced the study and the practice of information systems development. Chapter 6 discusses four key concepts that have vital importance for the study of information systems – information itself, the notion of systems, our understanding of technology, and the nature of human organizations. The chapter also explores some of the reference theories that researchers use to make sense of information systems phenomena. Chapter 7 then goes on to evaluate the principal model for viewing and organizing the development process – the systems development life cycle – and discusses some alternative perspectives including ideas of prototyping and of evolutionary systems development. Chapter 8 discusses variations of approach to information systems development which stem from different perceptions of information systems either as technological innovation or as socio-organizational reform. Chapter 9 evaluates information systems development methodologies as an effort to guide how organizations approach systems development tasks and how methodologies define and promote professional practice.

Part 3 of the book moves on to consider the problems of managing and resourcing information systems activities. In chapter 10 the question of how to establish and manage information systems activities within an organization's structures is discussed. Chapter 11 then considers questions of how an organization can seek to chart its way forward, to exploit and innovate with technologies and to achieve success through information systems. The concluding chapter of the book argues for a broad perspective for the study of information systems: a perspective which shifts the focus from the normative to the analytical and from the needs of discrete organizations to the extensive socio-economic changes taking place in countries throughout the world.

Chrisanthi Avgerou and Tony Cornford
Department of Information Systems
London School of Economics and Political Science, 1998

1 Introduction

- *The increasing significance of information systems*
- *The computer as part of an information system*
- *Four perspectives on information systems*
- *The approach of this book*

This is a book about information systems, that should be clear from the title, but we suspect that most readers will start to read with an implicit question in their minds, 'What exactly is an information system?'.

The full answer to that question has to be deferred, at least until the end of this book and probably until the end of many more books, but without seeking to provide a single definition, or a long and extensive discussion, we can start by using the term to refer to information and data handling activities in human organizations. Information handling in this sense is a purposeful activity sustained over time, and includes the activities of collecting information, storing it, directing it to appropriate places and people, and utilizing it in various tasks within the organization.

Of course this description just begs further questions as to what we mean by words such as *information*, *data*, and *human organizations*, but we will not go further down this route, and certainly not in this opening section! Rather we appeal to the reader at this point to apply some common sense in striving to interpret the phrase. For example, it should be clear that human organizations, from a multinational oil corporation to a local football club, need to handle various forms of information in order to continue operating, and that they will establish some long-standing methodical activities in order to do so. Such activities are the topic of this book. In so far as it discusses their establishment, then the topic is the *development* of information systems; in so far as it discusses the need to ensure their long-standing character, then the topic is the *management* of information systems. We have restricted ourselves to human organizations. A study of what makes an ants' nest, a beehive or a shoal of fish operate as a co-ordinated group could be approached in terms of sustained information handling activities, and hence of information systems. In this book however we consider only those organizations that are substantially made up of people.

There is of course a further strong theme implied in the subject matter of this book, and that is the involvement in information handling of some form of information technology, almost certainly based on the use of computers and telecommunications. It should not surprise anybody to learn that a multinational oil company or a football club might make use of computers; indeed we would

1

probably expect it. A football club will have a database of members and use it to mail out (or e-mail out) a list of fixtures or to keep track of those who have paid their annual subscriptions. An oil company will have systems to keep track of their inventory of oil products, to produce invoices for customers, to forecast demand for products in the months ahead, or to predict the price of crude oil. Each of these activities can be understood as requiring sustained information handling, including capturing information, storing information, processing information and displaying information, and each of these activities can be matched to some information technologies that can provide support for it.

Within all types of human organizations a wider and wider variety of such informational tasks is being undertaken with the aid of some technology. Note that we say 'with the aid of some technology', not 'by technology'. It is important to recognize that in the study of information systems we consider how computers and other information technologies help (or hinder), reinforce or reshape, essentially human and organizational activities, not just what the computers themselves do or how they operate. In this we are saying that an information system is essentially an organizational rather than technological phenomenon. Since organizations are populated by people, it follows that the concerns, attitudes and behaviours of people are at the centre of the study of information systems. Nonetheless, there is a strong link between understanding, developing or improving an organization's information handling capacity, supporting the people who make it up, and making use of computers and other information technologies. This is seen as so evident that many books written on the topic of information systems carry a strong implication that information systems necessarily involve computers, and some authors even use the term information system as a synonym for a computer application.

This is not the position taken in this text. It must be clear that information handling activities can be discovered in all sorts of organizations and are often carried out without any substantial technology, electronic or otherwise. The study of information systems is rather a way of understanding and exploring this essential characteristic of organizations and what technology brings to it, not a study of machines. Identifying the subject of information systems as being essentially to do with computers or even the use of computers in support of individual work tasks is wrong and leads at best to dangerous simplifications. Over-concentration on the computer and other technologies shifts attention away from the essential reasons for which we undertake information handling activities and the organizational context within which they are carried out. Losing sight of the context and the people does not help us to understand the full range of aspects of information handling that need to be considered if we are to be able to improve the way in which an organization operates.

While adding computers does not in essence change the fundamental pheno-menon of information systems as it has been sketched above, their presence in organizations can change in important ways the manner in which information handling is undertaken, and certainly leads to specific problems and pressures when computer-based systems must be developed and managed. This text therefore puts a particular emphasis on the effort required to understand, harness and control the power of information technology in order to achieve better and more successful information handling activities. The book considers the problems faced in building and using a technical infrastructure that aids information handling within human organizations, and the models and methods that can be used to assist in that end. However, throughout the book we try to keep in mind a broad vision of information handling activities, always acknowledging that there is a lot of information handling within organizations that is beyond the possibility of even partial structuring and support by information technology. Indeed, a great deal of information handling defies any methodical arrangement at all and the subject of information systems need to be seen as involving both *formal* (either manual or computer based), and *informal* activities.

By the concept of a formal information system we mean the explicit, acknowledged and designed information handling activities of organizations. The structure of a formal information system is usually relatively easy to understand, as are the flows of information and the purposes which it is intended to serve. An example of a formal information system might be a computer-based system designed to keep track of the stock of frozen foods in a supermarket. It records the arrival of goods, it records, through the bar-code reader on the check-out tills, the outflow of goods, and it provides information to the store manager via a terminal in his office. The information to which the manager can have access includes what goods have been sold and what goods are in stock. In this way the system allows the manager to make decisions about the reordering of goods and to determine which particular goods are selling well, and which are not. The computers, bar-code readers and communications equipment used in such a system would be quite easy to identify, and the outline logic of the programs to be run on the computer could be specified quite easily too.

It would make the subject of information systems much simpler, though much less interesting, if information systems only needed to be considered in this structured and formal manner. It would certainly be much easier to develop and manage them. Fortunately this is not the case, and information handling in organizations extends well beyond any formal and designed structures that are put in place. Thus, in the example given above, it could well be the case that, despite all the formal apparatus designed to keep track of frozen foods, the manager at times prefers to stroll into the shop and look in the freezer cabinet to check stock levels. This may be quicker than using the computer, it may give more up-to-date or accurate information, and it will almost certainly give the manager a richer picture, a fuller set of information, than would be available from the bald figures displayed on the computer screen. While the report on the screen may say that no frozen carrots have been sold, a walk into the store might reveal that nobody is buying frozen carrots because a pile of frozen peas is laying on top of them. It might also be appropriate for the manager to ask the person on the check-out about the sales pattern of frozen foods, and the insight that they can give as to who buys what would serve to build a still richer picture of what is really going on.

In the case of the supermarket it is probably true that the manager would see the need for both the more formal and the more informal sources of information. The formal system serves the needs of day-to-day activities in the store, keeping track of sales over a long period of time and maintaining the core set of data required to run the business. The informal system is equally essential to allow the manager to be able to place the information provided by the computer into a context and to develop the understanding he needs in order to be able to make important decisions (such as cancelling the order for carrots). We therefore need to acknowledge that around and throughout the formal information handling activities of organizations are a myriad of informal activities that duplicate, support and extend the formal.

In general, formal information systems are based on structured administrative procedures that can be explicitly set down and which capture, store and process essential data that an organization needs in order to be able to operate. Computers, databases and networks find a clear and obvious role in supporting this type of information handling activity. The informal information handling activities on the other hand are more probably the ones that rely on people observing the world around them, making decisions and inferences, and using and exchanging information in the course of more *ad hoc*, intuitive and sense-making activities.

Most of the day-to-day activities of people at work are of this latter type. They are not formally designed or structured to any great extent; indeed they almost defy design, since they are seldom well understood and the purposes they serve are often obscure, being more the territory of a sociologist or psychologist than a computer systems analyst. If this seems a strong assertion to make, consider what a teacher does, or a policeman, a shop owner or a delivery van driver. These are all common occupations, but a person in any of them will spend most of their day collecting diverse kinds of information and handling it in all sorts of creative and context-dependent ways that are not easy to pre-structure. Nonetheless, this type of informal information handling, undertaken by intelligent people, creates the essential fabric of real organizations, and any person who professes to understand information systems needs to be able to see the importance of informal information activities, just as clearly as formal or designed activities.

The role for computers and information technology in contributing to the effectiveness of informal information handling is a less easy topic to address. When the computer has to help a *person* to achieve some loosely defined task, rather than to implement (automate) a clearly predefinable process, our ability to understand how it might be done, what real help the individual would appreciate and what the outcome will be is less well established. This is one of the reasons why information systems are such a rich and interesting subject to study, and a rewarding field to work in. And while this opening section has not really answered to any satisfactory degree the opening question, *what exactly is an information system*, it has done its job if it can convince the reader that there is a subject here to be studied.

The increasing significance of information systems

In recent decades there has been an increasing recognition of the significance of information handling functions both in individual organizations and in the economy as a whole. Modern organizations, both commercial businesses and other forms of administration, devote a great deal of attention to how they set about capturing, storing and processing the information that they use in their operations and to inform their management decision making. In doing this they have come to rely more and more on the use of computers and telecommunications. More generally, the structure of the economies of industrialized nations has moved towards a growing reliance on information handling activities or 'service industries', including such important sectors as finance, transport, education and the media. This process is sometimes referred to as the emergence of a new and significant information economy, or an information society. Information technology has played a key role in this change of emphasis within developed economies. Recently it has become widely accepted that information, and the systems that handle it, are key resources of an enterprise or administration and can be used to distinguish success from failure or mere existence. Effective utilization of such resources can provide the *competitive advantage* for successful organizations and nations, allowing them to out-perform their rivals or raise the level and quality of their products and service.

Many commercial organizations have come to believe that their business prospects do not just rely on information handling and information technology at the margin, in terms of efficiency, better productivity or lower costs. Rather they have been persuaded that their long term existence depends on the successful use of information, and that their future is critically dependent upon the identification, development and management of new and innovative information based activities to support management and to deliver new products and services. Similarly, organizations in the public sector, such as government departments, health administrations and local authorities, have sought new ways to provide services to citizens through the use of information technology.

At the same time that organizations have become beguiled by the power of information systems to offer them new levels of performance and control, they have learned, often the hard way, that developing information systems based on information technology at whatever level of ambition is not a trivial task. It demands an extensive infrastructure of people and skills, and encompasses significant risks of failure. It is a process that naturally places great emphasis on getting computer-based information systems successfully installed and operating. How exactly this is done is the basis for much debate and discussion centring on the appropriate ways of organizing the technical specialists who analyze, design, and implement computer systems, and the approaches that they should use as they attempt to make changes within organizations while at the same time co-ordinating complex technology. Hence organizations have come to realize that emphasis is required both on the development of the technical structures and on the design and management of organizational change.

Facing up to this enhanced importance of information handling has become a crucial issue for many organizations in both the public and the private sectors. While they may be generally aware of the issue, determining how to proceed has proved less easy, particularly since over the years the existence of certain fundamental problems in thinking about, let alone developing, information handling activities have become apparent.

Organizations have learned that managing the technologies themselves is a complex and risky task that demands its own expensive specialists with attendant skills. One result is that most organizations of any size have within them a specific body of people, described perhaps as the data processing department, the information services department or the computer centre, which has a central role in initiating, developing and managing information systems, or 'buying in' the required skills and services. Organizations need to have available to them people who understand the technology and are able to make it work. But beyond this it has become painfully apparent that both gaining a full understanding of the current information systems that operate to support an organization, and planning how to develop them so that they contribute to specific activities and the overall goals of an organization, are not trivial tasks or ones to be undertaken lightly. Understanding the information requirements of a particular administrative or managerial task in both the formal and informal aspect is not easy, nor is assessing consequences of going ahead with some development. The more innovative an application, the more organizational change it will imply; the more bearing it has on overall organizational goals, the harder it becomes to predict outcomes with confidence. Organizations have therefore had to seek out people who can both understand the information needs of a business and can transform this understanding into plans for information systems development. This work of analysis has become a prerequisite before any attempt can be made to start designing or building a technical system. We might even say that it is exactly the emergence of this insight, that using computers effectively within an organizational context is about more than simply the efficient use of technology, that has given rise to the emergence of a distinct field of social science named *information systems.*

The computer as part of an information system

As acknowledged earlier in this chapter, this book is about information systems in a general sense, but addresses in particular the use of computers and other information technology for the information handling activities of organizations. It is therefore important to understand some of the general ways in which the advent of computers into information handling activities alters things in organizations.

Inflexibility

Perhaps the most common-sense observation to be made about computers is that they are inflexible. A computer is good at doing what it is told, but it is not in general able to use intelligence or insight in order to develop new ways of doing things or to handle situations that it is not prepared for. Despite all the efforts of the artificial intelligence research community, and the development of new ideas such as intelligent agents, this is a situation that is probably going to remain. In contrast to computers, people can and do exhibit intelligence in their activities, particularly in facing novel or trying circumstances. A further manifestation of the computer's inflexibility is that not only is handling unplanned situations a problem, but also that any change in an information system based around computers has to be carefully planned and prepared for. This is necessary in order that the computer component can be issued with new and unambiguous instructions, that is, be reprogrammed.

The importance of this characteristic of inflexibility has grown as the areas within organizations into which computers penetrate have extended. The traditional accounting and record-keeping functions that computers undertake do not in general change rapidly or often, but many of the newer management, decision and communication tasks that computers now support are less well embedded in the organization and are subject to more frequent and urgent amendment. Furthermore, information technology not only lies at the heart of more and more of the tasks undertaken in organizations, it also constitutes the linkages *between* individual tasks. As a result, computers have become a key part of any and possibly all proposed organizational change. Now, when organizations wish to alter or to develop some aspect of their service, their management or their product, they almost certainly need to consider the implications that this will have for current information processing, and the new information handling activities that such change will imply. This investigation needs to be undertaken at very considerable levels of detail if the cost and effort involved in a proposed change is to be sensibly evaluated. When a decision is made to go ahead with some change, then even more detailed preparation is needed to allow the technical apparatus to be developed in support of the change.

Remaking work

In evaluating and in undertaking change, computers demand that there is access to special and particular skills and knowledge, both in terms of specialists and in the general workforce of an organization. From the point of view of this general workforce the advent of a new computer-based information system can, quite simply, remake their jobs. Introducing computers puts a premium on new ways of doing things, ways that make the best use of the information that is processed. This can downgrade such qualities as experience and intuition, and bring a new focus on hard analytical skills that make the most, or even too much, of the computer's data.

When computers are deployed they have the characteristic of reallocating tasks, taking on some and providing the people who work around them with other new tasks. Consider for example how the job of a typist is changed when a word processor is introduced in place of a typewriter. The computer requires the learning of a whole range of new skills, but will probably also change the job content too. The typist may be expected to undertake many more revisions of documents or to accept rough drafts of text on disk to edit and tidy up. Good skill at spelling may become devalued with the advent of computer-based spelling checkers, while the importance of layout or design skills may be enhanced. A similar set of changes in the nature of work could be observed for a middle manager, a clerk or a chief executive.

Power and control

The effect of computers is not just seen in the way that they affect individuals in their jobs. Computers handle information and, while it is a cliché to say that information is power, it is nonetheless true and many relationships in human organizations are based on access to and control over information. Introducing computer systems into information handling may well have the effect of shifting access and control of information to different individuals or groups, and hence in establishing new power relationships. This general observation tells us very little about the actual way in which these changes come about. For example, cases can be cited that show computers centralizing control and giving greater power to senior managers. Equally, the opposite effect can be demonstrated where computer-based systems have provided a broader distribution of information and allowed a wider allocation of power.

The early studies that considered these issues tended to argue for an effect of centralization, and that whole levels of managers in organizations would be displaced, with power becoming concentrated in centralized decision-making bodies made up of technical specialists and senior managers. During the period that large, expensive mainframe computers were the main type of technology available to organizations it was perhaps inevitable that some centralization would be observed. By the mid 1970s technological change had begun to challenge this model of computing, and today with microcomputers and network-based distributed systems the impact of computers on the balance of power and control in organizations is a rather harder topic to get to grips with and one that needs to be assessed in each individual situation.

Four perspectives on information systems

In order to be able to develop information systems, whether based around substantial information technology or not, it is important to be able to perceive and describe them. This lies at the heart of the task of systems development, and in particular in the analysis and design tasks. There is no single or absolute way in which to describe an existing information system or to set down the design for a new one. Rather, there are a number of possible perspectives, each of which can reveal important insight or express significant detail. By using more than one perspective we can capture the details of different but essential aspects of any information system. Here, we outline four possible perspectives: that of the functional activity supported; the technical components used; the organizational context in which the information system is embedded; and the interests and requirements of the people involved.

- Functional – activities supported
- Technical – components and technologies used
- Organizational – needs and requirements served
- Human – people involved and influenced

Each of these perspectives is an abstraction from the complex reality of information handling, focusing on some aspects but ignoring others. The making of abstractions from particular perspectives is a powerful way to simplify phenomena, and makes it possible to undertake more detailed study of certain of their relations. It is a widely used scientific method. Throughout this book we make an effort to present the activities of information handling in an organization in all their complexity; but it is nevertheless useful to identify and investigate perspectives which shed light on particular issues concerning those who develop or are involved in them.

Function

Information systems are developed to do something; they support specific tasks performed in organizations. Thus we may have a medical records system in a hospital, a criminal records system serving legal and law enforcement agencies, payroll systems in almost all organizations, inventory systems in supermarkets, office automation systems and many others. The function by function perspective is very popular as an initial method of finding out about information systems. It is easy to describe an information system in terms of the tasks of the organization that it supports, and it is common for organizations to develop and maintain their information systems on a function by function basis. For example, different departments, charged with different tasks, may develop separate information systems.

One way to classify such functions for the purpose of studying information systems is in terms of the type of task they undertake and the information that they handle. At one end of the range is the limited types of information handled by transaction processing systems, with high volumes of regular data, low value per data item and simple well structured processing – essentially clerical replacement systems. Examples would include a payroll, a sales ledger or a system processing orders from customers. At the opposite end are tasks that require working with low volumes of high value information. Systems to support such tasks may be based around representation of concepts and ideas and be used to support a specialist in a particular task. Examples would be an economic model predicting the price of crude oil in five years' time or a spreadsheet used by a marketing manager to allocate an advertising budget.

Technology

In many information handling activities it is possible to identify some particular technology. The description, specification and construction of technology becomes a major part of the development of many new information systems. We can recognize different types of information system according to the different technology employed. It is common in this way to identify an information system in technical terms: a database management system (DBMS), a decision support system (DSS), an intelligent knowledge based system (IKBS), a computer aided design (CAD) system or an intranet. The development of information systems may at times be approached in terms of the application of such technologies; there are people who specialize in them, and the study and development of such technologies have become disciplines in their own right.

Information technologies have come to provide more and more of the key infrastructure of organizations. The convergence of computers with tele-communications, together with an ever more sophisticated range of office technologies, has given rise to a new technical foundation for information handling activities. At times the development of this *infrastructure* is an independent project without aiming to support specific organizational functions or needs. Thus the establishment of a communications network in a high street bank can be seen as laying the basis for many possible systems today and in the future.

The organizational view

The position and role that an information system occupies within an organization, defined by that organization's own structure and the goals that it pursues, provides another opportunity to establish a distinct perspective on information systems. Systems may exist or be built to serve a whole organization, or very specific parts, they may be of critical importance and contribute to the essential mission of an organization, or they may be rather more peripheral. They may help to sustain and reinforce a particular management structure, or they may operate to change traditional ways of doing things.

The past 20 or so years have seen the organizational role of information systems alter considerably. The availability of powerful and diverse technologies has demanded that organizations make conscious decisions about how information systems are going to become a part of their future shape and form. Now, for example, it is common to discuss how information systems can be established to help the most senior managers and directors in their jobs – so-called executive information systems. The organizational perspective illustrates a more general view, often expressed, which advocates approaching the development of information systems as part of the *business strategy* that organizations need to pursue in order to sustain themselves. More recently, this has been expressed in terms of business process reengineering; using information systems as part of a process of substantial organizational reform which reshapes the way things are done and emphasises efficiency. Other versions of the basic idea are expressed in terms of establishing better links beyond the organization, by exploiting information channels and adding information to other products and services.

A human perspective

Finally, we may choose to take a human perspective on information systems. We have already identified people as central to an understanding of what an information system is, and in developing information systems it is essential to have a clear idea of how both information and technology are used by people, and the type of results they achieve with them. A new information system will imply new working practices so that people can make best use of the informational product. The final and perhaps highest level of understanding of information systems is thus the human level.

The human perspective highlights various needs of the individuals who use information technology to perform their jobs. It examines, for example, what information should be provided to people to enable them to make the decisions involved in their job, how the equipment should be arranged in an office or factory to provide a suitable environment for those who work with it, what kind of training, supervision and control should be provided so that individuals receive adequate support and feel that they have adequate freedom. The human perspective considers also the needs of groups of employees who collectively perform some work and need to work closely with each other.

A human context is often introduced into discussion of the way in which information systems are designed, built and implemented. One such approach is in the careful consideration of how human computer interfaces are built and what qualities people look for in such interfaces. This is the field of human computer interaction. Another theme is that of arranging the participation of the ultimate users of a system in its development. This is advocated by many, and a variety of techniques to achieve this have been proposed. More recently the advent of microcomputers and more 'user friendly' software has given rise to the notion of 'end-user computing' – the construction of systems by their users. This, it is suggested, should ensure a closer fit of the technical parts of systems to those who will use them, as well as encouraging a smoother uptake of technology, and hence serving the organizational interest too.

The approach of this book

It may help the reader to know what kind of knowledge this book, and more generally the study of information systems at present, can provide. We did not start with a definition for the term *information systems* because we believe that the term cannot be defined precisely. Similarly, the remainder of this book does not offer a precise theory describing information handling activities in organiz-ations. The study of information systems is a relatively new field that does not (yet) have an adequate theoretical basis. Even the fundamental concept of 'information' is still very poorly understood, and we have no widely acknowledged theory capturing the behaviour of human organizations in all their complexity. Nevertheless, we can find a great deal of relevant knowledge and method in a number of established scientific domains, including psychology, organizational theory, sociology, computer science, decision theory, systems theory, semiotics, and anthropology. The study of information systems is, therefore, a multidisciplinary field.

This leads to two significant problems. The first is the sheer size of the body of knowledge that one has to master in order to acquire a good understanding of the various aspects of information systems and the confidence to develop them successfully. The second is that we try to combine knowledge from applied sciences, such as computer science or engineering, and from social sciences, such as organizational theory. There are differences between the two, in terms of methods of investigation and the types of knowledge which are considered valid. The former tends to apply scientific, mathematical or other formal logical methods, and aims at producing precise knowledge, often expressed as general laws or guidance as to appropriate practice. The latter favours interpretative methods and produces more qualitative knowledge, which aims more to explain, rather than to describe or prescribe the behaviour in a situation under study.

These are serious problems that have to be overcome by those who wish to study information systems. The uneasy mix of quantitative and qualitative methods implied by the four perspectives outlined in the section above is manifested in both the development and the management of information systems. For example, the investigation of the technical characteristics of a system usually results in numerical values such as for the speed of information processing, or the cost of a piece of hardware, while the investigation of the human requirements results in non-numerical values such as dissatisfaction with the quality of information that a computer system produces. It is particularly difficult to integrate these two types of results in information systems development and management practices, for example when we try to express the overall value of a new system that we propose to develop.

In this book we provide an overall, but not always detailed, study of many aspects of the subject of information systems. As we explore the multi-faceted nature of information systems we suggest many other disciplines which have interesting knowledge to contribute to the formation of better insights into information systems issues. We also make suggestions as to the sources of relevant material. With regard to the second difficulty, we set out to examine the biases that various methods which originate in science, engineering or social sciences imply when they are used in information systems development and management practices. We have to assume the need to combine methods from different domains flexibly, and argue that, to do so, we need to understand the limitations of the various methods. In this way this book does not have the intention to instil a narrow and ill-grounded body of prescriptive knowledge, sharply focused on information systems development and management. Rather, we wish to cultivate an ability for understanding issues related to information systems, together with a sense of judgement as to those courses of action that are appropriate under specific circumstances.

Finally, without being too pedantic we need to clarify a point of terminology. As explained above, the term information system is often used in the literature with a narrower sense, to denote the means for processing data. We have made clear that we consider this to be an impoverished perception of information systems, because it leaves out the most central players in information handling activities, people. When people are considered, they are often referred in an undifferentiated way as 'users' of an information system. Although, unfortunately, this is a widely used terminology, we will avoid it so far as we can and retain the concept of information system for the study of information handling in organizations, which always involves people. Furthermore, these people will serve in multiple and various roles, and have multiple and various interests. It is not sufficient to lump these all together under the vague term of users.

Exercises and discussion issues

1. Provide two examples of formal information handling activities, and two examples of informal information handling activities, for each of the following four occupations: a teacher, a policeman, a shop owner, a delivery van driver.

2. Consider the case of the supermarket information system to keep track of frozen goods introduced earlier in this chapter. Provide four simple descriptions, as diagrams or as text, which explain the system from the functional perspective; the technical perspective; the organizational perspective; and the human perspective. The material given in the chapter is very sketchy, so add any particular detail needed to complete the assignment. In doing this, and by comparing your image of the system with others, you will see how varied and complicated a full description of such a simple system can be.

3. Repeat the assignment of Exercise 2, but in this case go out and find a real system to describe. It may be in a college (admissions, halls of residence), in a public body (library, citizens' advice bureau) or in a commercial organization.

4. Tsuahxe Engineering is a medium sized company that produces replacement exhaust pipes for motor cars and sells mostly to small garages and to wholesalers. The company is organized into four main departments: manufacturing, which produces the products in a modern hi-tech factory; sales, which sells the product on the basis of a team of travelling sales representatives; development, which designs and tests new products; and administration, which does the accounting and keeps the business records.

   Suggest for each department activities that are a) highly suitable for support by computer-based information systems; b) potentially supportable; c) unlikely to be directly supportable by any computer-based system.

5. This small news item appeared in the 31 October 1991 issue of *The Guardian* newspaper:

   > The Exxon Corporation is suing the makers of an automatic steering device that the oil company says caused the wreck of the Exxon Valdez

   Can a machine cause such an accident? Could the machine be held totally to blame. If the machine is to blame, are its makers too? What responsibility, if any, should the users of such a machine have?

6. In this chapter we have used the word *information* many times, and the word *data* a few times. Using dictionaries, an encyclopaedia and other textbooks explore the various definitions of these two words. They clearly are not exactly the same, but what is the relationship? The book by Liebenau and Backhouse cited below provides one exploration of these concepts.

Suggested reading

Complementary texts that are suitable to be read alongside this book include the following:

Angell, I.O. & Smithson, S. (1991) *Information Systems Management: Opportunities and Risks*, Macmillan Press, Basingstoke.

Avison, D.E. & Fitzgerald, G. (1988) *Information Systems Development: Methodologies, Techniques and Tools*, Blackwell, Oxford.

Cashmore, C. & Lyall, R. (1991) *Business Information: Systems and Strategies*, Prentice Hall, Hemel Hempstead.

Cornford, T. & Smithson, S. (1996) *Project Research in Information Systems: A Student's Guide*, Macmillan Press, Basingstoke.

Curtis, G. (1995) *Business Information Systems: Analysis, Design and Practice* (2nd edition), Addison-Wesley, Wokingham.

Laudon, K.C. & Laudon, J.P. (1996) *Management Information Systems*, 4th edition, Prentice Hall, Englewood Cliffs, New Jersey.

Liebenau, J. & Backhouse, J. (1990) *Understanding Information: An Introduction,* Macmillan Press, Basingstoke.

Sprague, R.H & McNurlin, B.C. (1993) *Information Systems Management in Practice*, 3rd edition, Prentice Hall, Englewood Cliffs, New Jersey.

Stowell, F. & West, D. (1994) *Client-led Design: A Systemic Approach to Information Systems Definition,* McGraw-Hill, London.

Yourdon, E. (1989) *Modern Structured Analysis,* Prentice Hall, Englewood Cliffs, New Jersey.

More advanced material can be found in the following:

Boland, J.R. & Hirschheim, R.A. (editors) (1988) *Critical Issues in Information Systems Research*, J. Wiley, Chichester.

Dahlbom, B. & Mathiassen, L. (1993*) Computers in Context: The Philosophy and Practice of System Design*, BCC Blackwell, London.

Galliers, R. (editor) (1987) *Information Analysis: Selected Readings,* Addison-Wesley, Sydney.

Introna, L.D. (1997) *Management, Information and Power*, Macmillan Press, Basingstoke.

Walsham, G. (1993) *Interpreting Information Systems in Organizations*, J. Wiley, Chichester.

Part 1

The tasks of information systems development

The four chapters in this part explore the fundamental tasks required when information systems development is undertaken. These tasks, taken together, make up a complex and multi-dimensional process that is not at all easy to understand or to control. Even where the function to be performed by a new system is clear, which is not the usual case, development must involve the working out of the design of a number of sub-systems that encompass the information processing to be undertaken, the technical means to be used, the work procedures that people will follow, and consequent changes in the way an organization is managed. And all this has to be done in a more or less co-ordinated fashion and more or less in parallel!

At first sight the most prominent aspect of this process is the effort required to build computers and communications technologies into information systems. This includes attention to the design and programming of software, the establishment of data files or databases, and the choice and configuration of hardware and communication components. But the construction and implementation of such technical information processing components represents only a fraction of the effort needed to transform an idea or a perception of need into a high quality functioning information system. Before any such consideration of technology related issues, it is important that a new system's purpose be established and understood. Indeed the concern with *why* systems are built, who is going to be involved in their operation and what their interests are, must be seen as a major part of the information systems development process.

Even when the objectives and scope of a new system has been established, development still needs to concern itself with more things than just building a new information handling apparatus. For example, facilities for changing over from the existing means of information handling to the use of the new system need to be established; adequate security systems, back-up and recovery systems must be provided to restore operations when technology fails; appropriate work procedures for the people involved must be designed and communicated to all parties; and management and control structures are needed to ensure that the new system operates smoothly.

As the technical parts of a new system are developed, we need to consider how it can be linked with the organization's existing work procedures. New work procedures may need to be established, new jobs and work roles may need to be designed, and employees will need to be trained accordingly. For example, an information system for handling customer claims in an insurance company may involve receiving claims by post, possibly on specially designed forms, editing and entering the data into the computer system, dealing with errors or incomplete application forms, perhaps allowing employees to exercise discretion in complicated cases which are not adequately treated by the computer application, dispatching letters and payment orders to claimants. Such procedures require detailed planning which may involve specialists in management and administration working with information systems specialists.

All the activities mentioned above are interdependent and need to be undertaken more or less in parallel in order to secure effective functioning of a new information system. The configuration of the hardware has to satisfy the software design options, while certain parts of the software may be dependent on the hardware options. The design of the software and the selection of the hardware need to take into account the manual procedures that the organization wishes to adopt. The security, back-up, recovery and cut-over systems must not be left to be treated as secondary issues either, because the possible options regarding them condition both the technical and the organizational choices for a new system.

There are various ways to summarize this complex environment for systems development. It involves a technological activity, concerned with computers, databases and networks; it also involves a considered intervention in a social world. The bias of this book has already been declared. We elaborate on the latter perspective and emphasize throughout the social and organizational context of systems development. This is not, however, to ignore the technical and the more formal aspects of information systems, but to see them as a part of a broader landscape. The key for 'would-be systems developers' is to take their work forward in a manner that allows for the interplay of the technical and the social. Later in the book, in chapter 6, we explore in a more theoretical way this socio-technical frame of reference.

For the purpose of this first part of the book we can frame this concern to consider an information systems development activity in broader terms by turning our attention to the following five aspects:

Expectations: The reasons to embark on development and the aims that we acknowledge and pursue.
People: Those who have some interest in the development and in the shape that it takes.
Results: The quality and appropriateness of the items that are produced and the organizational changes that are achieved as a result of the development.
Process: The approach we take to development in terms of activities, their sequence and their interrelationships.
Project: The structures and resources we use to make the development happen.

There are many subtle interrelationships among these elements. For example, different people will acknowledge different expectations, and some accommodation has to be found between them. Equally, the process we adopt to take forward the development will usually be instantiated and resourced within a formal project. Despite these multiple aspects and their interrelationships requiring our attention and conditioning the outcome of development, we choose to base the broad structure of this part of the book around the concept of *process* as described in the next paragraph. Even so, the other aspects, or their synonyms, will turn up repeatedly in what we say.

The process of development of an information system, in a simple form, can be seen as a list of tasks, starting with the identification and launching of an information system's development project and ending with the maintenance of its operational components for a period, before the system is phased out or replaced. The exact names and the number of such tasks vary from one description to another. However, a typical sequence involves the following:

- identification of a problem, pressure or opportunity;
- determination of general requirements for change;
- feasibility study to explore possible approaches;
- systems analysis to model detailed requirements for technical components and organizational reform;
- systems design to work out how requirements are to be met;
- development or acquisition of software and hardware and their configuration;
- systems implementation within the organizational setting;
- operation and maintenance;
- phase out when the system is no longer needed or used.

This sequence, known as the information systems development life cycle, is intended to provide a strong logical insight into the activities required, rather than setting down an absolute sequence to be followed at all times. As will be explained in chapter 7, the information systems development process requires iteration between activities and the overlapping of tasks. It may even be appropriate at times to approach development without treating them as distinct activities at all.

Our choice of this life cycle perspective to structure the following four chapters should not be seen as intending to award the process perspective a particular primacy, but rather as offering an initial framework within which to explore development, and from which alternative perspectives can be developed. The following four chapters then elaborate on this basic sequence of systems development activities and outline some of the most frequently applied practices. Further, in the discussion, the simplifying assumption is made that these tasks are undertaken largely by professionals, mainly systems analysts. The role of the analyst is to lead an investigation to find out what new information system is required, and to establish how it will work. In this they are supported by systems designers and programmers who develop and implement the technical components of a new system, such as computer software, a computer network or a database. The task of project management may also be seen as a distinct and separate role. There are of course roles for other participants and specialists too. Those who request a change to information handling, those who sponsor or pay for a new system and those who work in the affected area will all need to become involved in development activity. Even so, for the purposes of the next four chapters we place the analyst at centre stage.

2 The conception of an information system project

- *Starting the information systems development process*
- *Case study: maintenance management in A.B. Smith*
- *Investigating the need for a new information system*
- *Some comments on Soft Systems Methodology*

Information systems change all the time. They are inseparable parts of organizations which are dynamic, ever changing entities. When an enterprise grows, its information systems need to change, in order to cope with a larger information load; additional clerical personnel may be hired, a more effective organizational structure may be adopted, a fax machine or a new computer may be installed. Information systems also change in a day-by-day way, usually informally, adopting relatively minor modifications of information handling procedures to serve the changing needs of the environment within which they operate.

In this part of the book, however, we consider those occasions which require more substantial information systems changes, circumstances when new systems cannot simply result from adjusting existing information systems. Such changes must be planned, designed and managed as something new in the life of the organization. This gives rise to systems development projects. Such projects are needed, for example, when an organization enters into new business activities by launching a new service or product, when a subsidiary or a new office starts operations, or when a decision is taken to reorganize or to exploit the benefits of certain new technologies. For one or another reason, information systems development projects occur frequently, and most organizations of any size will have several such projects under way at the same time.

Starting the information systems development process

Information systems projects may be launched for a variety of reasons and in a variety of ways. In some cases the need for a new information system is clear and the expected gains can be well expressed. In others, views about whether a new information system is needed, or the gains to be expected, are only vague. Information systems development projects may be conceived for three general reasons: to provide a solution to a specific problem, to respond to a pressure, or to exploit an opportunity.

Problems

Some information systems development projects begin with a widely recognized problem to be solved and a clear view of why and how the new system will contribute to solving it. For example, a company which starts facing problems in coping with an increasing number of sales may consider introducing a new computer-based system to process orders from customers, produce dispatch information for the distribution staff, produce invoices for the customers, maintain information on the inventory, and link all this to the accounts. The company's managers may be confident that the problem they are faced with is indeed an information systems problem, and that some new form of computer supported system will provide an efficient and effective solution. Another example of a project launched to satisfy a specific need was the information system to support the Eurotunnel project to build a rail tunnel between England and France. The firm responsible for the management of the construction of the Channel Tunnel required the development of an information system to meet the communication and decision making needs of this enormously complicated endeavour. The construction of the Channel Tunnel involved several construction consortia in England and France, operating from many different locations. Management of an ambitious construction project, such as this, involves decisions taken at various places, and by various partners. Information has to be communicated among these partners, and co-ordination of activities is of paramount importance. It seemed clear that the information system to support such a project could not be left to take shape informally from whatever means each partner of the consortia employed. A system had to be designed with the specific objective of meeting the sophisticated information communication and processing needs of the tunnel project.

A problem that many organizations face at this moment is ensuring the integrity of their information systems when the millennium comes, and dates change from 1999 to 2000. At first sight this may seem a trivial change, exactly the type of thing that computers should take in their stride. However, many studies have suggested that large numbers of existing computer systems are unable to handle the change and will cease to work on or close to 31 December 1999 – the millennium bug. For example, a system that works out which customers have outstanding debts by comparing invoice date with the present date may work on the basis of computing years based on the last two digits. Comparing 97 with 98 will give a correct result, but a comparison of 99 with 00 may well not. When such a system was developed, in the 1980s say, the millennium seemed a long way away; now it approaches fast and many systems have to be adapted. If adaptation is not easy, then this may be taken as the opportunity to develop new systems that are 'millennium compliant'.

Pressures

Information systems projects are sometimes a result of external pressures. They may stem from the government or other regulatory bodies, customers, or competitors. Government legislation on such affairs as taxes and national insurance often affects the information systems of organizations. For example, when VAT was introduced in Britain, all companies had to modify their accounting systems. More recently, in Greece, all small companies were obliged by legislation to introduce computer cash registers conforming to the government's measures for fighting tax fraud. For most of them this was the first time they had introduced any computer-based information handling. Also, some regulatory institutions, such as those existing now in all European countries to monitor organizations' compliance with legislation for the protection of citizens from misuse of data, make specific requirements for information handling in organizations.

Pressures may also result from the marketplace within which the organization is doing business. An organization may come under pressure from a major customer to develop a system that will allow them to take orders and make payments via electronic data interchange (EDI). It may also come under pressure to develop information systems which allow them to offer new or higher quality services, similar to those of their competitors. For example, ever since the first bank introduced automatic cash machines, all other high street banks have come under pressure to offer the new service in order not to lose their customers. A similar more recent set of pressures has been to provide telephone banking for customers, and now internet banking too.

Opportunities

On other occasions, information system development projects aim at introducing innovation in the way information is processed. It is not then a matter of solving a problem or responding to a pressure, but one of exploiting some new opportunity arising from advances in IT. In the 1980s banks introduced new ways of serving their customers through automatic teller machines (ATM); in the 1990s supermarkets are developing sophisticated and multi-function electronic funds transfer at the point of sales systems (EFTPOS) to speed check-out and provide increased levels of service and new products for their customers. In more and more sectors companies find new ways of doing business based on information technology. As is explored further in chapter 11, information systems projects often form part of an organization's strategy to secure or promote its competitiveness. In this way, one company's opportunity, to do something new and distinctive, can become in time a pressure for change for their competitors; a pressure to which they may or may not be able to respond.

Exploring perceptions of information systems needs

It may not be obvious whether a new information system is what the organization needs, or what are the benefits to be gained from it are. There may be concerns about the performance of certain parts of the organization, or even serious worries about the strength of some business areas, and there may be several ideas for technical innovation or reorganization but it may not be fully clear what the problem or opportunity is, or whether it is indeed a problem of information systems rather than of some other aspect of the organization. Views about the causes of a problematic situation are very likely to be in conflict. Also, a technical opportunity may not appear as immediately justifiable and different people in an organization may have varying degrees of enthusiasm or reluctance for some proposed innovation.

Intuitively, a manager or an information systems expert may feel that a change in a company's information system can offer considerable potential, but they may not be in a position to make a convincing proposal. In such cases a special effort is required to understand the nature of the problematic situation or the potential of new technology. The start of the information systems development process is not in general a straightforward case of an agreed description of a need for change with clear expected benefits, but rather the vague identification of some perceived problem or opportunity, which requires careful study before a decision about establishing an information systems development project can be made. The case of A.B. Smith described below demonstrates that an information system's project may begin with a vague, and even misleading, request.

Case study: maintenance management in A. B. Smith

A.B. Smith is a chain of supermarket stores. The company is well established, with a history of nearly two decades of successful business. For the last three years it has been growing substantially, and it now has over 100 stores throughout the UK. All substantial maintenance work for the company's stores is managed by the Maintenance Division of the Maintenance and Development Department, which is represented on the company's board of directors by the Director of Maintenance and Development – figure 2.1. Most maintenance projects are contracted out to specialist firms, and the main task of the department is to allocate funds to requested projects and to manage the contracting out procedures. In charge of maintenance project approval, funding, and monitoring, is the General Maintenance Manager. He is assisted by the Managers of Electrical and Refrigeration Services. He also has a force of 10 Regional Maintenance Managers, each responsible for the stores in a certain geographic area. These Maintenance Managers are not physically based in any office of the organization. They work from home and regularly visit the stores that they are responsible for.

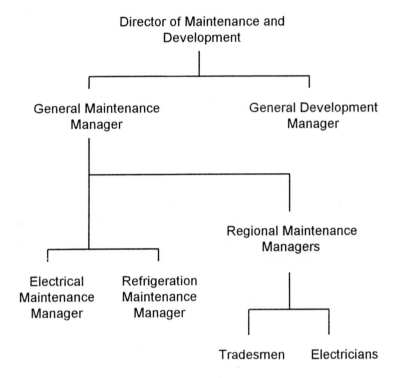

Figure 2.1 Maintenance Department organization chart

The 'problem' perceived

A new Director of Maintenance and Development had recently been appointed. He felt that the process of approving funding and managing maintenance projects was inefficient, and that a computer application for assigning priorities to requests for maintenance projects could provide the missing rigour in his department. The previous director, through many years experience, had developed the ability to appreciate the priority of maintenance projects and to keep track of their funding informally. The new director not only lacked the benefit of such experience, he also had to cope with increasing pressure on his department resulting from significant growth in the number of stores and the decreasing amounts of funds made available for maintenance. He therefore saw the need for a reliable system providing necessary information for the assessment and approval of requests for funding maintenance projects.

Project requests were made to the General Maintenance Manager by various means and through various communication channels. For example, maintenance requests could be made directly to the General Maintenance Manager by telephone from the managers of individual branches, or could be submitted by the Regional Maintenance Managers. Project requests also resulted from the regular inspections of specialists, such as pest controllers, heating and ventilation experts, or building safety experts, which were communicated to the general maintenance manager by means of their reports. As figure 2.2 shows, projects could originate from any of the following sources:

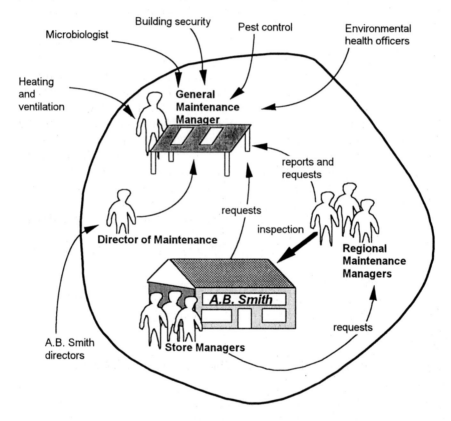

Figure 2.2 Maintenance projects request routes

- Report resulting from the visits that the General Maintenance Manager makes once a year to each branch. During these visits the General Maintenance Manager, the branch manager, and the Regional Maintenance Manager designated for the branch assess required maintenance work and make project suggestions.

- Project requests made by Regional Maintenance Managers to the General Maintenance Manager.
- Project requests made by branch managers either directly to the General Maintenance Manager or through the designated Regional Maintenance Manager.
- Reports from Directors' meetings or direct requests from various directors to the Director of Maintenance and Development, which he then communicates to the general maintenance manager.
- Project requests from specialist inspectors such as heating and ventilation, microbiologist, building security, pest control, refrigeration, and others.

Every six months, the General Maintenance Manager compiled a list of maintenance projects and estimated their cost. He did this without any systematic mechanism to record the various project requests. The Director of Maintenance and Development had officially to confirm that he would fund the projects on the list, but he was given little information about the overall demand for maintenance projects and the grounds on which the General Maintenance Manager chose the particular projects appearing on the list that he signed. Many projects were deferred with the intention that they would be included in the list compiled in the following six-month period, but often the General Maintenance Manager could not inform the applicants when, if ever, deferred requests or the work suggested in specialists' reports would be funded. By experience, the cost estimates of projects by the General Maintenance Manager and his assistants were impressively accurate, within about 2%.

An information systems analyst was called in to investigate the problem and specify the information system needed. At first, from the Director's brief, the 'problem' appeared to be clear enough and to require a straightforward computer-based system. This would be a new system to record properly and prioritize maintenance project requests according to the following project priority criteria:

1. safety of customers and employees; subject to statutory obligations;
2. trade bearing;
3. employees' comfort;
4. nice-to-do.

When a request was made by higher echelons of the company, as for example the director of another department, it was usually assigned the highest priority and was included in the work list of the next session.

What really was the 'problem'?

Despite this neat description, when the analyst tried to understand the process of project funding approval, she found that there were substantial grey areas, and it emerged that the lack of an efficient priority assigning mechanism was only part of a more broadly problematic situation. The importance of the recording of requests and priority assignment component was not so obvious as was initially thought. To assess what the real significance of a priority assignment system was, she had to understand the ramifications of the complex process of initiating and handling maintenance work projects. This included questions such as what information a system would need to handle, what information transformation it should apply, and how it would fit in with the practices of the people working in the Maintenance Division?

From the first interviews it became apparent that the meaning of 'project' was vague. Also, the overall management of maintenance projects was an unsystematic process. Different people had different perceptions of what a maintenance project was, and different views about the urgency of any specific project. Consequently, project requests were supported with different information and there was no consistency in applying the priority criteria. Most Regional Maintenance Managers were very good at presenting their requests convincingly. Each of them, however, was using his or her own interpretation of the criteria for the projects that they identified and put forward as urgent.

There was also a confusing division of responsibilities between the General Maintenance Manager and the Regional Maintenance Managers, with duplication of some tasks and loose co-ordination of some others. Project requests were an obvious area of duplication, as projects could be identified by many parties but often with different perceptions and justifications of urgency. Conflicting project perceptions and confused procedures for project approval often resulted in disappointment for the branch managers. Beyond this, the implementation of approved projects suffered from lack of co-ordination and accountability. The Maintenance Managers had the responsibility to supervise the implementation of projects, that is to find contractors, schedule when work was to be done and ensure that the work was completed to the satisfaction of the contract. However, when the General Maintenance Manager compiled the list of projects to be funded in the next six months, he had no means of considering the capacity of each Regional Maintenance Manager to cope with the project administration load in that period. In addition, the management of contracted out projects depended totally on the personal skills of the individual Regional Maintenance Manager, with no mechanism in the department for monitoring the effectiveness of maintenance projects and their results.

It therefore became increasingly doubtful that a computer-based system that would apply the priority criteria stated above could bring the benefits that the Director of Maintenance and Development expected. There was clearly a broader problematic situation of information handling which needed consideration.

While a formal information system recording project requests and assigning priority to projects was probably needed, it was unclear to what extent such a system on its own could improve the performance of the department. Questions remained about how it would fit within the overall process of maintenance project management, and what information processes it should include.

Investigating the need for a new information system

In a case such as that described above, reaching a decision about the launching of the information systems development process requires judgement, new ideas and a deep understanding of organizational needs. It needs expertise in both the business and technical information processing and depends greatly on understanding the organizational culture. To address these needs this chapter outlines an approach based on Peter Checkland's *Soft Systems Methodology*, for investigating whether and how an information systems development project can contribute to the improvement of a problem situation [Checkland, 1981; Checkland & Scholes, 1990].

Soft Systems Methodology (SSM) provides a way of reaching insights to illuminate unclear problem situations. It guides an analyst or 'would be problem solver' to view an organization as a 'human activity system'. Very often, problems related with human activities cannot be expressed explicitly enough for the analyst or anybody else to be sure of what their solution may be. In other words, the problem faced is unstructured and different people involved have their own views or feelings about what is wrong, and what might be done. Often this is manifested as a feeling of unease rather than as a clearly stated need or requirement.

In SSM, the first task of the analyst is to choose a system relevant to the situation under investigation – in information systems studies, the part of the organization where the problematic situation lies – viewed as a human activity system. Subsequently, the analyst's intervention in the organization should lead to a plan of action which will improve this system's functioning. As is explained in chapter 6, there is a substantial body of theories on systems which provides useful ways of perceiving a part of the world as a whole and studying its behaviour. Using such theoretical guidance, the analyst can develop models of activities that need to be performed by this part of the organization. However, a conceptual model of the human activity system's behaviour based on a theory of how systems function is not the same as an effective plan of action for improving a situation. The analyst also needs to ensure that a proposed plan is acceptable and implementable by the organization and by the people who work there; the models have to be compared with the actual situation. In other words, a plan of action must be derived, which is not only desirable or viable according to theories of systems (systemically desirable), but which makes sense to, and can be feasibly accommodated by, the organization in question (culturally feasible).

Figure 2.3 illustrates one version of how SSM attempts to achieve this. It represents SSM as a process with 7 stages. In the first two stages, the would be problem solver tries to find out what makes the situation problematic. To do this, it is useful to build up the richest possible picture of the situation studied, by observing the processes taking place, by interviewing participants, by examining reports and other organizational documents. A picture may be expressed in terms of structures, such as the power hierarchy and the communication patterns, or in terms of processes, such as those for decision making or production. It may also need to be expressed in terms of looser concepts such as interest groups and patterns of influence. It should capture both the formal and the informal aspects of the problem situation. In this way the rich picture should also prepare us to capture the various viewpoints from which the problem situation can be perceived. Particularly useful for doing this is the concept of *Weltanschauung,* the unquestioned image or model of the world that somebody carries, which makes some human activity meaningful. Conflicting views about a problem are likely to stem from different *Weltanschauungen.*

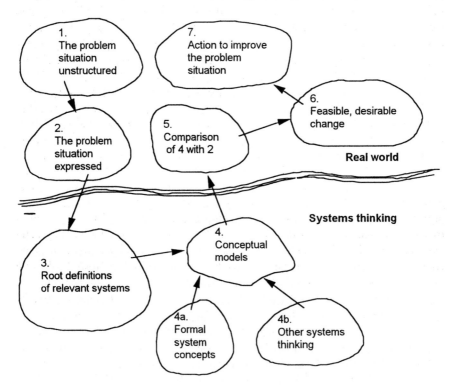

Figure 2.3 Outline of SSM [Checkland, 1981]

It is likely that owners, customers and participants of an organization will have different views on a problem situation because they hold substantially different beliefs. Displaying the situation in a way that reveals the different points of view helps in achieving some accommodation between the range of possible actions to follow.

In considering figure 2.3, and the following description, it is important to be aware that the numbering of stages from 1 to 7, and the implication of a single linear sequence, needs to be treated with caution. To explain SSM it is useful, but to do SSM requires that the model be recast to meet the particular situation under study. Aspects may be tackled 'out of sequence', omitted or iterated. In this way, the 7 stage model is a framework for thinking about how we can think through problems, and not a prescriptive method. We return to some of these issues in part 2 of the book when we consider the limits of prescriptive methodologies.

In the case of A.B. Smith's maintenance department the perceptions of the problem situation by the branch managers, the Regional Maintenance Managers, the General Maintenance Manager and the Director of Maintenance and Development were quite distinct. The views of branch managers varied; while many were pleased with the overall arrangements for maintenance work, some expressed frustration that their Regional Maintenance Manager failed to secure approval for projects that they considered important. It all appeared to depend on the Regional Maintenance Managers' ability to push a request through and find good contractors. Most Regional Maintenance Managers enjoyed the flexibility of defining informally what maintenance work to request, and of dealing with contractors locally without any restrictions from the maintenance department, but they did consider it problematic that it was becoming ever more difficult to know which of the projects they requested would be included in the project list for the following half year. For the General Maintenance Manager the main problem was the lack of a systematic procedure for recording and presenting project requests. The lack of a mechanism to keep track of requests was a frequent source of embarrassment. For the Director of Maintenance and Development, the whole process was unacceptably informal. He was not given enough information to be able to approve a work list with confidence. He had no means of knowing how effective his department was, as he himself had insufficient information about the urgency of the requested projects that he approved and the cost-effectiveness of the contracted out projects.

In stage 3 of SSM the analyst uses what has been discovered about the problem situation to define notional human activity systems which seem relevant to the problem, the so-called *root definitions of relevant systems*. Several root definitions can be developed, according to the various *Weltanschauungen* revealed in the rich picture of the situation, in order to produce insight for the investigation of the problem. A root definition must give a clear statement of a system being proposed or projected. From the SSM point of view, the idea of the system exists in the process of exploring the real situation, not in the real situation itself. Ideally, this system we choose to see should contain information about:

- the transformation performed by the system – the means by which inputs are transformed to outputs;
- the actors involved – the agents who carry out the main activities of the system;
- the ownership of the system –who has a prime concern for the system and the ultimate power to cause the system to cease to exist;
- the customers of the system – beneficiaries or victims affected by the activities of the system;
- the environmental constraints on the system – the features of its environment which affect its operations; and
- the *Weltanschauung* which the definition embodies – the particular way of looking at the problem that the root definition implies.

This set of requirements for a root definition is encapsulated by Checkland in the mnemonic CATWOE: Customers, Actors, Transformation process, *Weltanschauung*, Owner(s), Environmental constraints. However, this should be seen as a useful checklist, rather than a necessary and sufficient specification of any human activity system.

Since more than one *Weltanschauung* can be found relevant to a human activity system under study, either expressed by the actors in the system or supplied by the analyst, several different root definitions can generally be constructed. However, it is often useful to provide a definition which expresses the 'official' task assigned to the part of the organization studied, the so-called 'primary task' root definition. If the problem situation is controversial, this definition can provide the main basis for designing a model of activities to compare with existing activities. If there are different views of what the problem is, the model of activities based on the primary task can be compared against the models of activities implied by alternative views of relevant systems.

In the A.B. Smith Maintenance Department the different perceptions of the problem situation lead to different root definitions. According to the General Maintenance Manager's *Weltanschauung* a relevant system capturing the problem situation is:

A system owned by the General Maintenance of A.B. Smith and used by the Maintenance Department of A.B. Smith, which assigns request's priorities by means of supplied information in order to optimize the use of allocated funds. The system to operate under the financial constraints of the company's maintenance budget, statutory constraints, and within the expected performance standards of the company.

Customer: managers of stores

Actor: staff of maintenance department

Transformation: unprioritized requests in – prioritized and funded requests out
Weltanschauung: rational allocation of funds on company-wide basis
Owner: General Maintenance Manager
Environment: budget, statutory requirements, company performance standards

From the point of view of the Director of Maintenance and Development, however, the problem area comprises the overall management of projects and a relevant system was proposed as:

A system, owned and used by the Maintenance Department of A.B. Smith, for managing maintenance projects by improving communications and information sharing in the Company in order to ensure projects' timely and economic completion. The system to operate under the constraints of the company's maintenance budget, statutory constraints, department stores operational constraints, as well as within expected performance standards of the company.

As an exercise, it would be useful to develop a CATWOE analysis of this second root definition and contrast it with the first. In doing so, the particular distinctive transformation and *Weltanschauung* needs to be considered. Indeed, in using CATWOE to illuminate a root definition the key aspect is very often how the transformation embodies the *Weltanschauung*, or put the other way, how the *Weltanschauung* makes the proposed transformation meaningful. To do this it is also useful to think of a root definition in terms of 'do X, by means of Y in order to achieve Z'.

Although the Director of Maintenance and Development had initially expressed his perception of the problem as a 'project prioritization' problem, the analyst understood from the first interview session that his concern covered the much broader project management processes in his department. The definition she used to capture his concern was broad enough to allow consideration of many areas of problematic procedures. She chose to use this latter definition to compare against the concerns of other actors such as the Regional Maintenance Managers and the General Maintenance Manager, and to study the requirements for an information system that could effectively improve this problem situation.

In stage 4 of SSM, the analyst forms a model of activities for each root definition. An activity model is a description of the activities which need to be done for the system to perform the transformation process of the relevant root definition. The simplest way of doing this is to assemble and structure a list of verbs covering the activities which are necessary for the transformation of the system's inputs to its outputs.

At this stage the analyst can make use of relevant theoretical work which conceptualizes organizations as systems. As is explained in chapter 6, there is a plethora of concepts and frameworks in disciplines studying organizations, systems, cybernetics, and information, from which the analyst can obtain guidance for forming an activity model, or some reassurance that the model constructed is defensible.

The analyst in this case made a conceptual model of the maintenance project management system based on the second root definition as a system comprising the following activities: project bidding, compilation of project work lists, accounts management, administration and monitoring of project implement-ation, and outside the outer boundary in the diagram overall control of the performance of the maintenance department considering criteria of efficiency and effectiveness – figure 2.4. She further analyzed each of these subsystems in terms of yet more detailed activities. For example, the compilation of projects work lists was analysed to comprise the assessment of urgency of requested projects, a first assignment of desirable timing according to implementation restrictions such as availability of contractors, the maintenance manager's work schedule, and the operations of the store concerned, the calculation of required funds, and deciding whether to include a project in the work list for the next session, or a future session, or to defer it indefinitely until a new request is made – figure 2.5.

Interestingly, the analyst's model does not contain anywhere 'priority assignment' as an element. She found that this term could not adequately describe a particular set of activities in the logical system model that she produced. The activity 'compilation of project work lists' was introduced containing a number of related but clearly definable sub-activities. Similarly, it was considered necessary to identify the management of maintenance accounts as a separate set of activities, in order to secure accountability.

At stage 5 of the SSM, the analyst compares the conceptual activity models with what actually happens in the part of the organization under study. The objective of this stage is to learn from the differences between the model and the actual situation, and to tease out the complexities, contradictions and in-adequacies of the existing situation. Comparisons can be made in several different ways. One is through discussion. The analyst can use the conceptual models as a base for asking questions about the problem situation. Another way is to compare a conceptual model with a historical reconstruction of how the system studied performed on certain occasions. Care is needed to compare the activities described in the conceptual model with 'which' activities are happening, rather than 'how' they are done.

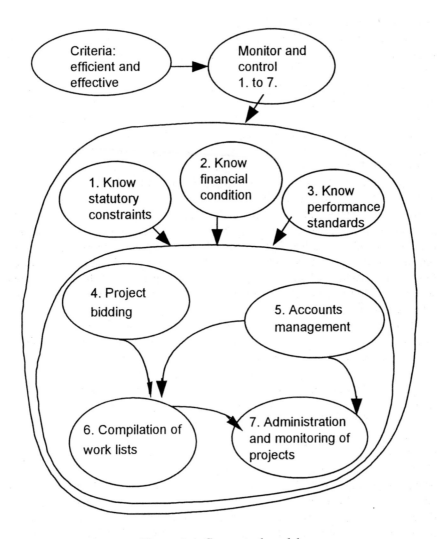

Figure 2.4 Conceptual model

In the A.B. Smith case, it was clear that the conceptual model of activities that the analyst produced had little in common with the way activities were organized in the maintenance division. Based on this model, the analyst formul-ated questions and stimulated discussions to find out which activities were missing from the practices of the division, and which were duplicated or intermeshed with others. She presented her model to the participants as a logical way to organize the tasks of maintenance management and she invited their comments.

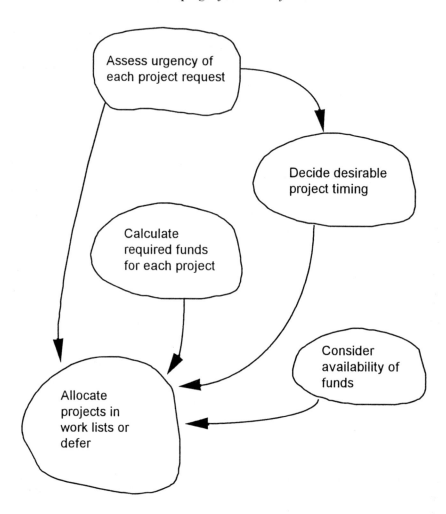

Figure 2.5 Activity model for the compilation of project work list

As the project developed it became apparent to all that there was little co-ordination between the Regional Maintenance Managers and the General Maintenance Manager. The approval of projects by the General Maintenance Manager and the Director of Maintenance and Development was largely separated from the implementation of projects by the Regional Maintenance Managers. It also became clearer that project priority assignment was a confused activity, which for some meant the assessment of a project's urgency and for others the whole sequence of activities leading to the allocation of funds and the scheduling of projects. Also, the way project funding was currently practised combined tasks which concerned two different main activities: the allocation of funds for projects to be included in the work list of the following six months; and the management of maintenance projects' accounts. It emerged from the discussions that this latter activity was becoming particularly significant as pressures for accountability increased. There were a number of different accounts for maintenance projects, with funds from different sources and earmarked for different purposes. Nevertheless, the General Maintenance Manager had the flexibility to use funds from different accounts in order to meet requests for urgent projects.

At stages 6 and 7, the analyst opens a debate about possible changes which can be made to improve the perceived problem situation. The objective is to find which of the suggested changes can be implemented. The actions for change must be compatible with the culture of the organization and acceptable to its participants. The analyst may seek a consensus solution with agreement on the validity and the utility of the proposed changes. Alternatively, we could suggest the need for accommodation, a negotiated trade-off of viewpoints among the stakeholders which is based on the learning they have achieved through the SSM process. In general, changes of three kinds may be decided upon: structural, such as of groupings of functions of the organization, procedural, which refer on the dynamic processes followed for doing the organizations activities, and changes of attitudes, such as the value attributed to certain situations or in the participants' expectations.

At A.B. Smith the analyst organized a debate in the maintenance division to decide which changes the participants would like to see implemented. Although the initial request from the Director of Maintenance and Development was for a formal information system to support a specific activity, the debate, stimulated by the analyst's findings, led to different issues. It was clear that most participants wanted to keep as much of the informal and flexible arrangements of project management as possible. They would all like to receive more information from the others and were willing to provide more information about their tasks, but they believed that a rigid formal system would be dysfunctional as it would curtail their flexibility to take the most appropriate actions. The following actions were finally decided:

- To examine further how to organize the co-ordination between the tasks of the main roles of Regional Maintenance Managers, General Maintenance Manager and Director of Maintenance and Development, allowing for as much autonomy as possible.
- To start longer term planning of maintenance projects by compiling maintenance project lists not only for the next six months but for following periods too.
- To ensure that the managers involved provided information about their activities and decisions to all others concerned. For example, the General Maintenance Manager should inform anyone who entered a bid for a project whether and when the project would be funded. The Regional Maintenance Managers would provide information about the contracts that they entered

into and their results to the branch managers, the General Maintenance Manager and the Director of Maintenance and Development.

- To examine the information needs of the reorganized activities of the division, and to develop computer-based information systems to support them.

Some comments on Soft Systems Methodology

We have already noted that, although figure 2.3 presents SSM as a series of 7 stages, this describes only a bare logical rationale for the methodology not an inviolable sequence. An analyst may find it appropriate to start with any stage other than the first, to work simultaneously at different stages or, while working at a certain stage, to go back and repeat some previous stages.

The wavy line in figure 2.3 indicates an important split between two different classes of activities. Those stages lying above the line involve interaction of the analyst with the organization concerned: interviews with employees, observations of procedures, consultation, and debates. The stages lying under the line are mental work, where the analyst applies and uses systems concepts in order to formulate and structure perceptions of the problem situation and then to conceptualize them in models of its functioning. In this the analyst may well be joined by other interested people, but these other parties will be asked to work within the particular frame of reference of systems thinking and may need help to achieve this. This distinction in modes of thinking is important as is the proposed broad sequence of the approach, starting in the real world, moving to a model based world of systems thinking, and then, most important of all, returning to the actual situation under study to validate and make use of the insights gained.

More recent work of Checkland has offered another perspective on SSM [Checkland, 1990]. In this the task of systems intervention is described in terms of two, parallel, streams of enquiry. The stream exemplified by figure 2.3 is the logic based stream of analysis, but this is complemented by a stream of cultural enquiry. In this latter perspective the problem situation is considered as a culture within which an intervention must be located. To appreciate the culture is vital, and pursuing this stream of enquiry requires continuous attention to the character of the social and political world within which an intervention is made. Furthermore, the analyst, or 'would be improver of the situation', is a part of that culture and cannot stand outside it as a neutral or unbiased player.

SSM provides a way of examining what information systems developments can contribute to the improvement of an organization, and which are feasible to undertake. More importantly, the commitment to building a rich picture of the part of the organization under study, of examining the required activity models from alternative points of view, and of aiming at interventions which are culturally feasible, can relate exploration of possible information systems development projects with other needs for organizational change, such as restructuring or changes to work procedures. The main value of SSM for analyzing the need for a new information system lies not so much in the problem structuring procedure of the seven stages outlined above. Rather it is in making analysts and other participants aware that unstructured organizational problems, which give rise to information systems projects, require attention to alternative points of view and the consideration of multiple versions of the activities implied or sought. The fundamental concepts of the methodology, such as the human activity system and *Weltanschauung*, are valuable tools for thinking about and making sense of complex problem situations. The analyst's search for systemically desirable and culturally feasible proposals for action proves in many cases to be the only viable start for an intervention.

The analyst's role

This discussion of the use of SSM in the A.B. Smith case study illustrates that the decision to develop an information system is far from trivial. It is likely that initial ideas as to what system is required will need to be explored, and may be challenged. How can analysts or IT specialists effectively take a leading part in such a complicated and political process?

Clearly this is not the kind of decision that analysts should make on their own. Their role is to provide information that will help others, those with a direct interest in developing and using the system, decide. Usually this responsibility lies with a small group of managers including the manager of the department or the office that will use the system, the manager responsible for funding the project, and the manager responsible for building and introducing the system. There may be others who wish to have a say too, for example, representatives of employees who will use the new technical system – perhaps their trade unions – and managers of other departments who feel that they will be affected by the new information system. It is therefore better to think of the conception of an information system's project as being the result of a negotiation process between people with different concerns. The analyst's role is not to determine alone what system is required, or to show which technical implementation is the best, but to support the negotiation process with as much information and insight as the participants need.

Exercises and discussion issues

1. The main library of the University of Human Sciences is under a double pressure: its budget is decreasing, while complaints about the adequacy of its services become more frequent and more severe. Various suggestions for changes have been heard from a number of places in the university: to

abolish its function as a research library and become a teaching collection only, with the research collection budget distributed to the various departments and research centres of the university; to preserve its function as a research library, but instead of continuing its effort to maintain a comprehensive collection of publications in the humanities, to introduce the most advanced electronic information retrieval facilities, such as on-line searching of catalogues and documents, and subscription to bibliographic databases of major institutions in the field. There are of course those who would not like to see any of these radical changes and who argue that the traditional library services have contributed immensely to building the excellence of the university. They suggest moderate technological modernization and better management of resources.

The director of the library feels that it is time to begin a thorough study of all possibilities. Try to apply the concepts of SSM to shed light on this problem situation. Think of relevant root definitions and work out activity models that capture the different conceptions of desirable library functioning. Open up discussion in class with different groups of students defending each of the different suggestions outlined above and others that you may identify. Try to reach a consensus decision, but also consider what might happen if no consensus is achievable.

2. This chapter has proposed that information systems development projects arise from three main causes: problems, external pressures and perceived opportunities. Do you believe that this is a sufficiently comprehensive classification? Are there any other causes that might be identified?

3. Analyze the SSM methodology in terms of its strengths and its weaknesses. Are there situations in which you believe that it would be inappropriate to use it? What particular qualities and skills would you expect an analyst practising this approach to have?

4. In the A.B. Smith case, how successful was the work of the analyst? Do you consider that the effort expended in arriving at the understanding of the problem was worthwhile, or would a more direct approach, building the information system that the Director first requested, have been just as fruitful?

References

Checkland, P.B. (1981) *Systems Thinking Systems Practice*, J. Wiley, Chichester.

Checkland, P.B. & Scholes, J. (1990) *Soft Systems Methodology in Action*, J. Wiley, Chichester.

Further reading

The best presentation of soft systems methodology is in Peter Checkland's books referenced above. Peter Checkland's second book on SSM contains many case studies which provide excellent material to gain understanding of how the approach can be applied and how it has developed. In the 1980s SSM became widely influential in Britain and the books listed below all set out to explain the SSM methodology to various categories of readers. The Lewis and the Stowell books in particular both apply SSM ideas to information systems development. SSM can be seen as a part of a wider movement to develop problem structuring techniques and the Rosenhead book provides a useful overview of a number of such methods.

Avison, D.E. & Wood-Harper, A.T. (1990) *Multiview: An Exploration in Information Systems Development*, Blackwell, Oxford.

Central Computer and Telecommunications Agency (1990) *Managing Information as a Resource*, HMSO, London.

Davis, L. & Ledington, P. (1991) *Information in Action: Soft Systems Methodology*, Macmillan Press, Basingstoke.

Lewis, P. (1994) *Information-Systems Development*, Pitman, London.

Rosenhead, J.V. (1989) *Rational Analysis for a Problematic World*, J. Wiley, Chichester.

Stowell, F. & West, D. (1994) *Client-led Design: A Systemic Approach to Information Systems Definition*, McGraw-Hill, London.

3 Launching an information system development project

- *Information requirements determination*
- *The feasibility study*
- *Limits to the feasibility study*

When a decision is taken that an information system does need to be developed, the next task is to understand the information requirements that the new system is to meet: what data the system should collect and process; what output it should produce; and how to make it available to the right recipients or users. An analyst can then propose various combinations of software, hardware, and organizational change to provide for them. An analyst must also support such proposals with adequate information so that the management of the organization can choose one of them and approve it for development. This requires careful consideration of the advantages to be gained and the risks associated with each of the proposals, a task which is generally known as a feasibility study.

We begin this chapter with a discussion of the various methods that can be used to determine information requirements. We then present the various aspects of feasibility that an analyst should explore and upon which decisions to go ahead might be made. Choosing to discuss establishing information requirements for a new system before judging feasibility may be seen as an inappropriate sequence. Indeed, there is a chicken and egg problem here. We cannot judge feasibility without some knowedge of information on requirements; equally, we cannot devote great effort to discovering detailed requirements if we have not made some decisions about what form the project will take or what 'product' it is to produce. In this chapter we choose to discuss requirements before feasibility issues, but it should be understood that these two aspects are more probably undertaken in tandem, or as a two phase process.

Information requirements determination

Requirements capture

The simplest way to find out the answers to questions of what is required of an information system is to ask the people who are going to be involved in the information handling activities. Unfortunately, people are very often not able to supply satisfactory answers about what information could better support a particular job, particularly if the intention is that the new system is to introduce new ways of working. It is likely that answers will be incomplete, inaccurate, or not expressed clearly enough for the analyst to understand them. People may not be able to remember all aspects of information handling in sufficient detail, or they may be biased, emphasising particular aspects while neglecting others.

Various methods can be employed to overcome some of the problems people have in expressing their own information requirements. In interviewing people analysts can engage in general discussion, discussion based on a basic set of issues and questions, or in a more structured manner asking 'closed' questions, defining for each question a set of possible answers. The more closed the approach the more this may help the respondent to consider possibilities that they might otherwise forget but it does rely on the analyst having a complete understanding of options available. The analyst might also spend time observing people at work, perhaps with the aid of a video camera. Observation of work going on may reveal important information that nobody would ever express directly. Observation also allows an analyst to become familiar with the culture and working style of a group of people, which may be critical in understanding what will be accepted, and what will not.

Brainstorming sessions or workshops can also be organized, where groups of people exchange opinions and options for a new system. This may lead to unconventional suggestions that individuals would not express if the analyst were to lead the elicitation process. More generally, a set of structured meetings can be organized in which different people representing different interests come together to work out requirements. This is sometimes undertaken as part of an approach known as joint applications development, or JAD. Approaches such as brainstorming or JAD sessions require, to some degree, that the analyst shift their role, away from the role of 'expert', and towards that of facilitator or catalyst. The extent to which analysts are actually able to do this is however debatable, particularly if they have had no training for the new role.

If analysts feel that they cannot rely wholey on people involved in information handling activities to specify their own information systems requirements, by what ever means, they can use one or more of the following three approaches: deriving requirements from existing information systems, discovering from experimentation with a prototype, and deriving from an analysis of the utilizing system [Davis, 1982].

Deriving information requirements from existing systems

Often, similar information systems to the one proposed for development already exist, and the analyst can get ideas from studying them. In particular the following possibilities exist as places to start looking:

The existing procedures that the new system is going to replace. This may be a totally manual system or some combination of manual and computer based procedures. In the early days of computer applications, most information systems development projects aimed at transferring existing manual operations onto computers and, therefore, the study of existing procedures was the main method to determine the requirements of a new system. When information systems projects aim less at 'automating' existing manual processes, and more at introducing new processes and at delivering new services and new products, this method is less effective. However, the new system will most probably have to fit into some existing procedures, and it is still necessary to understand those processes that it is going to complement.

Similar systems in other organizations. Unless the new system is intended to introduce an unprecedented innovation, systems that other organizations have already developed can be a useful source of ideas for information requirements. One does not need to look only in rival organizations of the same industry. For example, the development of a booking system for a theatre may have something to gain from studying existing airline reservation systems.

Standard software solutions. There is a huge range of packaged software applications available which seek to capture the requirements of a great variety of information processing situations. Even if buying a package does not seem likely to be a satisfactory solution, an examination of relevant software products available in the market can help in determining some of the requirements of a new information system. If buying a software package is a probable direction, it should be remembered that this does not solve the problem of establishing a new information system. Packages will introduce their own constraints and may imply more organizational change than a bespoke solution.

In the 1990s, the range of available packaged software is vast, and ranges from individual discrete applications to large, multi-function software suites. As one example, the German company SAP has had great success in selling its integrated software to medium sized and large companies as a comprehensive solution to core information systems needs. Customers include multinational oil companies, banks and manufacturers. SAP's success is in part attributable to the quality of the product as a technical solution to certain information handling needs, such as accounting and inventory management, but can also be seen as a solution to organizational needs. If such a package is chosen, then it will define many of the characteristics of the new system and of the organizational structures that surround it. This may be welcomed by senior managers, who at least get a definite model of the changes implied by systems development. That said, the configuration of any package, large or small, will require much detailed analysis of particular needs, and the requirements determination process is just as critical as in a bespoke development.

Descriptions of similar systems in books, and other publications. Many categories of information systems are well documented in the literature. Study of the great variety of publications available is a rich source of insight for as diverse applications as payroll and accounting systems, financial forecasting systems, expert systems, or point-of-sales systems. However, while analysts should avoid wasting effort by 'reinventing the wheel', they should also be careful to understand the special requirements of the case under study which may make the direct take-up of established solutions inappropriate.

Experimental methods

If the system under development is quite unlike existing ones and there is a high level of uncertainty about its required features, an experimental approach may be appropriate. After forming an initial view of requirements, the analyst can use programming facilities, such as fourth generation languages or database packages, to build a prototype of parts of the technical system. The prototype in this sense is not a complete information system, but is a combination of hardware and software exhibiting some of the features that the new information system is going to have, for example, data entry interfaces or generation of reports. A prototype can help the people who will work within the new system to visualize its features and refine their requirements. The prototype should be easy to change, and analysts and others can experiment with various aspects of the new system until they reach a satisfactory version which constitutes an expression of the requirements for the new information system. In chapter 7 we deal in more detail with the use of prototypes as part of a development process.

Analysis of utilizing system

A different way, and potentially the most powerful method to derive information requirements is by doing an analysis of the information needs of the parts of the organization that the new information system is intended to interact with. This approach is in some contrast to traditional analysis, which concentrates on how it is done today or how today's actors would like it to be done. Looking out, to the environment into which a system will fit, can help to ensure new thinking about requirements, unbiased by existing ways of working.

There are many methods an analyst can follow for this task. Here we outline a method which follows from the application of SSM [Wilson, 1990]. The analyst starts the study of requirements by using an activity model of the organization, or the part of the organization which is going to utilize the new information system. If SSM has been applied to identify a problem situation as described in the previous chapter, more than one such activity model may have been built to help the analyst and the participants to capture relevant views of the system. For the determination of information requirements, the analyst uses the model which describes the main transformation process that the organization performs. This is what was called above the 'primary task' model. From this model the analyst can derive the categories of information needed to support each activity and can trace from which other activities they can be obtained. The result is expressed as a table which relates specific activities with information categories as input and output. Figure 3.1 lists the input and output information categories required to support the compilation of the work lists for A.B. Smith.

A new information system does not need to cover the whole sequence of activities of the part of the organization under study. It is more likely that there are already adequate information processes that will remain unchanged and will co-exist with the information system under development. It may also be undesirable to embark on a large-scale project of change and a decision may be made to proceed with the development of some sub-part of the overall information handling system. By juxtaposing existing information processing procedures (IPP) in a table which shows the flow of information categories as input and output of the system's activities, the analyst can derive those information processes and information categories that a proposed new information system should comprise.

Activity / Information	Assess urgency of project request	Decide desirable project timing	Calculate required funds for each project	Consider availablitity of funds	Allocate projects in work list or defer
Inputs	Details of request Priority criteria Source of request	Implementation restrictions Degree of urgency	Details of request Maintenance cost list	Desirable project timing Cost estimate Type of account Degree of urgency State of account	Project timing
Outputs	Degree of urgency	Desirable project timing	Cost estimate Type of account	Account to be used Project timing	Work list entry Letter to applicant

Figure 3.1 Information requirements for the compilation of work lists

Wilson has developed a useful technique to map the information flows of the conceptual activities against the information flows of existing information processes, the 'Maltese cross'. Figure 3.2 shows the information requirements for the compilation of work lists in the A.B. Smith case in such a form.

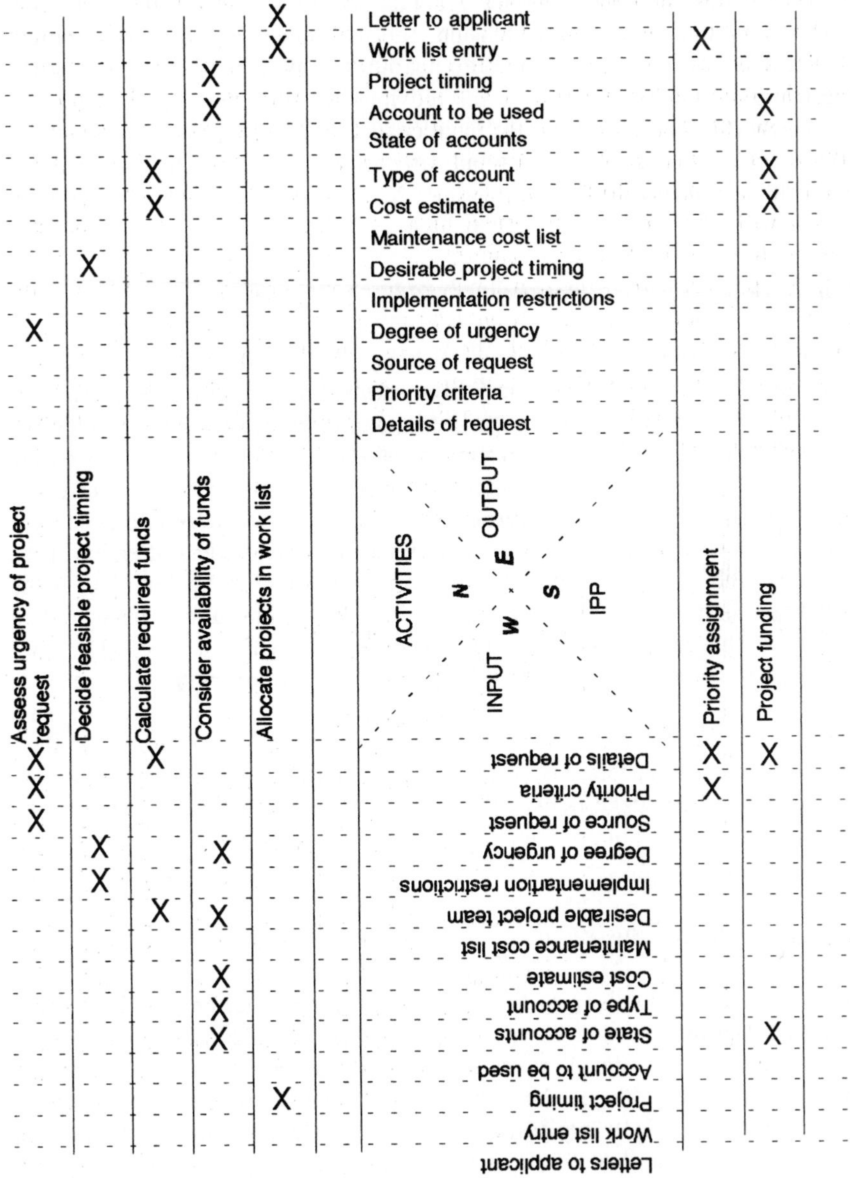

Letter to applicant — X — X (Priority assignment area)

Work list entry — X

Project timing — X

Account to be used — X (Project funding)

State of accounts

Type of account — X

Cost estimate — X

Maintenance cost list

Desirable project timing

Implementation restrictions

Degree of urgency

Source of request

Priority criteria

Details of request

ACTIVITIES

INPUT — OUTPUT

N W E S

IPP

Assess urgency of project

request

Decide feasible project timing

Calculate required funds

Consider availability of funds

Allocate projects in work list

Priority assignment

Project funding

Details of request

Priority criteria

Source of request

Degree of urgency

Implementation restrictions

Desirable project team

Maintenance cost list

Cost estimate

Type of account

State of accounts

Account to be used

Project timing

Work list entry

Letters to applicant

Figure 3.2 Maltese cross for the 'compilation of project work lists'

It becomes clear from figure 3.2 that the two established information processes in the maintenance division, the assignment of priority to project requests and the project funding administration, only satisfy a fraction of the information required according to the activity model that the analyst produced. If A.B. Smith decides to improve maintenance project management, they will need to develop means that will provide, in one way or another, for these various categories of information.

Which method for information requirements determination?

Which of the ways outlined above – asking, deriving from existing systems, experimenting and modelling – an analyst selects for a specific case depends on a judgement of the situation. If a new information system is going to assist some experienced employees in the performance of a stable process, the requirements may be fairly accurately supplied by those involved, and by examining the existing information handling procedures. If, however, the new information system is going to support the work of inexperienced people – inexperienced either in the tasks or in the new information system's formalities and technology – or if the new system is part of a deliberate effort to introduce innovation or change, then analysis of the needs of the utilizing system or prototyping are probably more appropriate. In practice the analysts will combine information requirements determination methods. It makes sense to ask the people involved what information categories and what information processing are required for their jobs, whatever the uncertainty of the situation may be. The analyst may then wish to refine their suggestions, either by experimenting with a prototype, or by further analysis of the information needs of the activities involved.

Requirements analysis

Finding requirements is just the beginning. Once requirements have been identified they then need to be analysed and classified. The traditional distinction is between functional requirements and non-functional requirements. Functional requirements are those that express what the new system has to do. As such, they are usually expressed in terms of the data holding of a system, the data transformations that it performs, and the reports and outputs that it can produce. Functional requirements are then the main basis for the subsequent crafting of the technical system. The Maltese cross, described above is one example of a means of expressing and analysing functional requirements.

Non-functional requirements express constraints, targets and control mechanisms. These may include performance requirements – say 20,000 transactions per day, security or access control requirements. Other categories include technical constraints, such as running on existing hardware or using existing networks; project constraints such as being implemented within 6 months; or organizational constraints such as being teachable to staff in one 3 hour training session.

Another important aspect of requirements analysis is some assessment of how the proposed system will be implemented. There may well be very specific requirements for a particular approach to implementation. It may be that the new system must be implemented in a single intense effort, or it may be that it needs to be run in parallel with old ways of working for some time. While implementation itself comes later in the life cycle, and is discussed in chapter 5, it is critical that some consideration of this issue is given at this time. If it is not, then it may be that a new system is designed and built, but proves impossible to put to work.

Requirements specification

To take us forward to the next phases of development it is important that what is learned about requirements is carefully documented. It is very easy to acquire good information at this stage, but to lose sight of critical aspects as the detailed work of analysis or design goes ahead. Requirements are conventionally written down in an information requirements specification document. It is usually appropriate to document the functional requirements of a proposed system using the tools and techniques of systems analysis that we will introduce in the next chapter. Thus a requirements document may include high level data models, data flow diagrams, and a data dictionary. The specification document should also include a suitable description of the non-functional requirements, appropriately classified. This will need also to include a statement of the business case for the system, which may be developed from previous problem analysis.

The requirements specification is intended to be a high level statement of what the new system is expected to do; it is not a detailed expression of how it will do it. Thus requirements specification should not include detailed specifications of algorithms or processing logic, or designs for inputs or outputs. That said, particular situations may dictate that requirements at this stage need to be quite specific in some areas, while quite vague in others. The important thing to remember is that the requirements document needs to serve a number of different audiences. Using the language of CATWOE, the problem owner(s) will use it to assure themselves that their interests are understood, the Customers will need to be assured that their needs are to be met, similarly the Actors. In this case Actors include those who will use and work within the new system, as well as those who will develop it, and those who will implement and maintain it.

The production of a requirements document is usually used as the basis for 'signing off' on a new project proposal. That is, those with life and death powers over the project (owners) use the requirements document as a vital check on the kind of system they are contracting for. In some cases this may indeed be as part of a legal contract, as when development is outsourced to a software house.

The feasibility study

Having established an initial version of information needs, an analyst can usually think of various information system proposals to meet them. One option always is to leave the existing situation unchanged. In the case of A.B. Smith, even though a decision has been made to improve the information communic-ation among those involved in the management of maintenance projects, the existing situation can serve as a basis for comparison for all other options. It is possible to propose a system which will aim to incorporate all the activities shown on the Maltese cross and to support all their information requirements. Various configurations of technology can be suggested to do that: to install a computer system in the maintenance division, which will collect and dispatch information from and to all those concerned; to develop independent micro-computer systems for the tasks of the Regional Maintenance Managers, the General Maintenance Manager, and the Director of Maintenance and Develop-ment; or to develop a network to interconnect the systems of the various users with each other and to allow them to share common applications and data. Alternatively, it is possible to undertake a less ambitious project for introducing some of the most necessary parts of these activities, with the possibility to extend them further when more money is available and as the affected managers become more confident that the changes introduced are beneficial.

Technologically, the range of choice has been enormously increased in the last twenty years, but the availability of technological options makes necessary the careful study of their appropriateness. The objective of the feasibility study at the beginning of the information system's development process is to examine whether the various options can be carried out successfully, and which of them it is preferable to develop.

Monitoring the feasibility of information system changes should of course be a concern throughout the development process. Most methods used for the various development tasks guide analysts' attention to consider the feasibility of the changes they propose or the systems they develop. We have seen that SSM leads to a debate about whether an information system change that may appear desirable is also feasible. Similarly, when more detailed analysis and design of the parts of the new system is under way, the feasibility of their implementation has to be reconsidered. The feasibility of the whole development project must also be examined in the light of more detailed understanding and new inform-ation obtained in later stages. Many projects have had to be abandoned at the implementation stage when it became clear that they were misconceived or that circumstances had changed since their conception, and the information systems they aimed at were not feasible any longer.

Even so, a formal feasibility study at an early stage of the development process is particularly useful. The aim of such a study is to state the information needs with the possible project options to meet them. Such a study will also make explicit the criteria for selecting one of them for further development. The feasibility study leads to the main decision point, which commits the organization to provide the resources required for the development project, and to work towards new organizational and technical arrangements. It also sets the basis for the evaluation of the success or failure of the changes that will be implemented. Such feasibility needs to be examined from a number of perspectives, including consideration of technical, legal, organizational, social and economic aspects of a project.

Technical feasibility

Technical feasibility refers to the question 'Does current technology support the proposed system?' Although the impressive advances of information technology in the last two decades have led to a great choice of technical options, this question still needs to be treated with great care. Many projects attempt real technical innovations, in hardware, the use of networks, database technology, knowledge based systems and others. It is not sufficient to know that a system is in general technically possible, for example that it has been built in the laboratories of NASA or put to work in another country. It must be established that the organization concerned can buy or build the technical system, and support it in use. Often information systems projects fail because they lack skilled staff to build the required technical components or to maintain them. As technology advances, all countries – from those which import information technology to those that pioneer it – face shortages of technical skills. In many countries the problem is quite severe and can only be overcome in the long term with greater efforts in education and training. In the short term the selection of technology has to be carefully undertaken to be certain that the organization can master and sustain it.

Organizations may find that the expertise of their information technology specialists is outdated and inadequate to handle a new generation of computer and telecommunications projects. Recruitment of the necessary technical staff is not always possible; for example, in Britain salary restrictions in public sector institutions place them at a disadvantage to private companies in attracting and keeping technical experts. Subcontracting or outsourcing sophisticated technical projects appears to provide a way out of such problems. Nevertheless, subcontracting is not an easy solution. Subcontractors often fail to comprehend the distinctive organizational aspects of their clients. To be able to gain from subcontracting, an organization must have adequate information systems project expertise to be able to control with confidence the information systems development process. Special attention also needs to be given to those technical aspects of information systems which cannot be resolved by the technical staff of an organization, such as telecommunications infrastructure or the interconnection with systems in other organizations. Also, despite the apparent flexibility and user friendliness of today's information technologies, hardware and software compatibility remains a problem. Efforts to agree on standards, such as 'open systems', which can make systems of different manufacturers operate together have been slow at producing universally accepted results.

Legal and regulatory feasibility

The consideration of legal and regulatory feasibility turns attention to externally imposed requirements or conditions that an information system must meet. There are many sources for such requirements and some classes of application may be intensively constrained by laws or regulations. For example, an accounting system will be expected to meet requirements set down in company law, the requirements of the company's auditors and requirements of the taxation authorities. Some of these regulations will be in the form of explicit rules to be followed or criteria to be met, but more often it will require some interpretation and judgement in order to explore and assess the imposed limits.

Another example of feasibility issues that emanate from the law are those relating to data protection. Across Europe it has become standard practice for countries to legislate on the rules and conditions under which data on people may be collected and stored. In some countries, as in Britain, this legislation is restricted to data held on computer, while in others there is no such limitation. The result is that any system that will hold such data needs to be assessed in the context of the very specific requirements and conditions which the legislation sets out. This may require that the use of personal data is restricted to a declared purpose, and that it is possible to supply enquirers with copies of their records, and to make amendments if required to do so [Edwards & Savage, 1986].

An area on which law and regulation increasingly impinges is the workplace itself. In most countries there are various laws relating to health and safety at work. These may impose general requirements such as the length of a working day or acceptable temperatures, or they may make specific requirements for information technology. In the European Union this kind of regulation is increasingly being undertaken by the Commission. For example, pan-European regulations on the ergonomic characteristics of computer workstations including the office furniture that they use have been set out. Public sector organizations face another legal constraint. Under the rules of the Community all public sector contracts with a value in excess of 100,000 ECU have to be put out to tender and should be based upon international or European standards. One consequence is that systems have to be specified in terms of a generic type or particular required functionality, rather than by name.

Organizational feasibility

Organizational feasibility refers to the changes that a proposed information system entails for the structure of an organization, its management procedures, and the way decisions are made. Until about the mid 1970s, economies of scale in the use of computer technology tended to reinforce centralization, even in organizations where decentralization was seen as politically desirable. Since then, microcomputers, telecommunications, and databases have provided increased flexibility in designing information systems. This means that the critical issues of management structures and the distribution of decision making authority have to be considered explicitly. One special category of such structural change concerns the management of information systems resources themselves, which can range from centralized services and facilities to full autonomy for the various parts of an organization to develop and manage their own applications. If an information systems project is intended to lead to structural change, such as to increase the decision making autonomy of certain units, it must be made clear that the new organizational scheme is manageable and acceptable.

The implication of this is that the development of a new information system requires management skills for the implementation of organizational change. The organization must be capable of adopting and managing new information handling, decision making and work procedures. Yet, many organizations are not very good at accepting or managing change; if the change implied is too radical for the organization, the new information system is unlikely to be effective. Two aspects of this which require particular attention are informal behaviour and the prevailing rationality of decision making. Analysts must assess the importance of informal functioning and the extent to which a proposed system will challenge it. Similarly, they must assess whether the decision making practices that a new system fosters are compatible with the management style of the organization. Many systems with sophisticated decision making models stay idle on managers' desks, while decisions continue to be made intuitively or by following orders from superiors.

The study of organizational feasibility should also examine whether a proposed system affects the integrity of the organization's functioning. All institutions have developed security mechanisms against intended fraudulent or malicious actions and unintended mistakes. Most such mechanisms are embedded in the organization's information systems, such as for example, regular control procedures by a supervisor, the need for authorization of certain decisions, or cross-checking the results of calculations before issuing payment orders higher than a certain amount. The change to a new information system may eliminate some necessary security procedures or it may introduce altogether new risks. For example, since the late 1980s computer viruses and hacking have posed a significant security threat to which organizations must respond. Open network based information systems tend to leave organizations particularly vulnerable to this risk. Achieving appropriate levels of security depends partly on technical features, such as a system's architecture, encryption, passwords, and the safety checks built into software, but more importantly on organizational characteristics such as work procedures and the assignment of responsibilities among employees. The various options with regard to security and integrity, their feasibility and their costs, should be clearly stated at this stage because they will have to be an inseparable feature of any new system.

Social feasibility

Social feasibility refers to the acceptance of changes in work conditions, power structure and relations by those who will work within a system. This will generally concern an organization's own employees but may also need to consider other groups affected, such as its customers. If information system changes are unwelcome to employees and customers then the new system is very likely to fail. The introduction of new technology and organizational changes can have profound effects on the work conditions for employees. Information technology has the potential for eliminating hazardous, tedious and routine work; unfortunately it often causes opposite effects. At the most basic level, there are still unresolved questions regarding health risks in connection with computers. Miscarriages, eyesight problems, and repetitive strain injury have on occasions been related to computer use. On the other hand, the introduction of a new computer system can be taken as an opportunity for general improvement in an office, such as rearrangements of furniture, improvement of lighting or the introduction of flexitime.

Computerization projects often cause fears of work specialization where employees are restricted to the execution of meaningless and trivial operations. They may threaten to reduce the scope of human communication within work groups and to destroy socially fulfilling and organizationally effective informal aspects of work. Changes to work opportunities and work conditions may threaten the career development prospects of employees. They may also cause shifts of power in the organization, threatening to weaken the position of certain groups while disproportionally favouring others. Indeed, many information systems projects aiming at utilizing computers to achieve efficiency gains have led to undesirable work environments, which render the change counter-productive. It has to be remembered that information systems do not automate information handling; effective performance by people remains a crucial productivity factor. Many organizations do recognize information systems projects as opportunities to improve work conditions and career opportunities, and encourage employees to develop their personal skills and talents. Whatever the case, the feasibility study must assess the social changes that a proposed information system will entail and the likely impact of these changes on overall organizational effectiveness.

Another equally important aspect is the likely changes in the relations between the organization and its customers. Information systems projects will often concern aspects of communication with people beyond the organization's boundaries, such as the taking of orders, offering of new services, or new electronic means for the delivery of existing services. A feasibility study must check whether those that an organization interacts with will indeed approve of and accommodate the proposed changes. Different groups may respond in different ways to innovative services from the organizations they deal with. For example, while many consider direct debit and credit through a bank account as an efficient way for regular financial transactions, some social groups, such as pensioners, find these practices alienating, feeling that they lose control of their financial affairs.

Economic feasibility

Finally, the study of economic feasibility examines whether a proposed information system is financially affordable and if it is going to lead to economic benefits. Most information systems projects are expected to yield economic benefits by improving business performance or reducing costs, but in developing them organizations incur costs and risks. For an investment in an information system project to be justifiable, the overall economic value of the new information system needs to be positive. Most companies scrutinize proposals for new investments by applying some kind of cost-benefit analysis or investment appraisal techniques. For each alternative system proposal, they estimate the financial benefits that are expected to be accrued during the system's life time, and subtract its development and operations costs. Alternative proposals are then compared and ranked by ordering the results of the cost-benefit analysis. However, the expected costs and benefits of information systems projects are notoriously difficult to estimate as we explain below, and more sophisticated ways are needed to judge the economic value of information systems.

In an organization which already has some computer infrastructure, an estimate of the cost of an information system development project will involve judgement of the extent to which the new system will use existing resources for development and operations. This will include consideration of the extent to which it will share administrative and staff resources with other projects, as well as estimates of the additional costs for hardware and software purchase. Estimates of risks need to involve judgements on the losses that an organization may suffer in the event that the transition to the new system causes problems to its normal functioning, and the possible ways in which a new system may fail.

Information systems projects may aim at various benefits, some of them being straightforward efficiency and cost displacement gains, which are quite easily quantifiable. Others are more elusive, such as the gains expected to be made from improvements in decision making or advantage over market-place competitors. In general, benefits can be classified into three types: monetary tangible, non-monetary tangible, and intangible. *Monetary tangible benefits* can easily be measured in monetary terms, for example, savings from staff reduction. *Non-monetary tangible benefits* are those benefits which, although not directly expressed in monetary values, are possible to convert to monetary terms; for example the gains expected from speedier processing of orders and dispatch of invoices. *Intangible benefits* are those which are expressed as improvements in effectiveness rather than efficiency; for example, improvement in the quality of management from the use of a decision support system.

Over the years, there has been a shift in the main objectives of information system projects from achieving tangible efficiency benefits, to aiming at improvements in business performance of a broader and more intangible character. Organizations may now explore a variety of possible ways to gain value from improving their information handling procedures, and yet many such improvements are hard to quantify. Such information systems projects might include objectives such as competitive advantage, management information support, competitive response or providing a flexible information systems infrastructure.

Consider, for example, a retailing company which examines the feasibility of introducing electronic funds transfer at the point of sale, with bar-code readers at the checkouts of its stores. The company will have to assess a number of potential benefits: better inventory control will bring savings in stock holding, money invested in inventory, and possibly personnel. These are perhaps quantifiable by the managers of the retail outlets. It may also be expected that EFTPOS will reduce the number of special deliveries and negative responses to customers' requests, and such gains may be estimated by experienced and perceptive managers. In addition, it may further be expected that the new system will improve goodwill from customers and suppliers, or may establish a technological infrastructure, in the hope of achieving some competitive advantage, or to pave the way to other desirable applications such as electronic data interchange (EDI). This last category of benefits, although perhaps one of the major objectives for the project, will be far harder to quantify in a single monetary value.

As information systems have become more ambitious, aiming less at increasing the efficiency of operations in back offices, and more at achieving other objectives for organizations, feasibility estimation techniques which require quantification of costs, risks and benefits in monetary terms have become inadequate to assess the value of information systems. Such techniques tend to favour cost-reduction projects and may exclude vital projects for the development of infrastructure or innovation. On the other hand, frustration with the limited capability of these traditional techniques for investment appraisal has led some organizations to invest substantial resources in information technology without examining the economic feasibility of their plans. Unfortunately, there is now substantial evidence that increasing investment in information technology does not necessarily improve an organization's performance [Strassmann, 1990]. This does not however mean that we should abandon the task of assessing the economic value of proposed information systems. On the contrary, we need to approach this task in a more sophisticated way.

Enhanced cost benefit analysis for information systems projects

For these reasons, the study of the economic feasibility of proposed information systems projects needs to take a multi-phase approach: .

Calculation of investment accounting measures for tangible benefits. To begin with, the analyst must make an effort to determine the costs of the development and implementation of the proposed systems, and the expected tangible benefits. These costs and benefits can then be charted for the year in which they are anticipated, to ensure that funds will be available at the time needed. The moment in time at which accumulated benefits will exceed accumulated costs establishes the point when the investment on the new information system will break even and will start yielding a return.

It is useful to produce several accounting measures describing the financial performance of an investment; the most frequently used ones are the *return on investment*, the ratio of the average net income of a project divided by the investment in the project, and the *net present value*, the benefit that a project is expected to yield, expressed in current money value. The calculation of such measures requires considerable expertise in accounting techniques which involve a number of judgements and information systems analysts need to work with business finance experts for this task.

Adjustment of the above measures. After quantification of non-monetary tangible benefits and risks, adjustments need to be made [Parker *et al.*, 1988]. This involves the assessment of several categories of possible benefits and risks, such as the effects of a project on the functioning of various parts of the organization, and the effects of restructuring employees' jobs. It also involves the evaluation of innovation risks, for those projects that attempt novel IT applications. The analyst can use several techniques from economic theory for analyzing and quantifying such effects in monetary terms; value linking, value acceleration and value restructuring. Estimates of this category of benefits and risks can then be used to adjust the simple calculation of return on investment produced in the first step.

Qualitative assessment of intangible benefits and risks. This involves an analysis of those economic benefits and risks which, although not possible to measure, may override decisions based on the numerical results of accounting estimates of investment value. For example, it may have to be established how a proposed project is going to contribute to corporate strategic goals, whether and how it will provide an advantage in the market-place, what contribution it is going to make to management activities, or how serious are the risks of losing market share from not undertaking a project or not introducing applications similar to those of competitors.

The decision as to which of a set of proposed information systems is better in economic terms is not, therefore, a simple matter of measuring and ranking financial values. Different measures will usually produce different rankings. One project may yield a higher return on investment than another, but may involve a longer payback period and (subjectively assessed) higher risks. A proposed information system may hardly appear from the accounting measures to generate revenue at all, although the assessment report on its value may suggest that it is crucial for staying in business in the long run. Instead of trying to resolve the question of economic feasibility by providing an indisputable numerical ordering of alternative proposals, the feasibility study report must provide various relevant indicators as well as explanatory analysis of potential short-term and long-term gains and losses which are not measurable.

Limits to the feasibility study

The feasibility study should provide information on the viability of the systems that are proposed to meet certain requirements. To that end, it scrutinizes how well each proposed route for the project fits within the current technological, legal, organizational, social and economic conditions. However, as the discussion of such aspects of feasibility in this chapter suggests, a feasibility study also involves a degree of forecasting of future trends and changes. The analyst needs to examine the vulnerability of proposed systems to future changes in the organization and its environment. The expected life of an information system depends on the pace of change in its environment. In most cases it is possible to design a certain degree of flexibility and adaptability into a system to cope with future changes, but flexibility comes at a cost.

Prediction of future trends and changes is not easy. In environments with a high degree of uncertainty it may be better to plan for a system with a relatively short life-span. However, the analyst may be able to increase the life span of a system by anticipating future changes such as:

- technological trends;
- changes in legal and regulatory requirements;
- trends in the industry within which the organization operates;
- changes in the broader economic environment;
- changes in attitudes, expectations, tastes, or climates of opinion;
- changes of structure and style of management within the organization.

To make these predictions the analyst may need to consult several experts both within the organization and outside it. It must be clear by now that the decision on an information systems project inevitably involves a great deal of risk and subjective judgement. The objective of the feasibility study is to provide relevant information to guide the management and the employees of the organization to avoid costly mistakes and form realistic expectations.

Exercises and discussion issues

1. You have been asked to examine the information requirements for the following systems:

    A system to produce and maintain the timetables for students' classes, lecturers' teaching hours, and lecture room occupation in a higher education college.

    A system to keep data on a bank's customers and to assist local branch managers in making decisions about loans.

    A system for making reservations at the hotels and boarding houses of a tourist resort.

    In each case consider what methods you could employ for your analysis of information requirements.

2. A hospital is considering the development of a computerized information system to help manage its ambulance service. Outline some of the possible configurations to do so and examine their technical, organizational, social and economic feasibility.

    There are several groups directly interested in the new system: the health authority administration that is going to fund the project; the hospital management who are keen to improve the services of the hospital, but also to demonstrate efficiency; the ambulance service employees; the local community who need to secure ambulance services both for emergencies; and for the chronically ill who require regular attendance at the hospital.

    Open a discussion about the different concerns of these groups and suggest what information the feasibility study needs to supply in order to address them.

3. The managing director of a medium-sized chain of high street travel agencies is concerned that the introduction of new computer based systems into these offices will lead to his staff gaining new skills. He believes that the medium-term result will be that they will leave their jobs for better paid positions with rival companies. On the other hand failure to introduce new systems will leave his company offering a poorer and poorer service compared to their rivals.

    Discuss the attitude of the managing director. Is his fear justified?

References

Davis, G.B. (1982) 'Strategies for Information Requirements Determination',
    IBM Systems Journal, Vol. 21, No 1, pp. 4-30.
Edwards, C. & Savage, N. (1986) *Information Technology and the Law*, (2nd
    edition), Macmillan, Basingstoke.
Parker, M., Benson, R. & Trainor, E. (1988) *Information Economics – Linking
    Business Performance to Information Technology*, Prentice Hall,
    Englewood Cliffs.
Strassmann, P. (1990) *The Business Value of Computers – An executive's guide*,
    Information Economics Press, Connecticut.
Wilson, B., (1990) *Systems: Concepts, Methodologies and Applications*, (2nd
    edition), J. Wiley, Chichester.

Further reading

Several books on information systems cover the beginnings of information
systems development projects, although few of them treat the subject extensively. Relevant material is contained in the following.

Ahituv, N., & Neumann, S. (1990) *Principles of Information Systems for
    Management*, (3rd edition), W.C. Brown, Dubuque, Iowa.
Davis, G.B. & Olson, M.H. (1984) *Management Information Systems:
    Conceptual Foundation, Structure, and Development*, McGraw-Hill, New
    York.

Techniques for estimating the economic feasibility of information system
changes are not usually contained in information systems texts, one has to
search the literature of business economics. An exception is the old classic by
Gildersleeve. The text by Parker *et al.* referenced above is also recommended.

Gildersleeve, T.R. (1978) *Successful Data Processing Systems Analysis*,
    Prentice Hall, Englewood Cliffs.

Detailed description of a future analysis method is contained in:

Land, F.F., Mumford, E. & Hawgood, J. (1980) 'Training the Systems Analysts
    of the 1980s: Four analytical procedures to assist the design process', in
    Lucas, H.C. *et al.*, *The Information Systems Environment*, North-Holland,
    Amsterdam.

In recent years the software engineering community has developed an increased interest in issues of requirements, developing a distinct area of requirements engineering. The following two texts provide an introduction to this perspective.

Macaulay, L.A. (1996) *Requirements Engineering*, Springer Verlag, London.

Sommerville, I. & Sawyer, P. (1997*) Requirements Engineering: A Good Practice Guide*, J. Wiley, Chichester.

4 Construction of an information system

- *The analysis task*
- *Case study: South East Employment*
- *Analysis approaches*
- *Structured systems analysis*
- *Object oriented analysis*
- *Systems design and programming*

The aspects of the development process described in the previous chapters are intended to arrive at a clear understanding of what system, if any, is to be built. This understanding is established in terms of the requirements for a new system, and the 'business case' for going ahead with development. The next set of tasks is to undertake detailed analysis and design, to establish the revised organizational arrangements required, and to build the technical systems needed. A number of different approaches may be taken to the construction of the various parts of information systems. However, it is usually possible to distinguish the basic tasks of analysis, design, and programming. In this chapter we discuss these tasks, and present some of the most commonly used methods.

Systems analysis aims at achieving understanding in 'logical' terms of the human activities, events and actions, information transformation processes and data resources relevant to the environment of a new system. This is achieved, by describing in some detail the kind of processes and data that a system will deal with, and the relations among them. Doing this in logical terms means that, rather than naming the 'physical' components, such as documents, people, offices, machines, or software items, we seek to present a higher level view that is independent of particular physical implementations. This latter task is done at the subsequent design stages or in a separate hardware study.

Analysis is about building a model of the proposed system, operating within its environment. From this model a specification can be derived which will contain information about what the new system is intended to do and how it should operate. It is then the task of the system's designer to consider how each component will be constructed, to specify exact data file or database structures, the paper forms and screens to be used for data capture, the computer programs, the hardware and communications configurations, and the operational details of the security procedures.

The distinction between analysis and design is well made by Rubin and Goldberg [1992]:

Analysis is the study and modelling of a given problem domain, within the context of stated goals and objectives. It focuses on *what* a system is supposed to do, rather than *how* it is supposed to do it (which we consider the design aspect). In addition, it must embody the rule of traceability (*why*) which justifies the existence of a given result by tying it back to the stated goals and objectives. The components of the problem domain can be described as anything that end-users of the system, both human and machines, view as part of the problem context. This may include technical issues, if the users view such issues as part of the problem.

As their last sentence indicates, the distinction between analysis and design is easy to make on paper, but not always so easy in practice. It is very tempting to get down to detail as soon as possible, and to start defining elements of the new system. Equally, it may be that important issues are ignored, but come to haunt us later on. Experience seems to teach us that a more structured and progressive approach will yield better results – results with fewer errors, less need for rework and a more coherent and maintainable system at the end. By first studying what the new system should do and then how it should do it – in other words by separating consideration of the logical and the physical specifications – a new system is more likely to match the requirements that it is intended to meet, and to survive longer. In this way, a new system should be rooted in a firm understanding of the nature of the information handling requirements it sets out to meet, rather than being constrained at the outset by premature decisions on how some parts of it will operate.

The analysis task

At this stage, and in broad terms, we know what system we aim to develop. A problematic situation has been explored, information requirements have been collected and assessed, and certain routes for improvement have been evaluated, and one direction has been selected. The main aim of systems analysis is now to discover, and in the end specify, what data the new system will deal with, what kind of changes (transformations) this data will undergo through computer or manual processing, what output it will produce, and the procedures that have to be organized to that end. This last aspect, considering in detail the new types of procedures and the new jobs and work roles being created, is referred to here as organizational analysis and needs to be taken alongside a more formal and technical systems analysis.

Taken together, these two streams of analysis aim at producing a detailed description of the functions of the new system, the roles and responsibilities of those who work within it, its boundaries, the data transformations within it, and its interaction with other information systems and elements in the environment in which it operates.

The output from analysis is sometimes spoken of as the functional specification or software requirements specification, but the results of analysis also have to include many more aspects, including detailed proposals for required organizational change and new employee roles, and to specify the required auxiliary systems, such as those for security, back-up and recovery.

Organizational analysis

Analysis for a new information system will almost always involve the reconsideration of existing organizational structures, procedures and employee responsibilities. The analyst has to investigate what changes are needed in the way tasks are allocated within the organization, the way they are differentiated by horizontal and vertical levels, and the way they are co-ordinated and controlled. The following aspects of organization need to be considered:

- *The way jobs are broken down as specializations.* In many organizations, over-specialization has deprived employees of a context or basis for responsibility in their work. A new information system may offer opportunities to redesign the allocation of tasks in individual's jobs and improve the overall results.

- *The way jobs are grouped together and managed in units.* There may be opportunities for integrating hitherto separate functions or the opposite, if required, to split dysfunctionally linked procedures. For example, new communication technologies provide a great deal of new scope for linking up geographically separated units and thereby redistributing decision making in organizations consisting of several sites.

- *The way control and co-ordination are maintained.* Current structures of management and control may have to change with a new system if it alters the distribution of information and decision-making authority. In general, over the years the implementation of computer-based information systems has led organizations to eliminate middle level supervisory tasks and therefore to adopt a flatter structure.

- *The way information is shared and exploited and issues of ownership.* A common goal of a new system is to improve information sharing and to allow the organization to exploit the knowledge of its various members. Such aims raise subtle questions of who owns information, who can control its use, and the incentives to share.

- *The way overall growth and development of the organization is supported.* The new information system may be able to contribute to better overall steering of the organization. To that end, the analyst should consider not just the particular task at hand, but also aligning this development with the overall aims and goals of the organization.

While worrying about the shape and form of an organization is perhaps the job of senior managers and management consultants, the information systems analyst may need to collaborate with such people in the redesign of an organization's structure and work procedures, or at very least reflect goals set by others.

Land, Mumford and Hawgood [1980] describe a method that systems analysts can apply to identify those organizational aspects that a proposed information system might aim at improving. They suggest modelling the part of the organization under consideration as interlinked units of operations. A unit of operations being a set of tasks which logically fit together and requires to be performed as a whole. In modern parlance, this might be termed a 'business process'. After identifying the logical units of operations, the analyst then goes on to identify the following categories of activities, and the employee roles and skills they require, according to the 'Viable Systems Model' suggested by Stafford Beer [1972]:

- operational activities, within each unit of operations;
- co-ordination activities, between units of operations;
- control activities, monitoring the performance of the whole set of units of operations according to the organization's objectives;
- development activities, aiming at securing long-term survival and growth of the organization.

Land *et al.* suggest the use of this model to examine which areas of the current organizational arrangements are weak and tend to deviate from a desired standard of performance. Often, such weaknesses occur in the interface *between* unit operations and this requires redesign of co-ordination tasks, or possibly the combination of units. Such analysis may also lead to decisions on how to redistribute responsibilities for various activities, decision making capacity, and required information.

This method does, however, convey a rather limited approach to organizational change. It is reactive to the problems of existing arrangements. The development of a new information system may provide opportunities for radically new ways of structuring an organization by utilizing new technologies. It might be foolish not to consider such possibilities explicitly, or to leave organizational forms to emerge as a random consequence of adopting new technologies. Information systems analysts therefore need to collaborate with business management to work out parallel plans for feasible and desirable organizational changes enabled by information technology based systems. This perspective is reflected in its own way both in the discussion of SSM in chapter 2 and in the approach of business process reengineering, discussed in chapter 11.

Case study: South East Employment

South East Employment is a recruitment agency that specializes in industrial and secretarial recruitment. It has expanded in recent years and has sought to offer an increased variety of services. At the time of the study the company was already fairly large, with thirty-four branches spread across South East England. The company operated in a largely decentralized manner through branch offices. Each branch office was headed by a branch manager, while the company as a whole was headed by its owner. Operating procedures in the company were fairly standardized, allowing the branch managers adequate authority to run their branches but expecting fairly similar structures to be adopted in each branch and data of a common type to be reported from each branch. Accounting was done centrally in the head office.

Branch managers were responsible for the operation of their branches. Working with them were from 3 to 8 consultants, a clerical assistant, and a location administrator. The consultants dealt with client companies – called simply 'clients' in the agency's jargon – and applicants for employment – called simply 'applicants' – trying to meet their requirements and match personnel to job vacancies. There were two types of consultants: recruitment consultants, dealing with recruitment of permanent personnel; and temporary controllers, dealing with placements of temporary personnel. The clerical assistant did mainly routine work, such as filling out time-sheets and compiling wages figures for the temporary personnel placed by the office. The location administrator did mainly typing jobs, such as preparing an applicant's *curriculum vitae* to be sent to clients, or typing reference letters.

The agency had decided to take actions to improve the way it handled the task of temporary personnel placement. This business area was growing rapidly, and the agency anticipated and planned to increase considerably the volume of temporary placement business in the following two years. Yet, most branch managers felt that information handling for temporary placement was inefficient, creating tension within the branches as well as contributing to a growing reputation for poor service. They considered the improvement of information handling to be a necessary prerequisite for the planned expansion.

Each branch had one or two word processors for typing letters, but all data on clients, applicants, and the employment of temporary personnel was kept on paper files and was processed manually. South East Employment tried to build the reputation of a company with a personal touch when dealing with clients, committed to finding 'the right people for the right job'. A great deal of the business was done through informal communication between consultants and clients or applicants. However, following a feasibility study, it was believed that a computer-based system storing information on applicants and clients, and employment details on the currently located temporary personnel would facilitate the tasks of the branches. To be safe, it was decided to develop the new system experimentally, in one branch only. In this way it would be possible to monitor benefits and to sort out difficulties before extending use of the system to other branches.

The analyst who was hired did a detailed study of the operations for the temporary recruitment service in the selected office and discovered the following:

Every morning the temporary controllers went through the client file, collecting relevant information and telephoning clients to canvass for business. If a client responded by saying that they needed temporary staff, the controller checked through the file containing details of applicants, trying to find those available who possessed the skills required by the client. She then phoned them, asking if they were interested in working for the day, week or the entire length of the booking, and arranged a placement if there was an agreement. The controller also compiled reports on temporary staff, based on feedback inform-ation received from clients.

At the end of the week temporary personnel returned their time-sheets to the branch office, signed by the client company, collected another time-sheet for the coming week of their booking and collected their previous week's pay. All the submitted time-sheets were despatched on Saturday mornings by courier to the accounts department at the head office, and the preparation of wages started the following Monday. In this way, temporary personnel were paid on Fridays, one week in arrears.

There was no formal method of documenting the temporary personnel's performance in the various placements made by the agency. The reports received were usually informal comments received over the telephone, and were not systematically recorded. Similarly, information about client contact persons, special company policies, special applicant skills and requirements were often unrecorded. The controllers managed to develop very good knowledge of regular clients and applicants. However, there were often periods of time pressure, confusion and frustration. The task of going through the clients' file and the applicants' file while canvassing was a tedious process and involved skilful negotiating with applicants. At the same time as canvassing and trying to satisfy client's requirements, the controllers also had to service applicants waiting in the branch office for work.

On Fridays, when a large number of temporary personnel came to the office at the same time to collect wages and time-sheets, the place was in chaos, with the controllers having to do three different tasks at the same time. The rest of the staff helped out; however, their involvement was very limited because only the controller had full knowledge of requirements and arrangements. As a result, the controllers felt a great deal of pressure and responsibility, while the clerical assistant and the administrator were frustrated by being restricted to clerical support tasks, unable to participate in serving applicants, and with no opportunities to develop the necessary skills to undertake more responsible functions in the office.

Not surprisingly, the branch manager felt that the present information handling arrangements did not allow her to use the branch's staff effectively. She expected the new information system to allow for a more flexible deployment of staff. Thus, in parallel with designing the computer-based information system the analyst had to design new organizational procedures.

The analyst distinguished three main units of operation related to the business of temporary personnel placements:

- registration and maintenance of applicants' files;
- canvassing clients, negotiation with applicants and matching of applicants to clients' jobs;
- administration of payments.

Clearly, specialization along the lines of these three units needed to be avoided if the offices were to retain the ability to match successfully clients' requirements with applicants' skills and aspirations. All staff needed to communicate with both clients and applicants, and thereby acquire a good understanding of applicants' details; it would be dysfunctional to separate the task of gathering information on applicants from the task of negotiating possible placements with them. Collection of time-sheets for payment might be seen as a separate job with specialised staff. However, the collection of time-sheets on Fridays was more than a simple administrative procedure. It provided an important contact with applicants and formed a vital information link. The branch manager felt strongly that the ability of her staff to communicate face-to-face with the applicants they served, to understand their aspirations, talents and complaints needed to be retained. Therefore, the analyst agreed with the office staff to propose to the central management of the company the following three recommendations.

- All members of staff engaged in temporary placement operations should develop the mix of skills necessary to carry out all the tasks of the three units of operations. To begin with, the current clerical assistant and the administrator should gradually undertake responsibilities for placements. If more staff were hired later, as was anticipated, then they should be trained to carry out the operations of all three units.

• . Work would be divided on the basis of groups of clients. Each member of staff would be responsible for a number of clients but would draw from the same general 'pool' of applicants, and all would contribute to the management of information on applicants: they would deal with registration of new applicants according to availability of time; they would update applicants' files with information on performance in the various placements they arranged; and they would deal with payment claims. In this way, it was expected, all staff would develop the necessary understanding of applicants' skills and qualities to be able to decide on appropriate placements for the clients they served.

• A new computer-based information system would need to facilitate this work structure, providing a common formal information basis and appropriate structures for information utilization and maintenance. It also would need to support appropriate links between informal information channels such as telephone conversations, and formal information channels, such as registration forms.

Analysis approaches

There are many different ways to undertake the technical aspects of the systems analysis task and to present the logical specification of a proposed new system. Some systems analysis methods put more emphasis on the study of the data that the system will handle, others focus primarily on the investigation of the processes to be applied to the data, while yet others start by considering the events which initiate decision processes and data transformations. Such differences of methods are significant because they direct attention to different aspects of a system, and they are discussed further in comparative terms in part II of the book. However, all practical analysis methods combine techniques for studying and specifying both the data and the processes of a new system.

This chapter describes some of the most commonly used techniques, presenting two distinct approaches. First analysis is presented using an adaptation of DeMarco's structured systems analysis method [DeMarco, 1978], with some additions of data modelling. The DeMarco method is chosen as a basis to demonstrate the systems analysis tasks because it is simple and widely applicable. It is nearly 15 years since DeMarco presented this method and tools, and in the meantime many elaborations of the methods have been proposed and used, and structured systems analysis should be seen as a family of methods which include, for example, SSADM and Yourdon Structured Analysis [Downs et al., 1992; Yourdon, 1989]. When other methods within the family are encountered it will be apparent that the particular format of the diagrams and tools used varies, but the essential approach is consistent.

The second approach presented here, object oriented analysis, is of more recent origin. The version we use is based on Coad and Yourdon [1991]. This version of object oriented analysis is chosen, not so much because it is very widely used and it may well not scale-up to large projects, but because it presents the object oriented approach in a clear and simple manner appropriate to a text book such as this. Industrial users of object oriented approaches, particularly those who take a more software engineering approach, may well use more sophisticated object oriented analysis approaches.

Structured Systems Analysis

Data Flow Diagrams (DFD)

The starting point for the DeMarco method is the study of the way data travels and is transformed within an information system. The basic tool to describe this is the *Data Flow Diagram* (DFD) which describes in a pictorial way how data flow among processes, files, and external data sources or data recipients. To be able to 'read' DFDs, all one needs to know is the following set of definitions of the elements and conventions for the symbols used to depict them [DeMarco, 1978]:

- data flow is 'a pipeline through which packets of information of known composition flow', and it is represented with a vector;
- process is 'a transformation of incoming data flow(s) into outgoing data flow(s)', and is represented with a circle ('bubble');
- file or data store is 'a temporary repository of data', and is represented with two parallel lines;
- data source or sink is 'a person or organization, lying outside the context of a system, that is a net originator or receiver of system data', and is represented by a rectangular box.

Each element on a DFD must have a clear meaningful and unique name so that the diagram makes a self-explanatory picture. Indeed, the most valuable property of DFDs is the simplicity with which they can be drawn and read. This makes them a useful means for communication between systems analysts and others involved in the development process. For most systems, analysis relies heavily on the ability of various parties to contribute information about existing procedures and desirable changes, to comment and correct the systems descriptions that the analysts produce, or to make suggestions of features that they want the new system to have. DFDs, although they are primarily tools for the analysts, can be easily understood and can form the basis for such communications. For example, it should be fairly easy to understand the DFD in figure 4.1 which describes the data flow in the process of recruiting and dealing with temporary staff in an office of South East Employment.

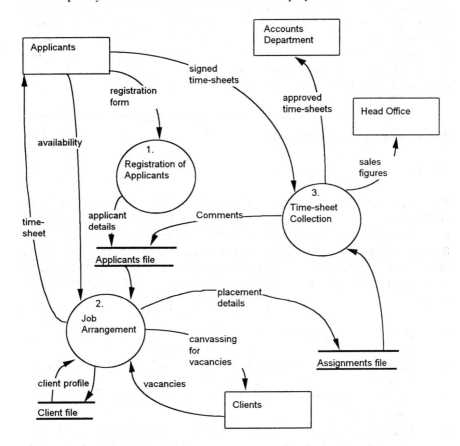

Figure 4.1 DFD for temporary staff recruitment in South East Employment

To draw a DFD the analyst should follow the following guidelines:

- identify all net input and output data flows;
- fill in the DFD body by concentrating on data flows first, and then putting bubbles at the points where they are to undergo some transformation;
- label data flows with meaningful names;
- label bubbles to indicate the action taken to transform the in-coming data flows to the out-going ones.

It must be noted that basic DFDs do not depict flow of control, that is decisions responsible for the transformation of data, and a data flow diagram is not the same as a conventional flow chart. Information on control and decision making will be found in the transform descriptions or minispecs that are described below.

In systems of any real significance a single DFD will soon become too big to handle; size defies simplicity and it becomes difficult to follow the data flows and cumbersome to make changes. Instead of drawing one large flat diagram, the analyst should draw a number of small ones, structured as a set of levelled DFDs. As a rule of thumb, no more than 7 to 9 bubbles should be allowed on any one diagram if they are to remain legible and meaningful. The top level, called a context diagram', does not contain details but delineates the whole domain of study with one bubble, assigned a name which indicates the function of the system, and the overall input and output data flows. The context diagram for the data flows in the South East employment is as shown in figure 4.2.

This is then decomposed into a 'child' DFD, as already seen in figure 4.1 above, containing a few bubbles and decomposed data flows corresponding to the data flows appearing on the context diagram. The decomposition process continues by adding more detailed lower (child) levels for each bubble (parent), until the analyst judges that an adequate degree of detail for the purposes of the analysis has been reached. For example, the process 'job arrangement' can be further decomposed as in Figure 4.3.

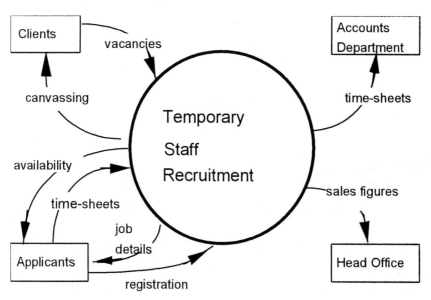

Figure 4.2 Context diagram for temporary staff recruitment in South East Employment.

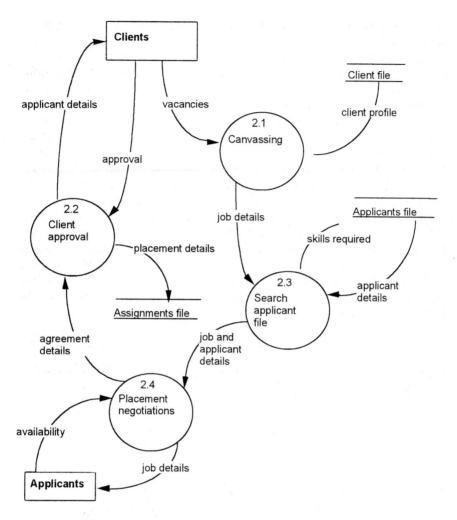

Figure 4.3 DFD for the process 'Job Arrangement'.

The processes contained in this lowest level are called 'functional primitives'. The order of the levelled DFDs is followed by numbering bubbles in a way which identifies their origins on parent diagrams. This structured set of DFDs helps to concentrate on detailed descriptions of parts of the system, while it also provides the ability to perceive the whole system and the relations of its parts with each other.

This use of levelled sets of DFDs is an example of the use of top-down functional decomposition in the development process. That is, the analysis starts with a high level description of the system, and then proceeds to break this up into separate and more or less independent sub-units that undertake specific functions. The procedure continues until it is judged unnecessary to break down the tasks any further. This is a powerful approach of 'divide and conquer', it also ensures that the analyst starts the job with a clear view of the whole system, and not with undue concentration on one particular part.

Data analysis

In the period since DeMarco wrote his seminal work there has emerged another influential perspective on the systems analysis task, data modelling, and this now comprises a part of most of the structured methodologies that have build upon DeMarco's approach [Yourdon, 1989; Downs *et al.*, 1992]. This move is reinforced by the widespread uptake of database technology that requires that data storage be addressed as a whole, rather than on an application-by-application and file-by-file basis.

While the data flow diagram seeks to capture how information passes through a system, and what is done in the various processing stages, it does not concentrate on the actual detail of the data itself or on the overall coherence of data. It is important to remember that data stores in the DFDs are described as *temporary*, yet we know that information systems must have permanent resources of data. Therefore a deeper analysis of the data to be used and processed by a system should be undertaken. This is known as data analysis or logical data modelling [Bowers, 1988; Flynn & Frangos Dias, 1996]. The intention in data analysis is to provide a clear picture of the relevant part of the world within which an information system will operate and about which it needs to hold data. This picture will show the real world items or objects which the information system needs to deal with and how they are related one to another. Such a description is useful in its own right as a map of the world into which a system will fit, and can also become the starting point for the design of an actual database.

The basis for the data analysis task is the development of an entity-relationship model (E-R model) of the domain under study. The purpose is to identify and structure all the items that the systems will need to hold data about, and to describe it in a *logical* manner that is independent of any particular technical means of storage. Data analysis also has to meet the general requirement that the models and descriptions produced should be understandable by all parties involved, both analysts and those they work with.

In data analysis the starting point is to identify and name the main classes of item about which information will be stored – these are the *entities*. In this sense the word entity is used to refer to a class of items, not an individual item. The analyst also has to understand how the various entities are related to each other – the *relationships*. Just as with entities, relationships should be given meaningful names. The usual way of approaching this task is to draw an entity relationship diagram (E-R diagram) such as that shown in figure 4.4.

This diagram is made up of rounded boxes representing entities and lines linking them representing relationships. The crow's feet on the lines indicate the *degree* of the relationships, that is *1:1* a plain line, *1:n* (*n* standing for many) with the many end of the relationship represented by the crow's feet, or *m:n* (many to many) with crow's feet at each end. It is also useful to show if a relationship is optional or mandatory, that is whether every occurrence of one entity type must have that relationship with another entity type. A mandatory relationship is shown by a solid line, and an optional one by a dashed line.

Relationships of the *m:n* type should be viewed with suspicion and can pose certain problems in actually building database structures, but at this analysis stage they are allowable in so far as they do describe the real situation. Consider the example of the entities *Client* and *Applicant*. One client may hire many applicants, and one applicant can, over time, work for many clients. In this sense it is correct to describe the data in terms of an *m:n* relationship and as an optional relationship, since we can have clients without applicants and applicants without clients. But it might be worth taking another look. The *m:n* relationship between the two entities can be elaborated into two *1:n* relationships, with a new entity *vacancy* – as shown in the second E-R diagram in figure 4.4.

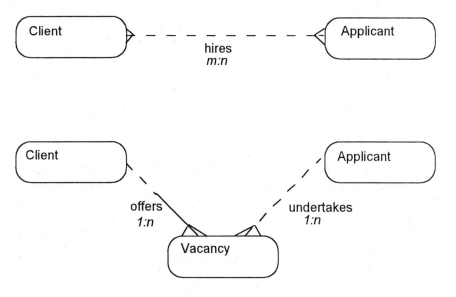

Figure 4.4 Two versions of an entity-relationship diagram showing removal of *m:n* relationship.

In this way the clients and their attributes (name address etc.) can be represented once only, as can applicants and their attributes (name, address, telephone number, tax code etc.), while the vacancy entity represents a particular period of work that is on offer from a client, and which an Applicant may undertake. Every vacancy must have a client, but every client does not necessarily have any vacancies, and hence notice how the optional and mandatory relationships have altered here. The second version will almost certainly be closer to what is required, though it still leaves open the question of whether more than one applicant could work to fill a particular vacancy.

The procedure for developing an entity-relationship data model can be described as follows, though each step will have to be returned to a number of times as further insight is gained.

- define the major data areas addressed by the information system;
- identify and name the entity types;
- identify, name and define the degree of the relationships between entities;
- draw the entity model in diagrammatic form;
- for each entity identify the attributes (data domains) that the information systems needs to accommodate.

The last step, identification of attributes, is important in that it sets out the details of the identified entities that are stored and used in an information system, those that are used in the DFD functional primitives. For example the entity Applicant is identified, but what are the relevant details to store – sex, age, hair colour, height, tax code, typing speed, mother's maiden name? For each of these we need to define the domain from which they are drawn, if we do store height, what are the units used – feet or metres? Of course answers to all such questions depend on the application.

A further step of *normalization* is often then undertaken to refine the data model and ensure that it represents a minimum coherent framework for storing and accessing information [Kent, 1983]. For the purposes of the analysis task normalization is not essential and it may be deferred until the design stage.

Figure 4.5 shows a refined version of the E-R model for South East Employment, but this only represents one version of the relevant entities and their relationships. Once the relevant entities have been established and their relationships described and named then the attributes of each entity can be set down. In this way data analysis sets out to provide a clear overview of the aspects or elements of the world that a system interacts with and will store data about, the detail of those data, and the relationships between these elements. In subsequent stages of development this data model can form the basis for the task of actually establishing data storage structures, be it in paper files or by use of the software of a database management system.

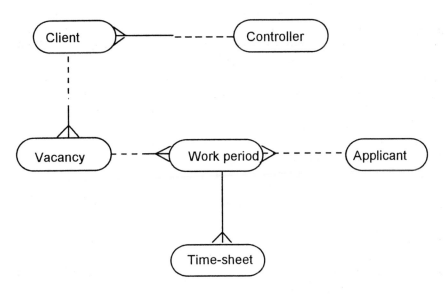

Figure 4.5 Refinement of the E–R model.

Modelling behaviour

So far we have modelled processes, data and data flows. There is one other aspect of a system that the analyst will wish to include in the model, that is the behaviour of the system – how it reacts to events in its environment. In the early structured approaches this behavioural dimension was never formally addressed. However in later versions it has been given greater prominence. At the very least it provides an opportunity to map between the data and process view.

One tool to achieve this is the entity life history, as used in SSADM. This modelling approach takes an entity from the data model and traces out the stages in its life, from 'birth' – entering the system, to 'death' – leaving the system. A tree structure diagram is used, with the birth events on the left, and the death events on the right. Within the 'life' of the entity the various episodes that happen are depicted in terms of 'iterations' – repeated sequences, and choices. Figure 4.6 shows a simple entity life history for the entity Applicant.

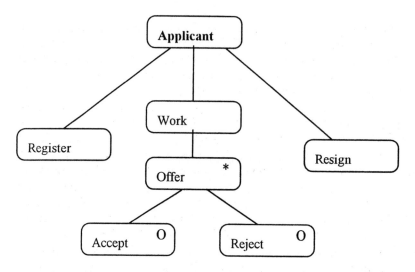

Figure 4.6 Entity Life History.

The * alongside Offer in the diagram signifies a repetition of that part of the life history, thus the period of Work consists of a sequence of Offers. The **O** in Accept and Reject signify that one or the other course is followed. The power of the entity life history is that it allows the analysts to 'tie together' the entities in the data model with the processes in the data flow diagram. In this case we can see that we must have a process to handle registration, resignation, acceptance and rejection of an offer of work. Another way to look at the diagram is to identify four significant events that a person can initiate.

Data dictionary

Taken together, a data model, a set of levelled DFDs, and entity life histories provide a co-ordinated set of tools for the analyst to use in setting down an understanding of how a system operates and the data that it uses. It is of course important that they are co-ordinated and, for example, every data flow and data store in a DFD needs to be composed of data items that are represented in the data model, and the DFD has to indicate how events in the life of entities are handled by the system. The linking of the techniques is made easier by the use of a data dictionary. This stores information about the elements that appear on the DFD, entity life histories and in the data model. DeMarco describes it as 'a repository of data about data', but it is really more than that when it includes processes and event descriptions. Specifically, the data dictionary contains definitions of data flows, data stores, processes, events, entities, attributes and relationships at the most decomposed level. Each entry in the data dictionary begins with the name of an item, defines which of the above categories the item belongs to, and states its synthesis. A data dictionary may contain additional information about the items defined, such as frequency, volume, size, affected users, security requirements and implementation restrictions. DeMarco, however, warns against the practice of loading the data dictionary with too much such comment, because of the risk that this will make the dictionary more difficult to maintain.

Indeed, maintainability is an overall objective of using the structured systems analysis tools. Such is the nature of the systems development process, that changes are certain to be made to the DFDs, data models and data dictionary, or any other model the analyst applies to specify the system under development. It is therefore necessary to have flexible tools, which allow changes to be made easily. It is equally necessary to be able to preserve consistency of the overall system specifications. To preserve consistency, DeMarco suggests that the tools used to model the system should complement each other without containing redundant or duplicated information. To change a feature of the system being modelled the analyst should only need to change those parts that define the elements involved. Comments such as which data flows particular data elements are part of, or which processes particular data flows are produced by, are redundant; this information can be found by looking at the DFDs. While it may be convenient to have additional reminders such as these added into the specification of the system, the problem is that it is too easy to forget to alter such comments when a relevant change to the logic of data flows or data structure is made and then the comments become misleading and the whole becomes inconsistent.

When computer based tools (CASE tools) are introduced to help in structured analysis, as they often are, then the data dictionary becomes central. With computer support not only are the diagrams easier to draw and modify, but the interlinkage of elements of the model can be traced and maintained. A modern CASE tool can offer multiple 'views' of the analysis model, accentuating aspects that are of particular interest or concern. They can even 'impose' standards on the analysts; for example, not allowing a lower level DFD to have more inflows and outflows than its parent bubble.

Specification of information processes

Although DeMarco's approach begins by identifying data flows, it systematically moves towards identifying the processes which alter the data and finally produce the various outputs of the system. Processing itself only needs to be specified in procedural terms at the lowest, most detailed, level of DFDs. Each functional primitive is then described with a mini-specification as the relevant entry in the data dictionary. It must be stressed that the descriptions of processes during systems analysis are different from the specifications of computer programs. They are intended to describe the required actions and decisions without consideration of how they will be implemented, by a computer or a clerk. It is, as DeMarco explains, like stating the policy which governs some actions and decisions, rather than describing the way the policy is implemented.

A number of different techniques can be used to write mini-specifications: structured English, decision tables, decision trees, or flow charts. Structured English produces descriptive text by making use of a limited syntax, consisting only of simple declarative sentences, closed-end decision constructs and closed-end repetition constructs. To avoid ambiguity, the vocabulary is restricted to verbs, objects and qualifiers, conjunctions, such as *IF*, and *WHILE*, and relational attributes such as *EQUAL*, and *AND*. The presentation of the text is structured by following formatting and indentation conventions, which make the text easier to follow as they show the actions and decisions involved in a process.

FOR EACH job details
    WHILE applicants in **Applicants File**
        Read next *applicant details* from **Applicants File**
        IF skills-required MATCH *applicant-skills THEN*
            COPY *applicant-details* to **Possibles**
    END WHILE
    IF records in **Possibles** > 0
        OUTPUT job details
        OUTPUT **Possibles**

Figure 4.7 A mini-specification for the 'search applicant file' process.

A mini-specification in this form is illustrated in figure 4.7. The data dictionary would show that *applicant-skills* is part of *applicant details*. Alternatively, the structures of the mini-specification can be represented on flow charts, by making use of graphical symbols to denote the flow of actions and decisions. Decision tables and decision trees can be used to clarify what action is to be taken when a number of possible actions depend on complicated conditions. They define the relation between a number of possible actions and a set of conditions with logical precision. They prove particularly useful when analysts try to comprehend the logic of complicated action patterns from verbal descriptions which are often incomplete or contradictory.

The steps of structured systems analysis

The analyst will certainly need guidelines as to how to apply these techniques when investigating the required changes to an information system. The following steps are one suggestion, though different projects will demand different weights be given to the various tasks.

- Study the current physical system that the new system is intended to change. Look at the existing information handling arrangements from the viewpoint of data and draw the current physical Data Flow Diagram (DFD).

- Sketch an E-R model of the environment of the current system.

- Derive the logical equivalent of the current physical DFDs. Substitute physical aspects such as specific names of people, offices or documents with names which denote the nature of the data communicated and the processing that takes place. Remove the restrictions from current physical and organizational procedures, while retaining the logic of the data processing that takes place. It does not matter who process data or how, the important thing to show on a logical DFD is what data is circulated, where it is stored and what data transformation takes place.

- Model the new logical system by incorporating in the DFDs of the current system the changes from the feasibility report. Write the data dictionary and the specifications of information processes.

- Refine the E-R model for the new system, developing it to a level of detail at which all key entities are identified and $m:n$ relationships are reduced so far as possible to $1:n$.

- Investigate the boundary of the computer-based system under development and establish the interface between the computer system and the activities of the people in the organization. Consider how the new computer-based system will fit in the organization, and what organizational arrangements are required.

- Identify different options regarding the extent of the computer-based system, select the genre of hardware and reconsider feasibility. Having more detailed information about possible options the four aspects of feasibility must be re-examined in order to confirm that the broad feasibility study results still hold true and in order to make further specific choices.

- Package the structured specification of the selected option. The building of a model of a new system is the direct product of the techniques outlined above. It is a model in the sense that once constructed it can be reviewed, analyzed, reshaped and discussed. When the model has served the purpose of allowing the exploration of system options and the understanding of system operations it will also provide the basis for a specification that can be handed on to systems designers. The structured specification or software specification of the system is a package of DFDs, data models, a data dictionary and mini-specifications, together with a linking commentary.

In this way, the analyst proceeds systematically from modelling the existing information handling procedures as a DFD, to a package of models for data flows, data structures, and information processing specifications for the proposed new system. The procedure outlined above can be seen as a modelling process that moves from the current physical systems, to the current logical, the proposed future logical and finally, in the subsequent systems design stage, the future physical. This sequence has aroused some debate over the years. When most computer systems were replacing and largely replicating existing manual systems it made great sense to put considerable effort into describing the current way of doing things; that indeed would form the basis of the new system. However, if a new system is really new, and does not closely follow existing procedures, it may well be foolish to lavish huge resources on modelling a system that will be totally replaced. Thus some argue, for example Yourdon [1989], that consideration of the current situation should be restricted to the extraction of the essential information required, but not be undertaken in great detail. The main focus of systems analysis is then on modelling the future logical system.

Object oriented analysis

The approach of structured systems analysis described above is based on top-down decomposition. The problem domain is modelled in terms of fairly distinct aspects of process (in the DFD) and data (in the data model). These two are tied together in the data dictionary, but essentially the two streams of analysis go forward independently. This has advantages in that different people may undertake the two streams, and issues of data and process are considered on their own terms. However, there are problems associated with such an approach and object oriented approaches seek to build the model of a new system in such a manner as to keep data and process closely integrated.

In the late 1980s the ideas of object oriented analysis (OOA) arrived out of work in object oriented design to serve programming in object oriented languages. At the same time developments in user interfaces, in particular window based operating systems on microcomputers, also led to the need for a more coherent means of describing systems which closely coupled data and actions. Just as structured analysis grew out of structured programming, so object oriented analysis grew out of object oriented programming.

The OO approach claims to provide a more powerful and coherent set of ideas for managing and modelling complexity in systems. Coad and Yourdon [1991] suggest 7 aspects of complexity that analysis needs to address, and which the OO approach embodies. Remember though that they are evangelists for the approach!

Abstraction – ignoring irrelevant detail, focusing on relevant aspects needed for both procedural and data aspects.

Encapsulation – hiding information/detail that is not pertinent – see also scale.

Inheritance – thinking of specifics in terms of generality.

Association – linking things together to explain particular events or circumstances.

Communication – passing of messages or signals.

Pervading methods of organization – using structures that people can easily comprehend; Objects and Attributes; Wholes and Parts; Classes and Members.

Scale – moving smoothly between a view of the forest and a view of a single tree.

Categories of behaviour – how or why things happen, immediate causation; change over time; similarity of functions

The main modelling element in OOA is the *object* and the *object class*. An object is an individual 'thing', an object class describes the generality of such things. An object class can be seen as an abstraction of a set of real world things – tangible objects (car, boat, plane, time-sheet, invoice, product), but may also represent roles (consultant, customer, reviewer), incidents or activities (election, earthquake), interactions (sales contract), or specifications (orders, recipes). An object class will specify *attributes* that members of the class have; a car has a registration number, a customer an address, a dog a name. But because we want to model dynamic behaviour too, an object class will also have *services* (otherwise known as methods or operations) – procedures that are bound to the object, things the object can do, or stimuli that the object should respond to.

The set of principles that are used to build models around the concept of an object might be summarised as follows:

Identity – an object knows *who it is*, book number 0-333-57726-4, or the third item ordered;

Classification – an object belongs to a class, it knows *what kind of a thing* it is and can inherit the characteristics of the class. For analysis this class level is the primary level; we are interested in clients not a client, books not a book, orders not an order.

Inheritance – there is sharing of attributes and methods among object classes, based on a hierarchical relationship. A passenger vehicle is a kind of motor vehicle and inherits the general characteristics (attributes and services) of any vehicle (a super-type, sub-type relationship);

Polymorphism – the general characteristics and methods of a super-type can be added to or overridden if need be. A passenger vehicle may have particular properties (attributes or services) that are not common to all vehicles;

Encapsulation – as a modelling construct, objects allow a lot of the detail to be hidden inside themselves, and other parts of the model only need to see a carefully defined interface of 'public' attributes (data) and services. The model is then tied together by message streams that flow from the outside world to objects and between objects. Such messages flow to the services of an object.

An OO approach to systems analysis

Coad and Yourdon present OO analysis in terms of five analysis activities, and we can take them in sequence, at least at first. These are:

Finding Class-&-Objects. Their phrase 'Class-&-Object' refers to things expressed as both individual objects and the class that they belong to.

Identifying Structures. These are the hierarchical relationships that allow inheritance to operate.

Identifying Subjects. These represent the main areas which the model covers, and allow navigation through a complex set of structures.

Defining Attributes. Attributes are the items of data that an individual object will hold and remember.

. *Defining Services.* These are the actions that an object can perform, and the events or messages to which it can respond.

If we go through these five activities we should end up with an OO model of our system. The model itself can be seen in slightly different terms – as a set of layers of understanding, from top to bottom. These layers can be taken on their own, or combined to give particular views of the model under development.

Subject layer – the kinds of things we are dealing with.

Class-&-Object layer – these things expressed as individual objects and object classes.

Structure layer – the object classes organized into a hierarchy with inheritance.

Attribute layer – the attributes needed, distributed within the Class-&-Object hierarchy.

Service layer – The messages which allow one object to communicate with another.

We can now apply these ideas to the case of South East Employment and start to build up an OO model of the new system. The first task is to find Class-&-Objects. To do this we can start by looking for nouns in the description; these might well be relevant objects. By convention we name Class-&-Objects in the singular and possible candidates include applicant, client, consultant, time-sheet, vacancy, and work period. Having already done a data model for this example, we have some help in finding objects, and indeed data modelling is similar in this respect to the early stages of building an OO model.

Having found candidate objects, the next task is to place these into some classification structure. To do this we look for general-specific structures – Gen-Spec as in figure 4.8 – and whole-part structures as in figure 4.9. In doing this we also need to distinguish Classes, from Class-&-Objects. For example, in South East Employment we recognize Consultant as a class (a role for employees), but there are no objects (people) of this class; rather if we read the original description of the arrangements in the offices we have two 'sub-classes', Recruitment Consultant and Temporary Controller. This relationship is represented in diagrammatic form in figure 4.7, the Class shown with the single bold outline, and the Class-&-Object with a double outline. What this indicates is that both Temporary Controller and Recruitment Consultant share or inherit some common characteristics from the class Consultant. Since they are both roles for employees this might include attributes such as training received, bonuses earned. It would not however include details such as salary, tax code, home address, or telephone number. These would be naturally attributes of another object Employee. This may seem over complex, but it may be very important to separate out people and the roles they fulfil.

Figure 4.8 shows the three main diagram elements for a Class and Class-&-Object. The top part is where the name is shown, 'Consultant', the middle part is where the attributes of the class are shown, in this case 'Training Status', and the bottom part is for the services.

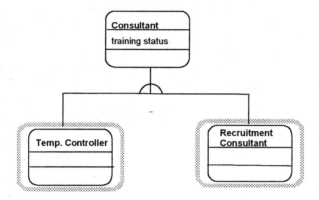

Figure 4.8 An example of a general specific (Gen-Spec) structure

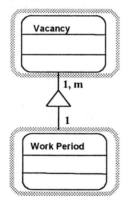

Figure 4.9 An example of a Whole-Part structure

Figure 4.9 shows that a Vacancy consists of 1 or more Work Periods (marked 1,m on the diagram). Similarly the diagram shows that there can only be one Vacancy associated with any Work Period. This may or may not be appropriate, but at least the model makes it explicit.

Taking the analysis on, we may arrive at the version shown in figure 4.10. Here we have identified a number of classes, and placed them into appropriate structures. As you can see, the figure is starting to become quite complex, and real life analysis will almost certainly require more than one page to display the work, and probably a computer tool to keep track of it. In part we address this problem by identifying subjects as shown in the large grey rectangles. Subjects are a mechanism for guiding through a large complex model and from here on one may well deal with one subject at a time. To achieve the Subject breakdown Coad and Yourdon say, 'promote the uppermost Class in each structure to a subject'; 'promote each Class-&-Object not in a structure to a subject', then name the Subjects. This is then the highest level view of the OO model.

The next step is to define attributes – the state information for which each object in a class has its own value. To find the attributes we can ask questions of each identified class such as: how am I described or identified, what do I need to know to be me (behave like me), what do I need to remember over time, and what states can I be in? Each attribute should be an 'atomic' concept not capable of being further broken down. We then position the attributes within the structures, with a preference for attributes being defined higher up and inherited through Gen-Spec structures.

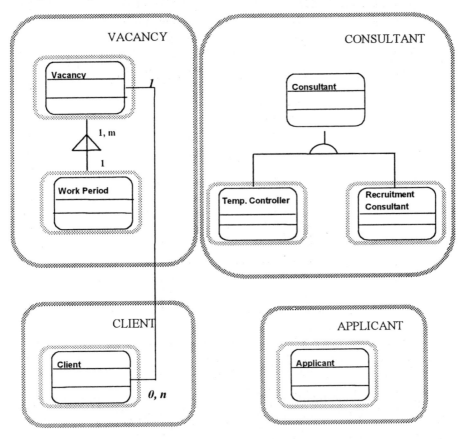

Figure 4.10 The Class-&-Object, Structure and Subject layer

Finally, we define services – specific behaviour that an object is responsible for exhibiting. This will include services to create or delete an object, to allow changes of attributes; to respond to stimulus; to report attribute (or state) information; to calculate and report some value. As noted above, an object will need to be created, that is a new object of a class introduced, similarly objects will need to be deleted. When this is done there is a need to assure that the object is 'allowed' to be created or deleted. For example, we would not want to create a Vacancy if there was not a corresponding Client (in data model terms this is a mandatory relationship). Similarly we should not delete a Client if they have some vacancies. To show this the model shows instance connections, as in figure 4.10, between Client and Vacancy. This shows the degree of the instance relationship between particular objects. The degree of the instance connection is shown by small numbers written on each end of the line. In this case, a Client can be associated with zero or more Vacancy objects, but a Vacancy must be associated with only 1 Client.

More generally services are the means by which one object can request some action from another. Figure 4.11 shows an example of attributes and services for the object Applicant. The two services shown allow the applicant object to report its availability at a given time and to return a time sheet for a given week. Message Connections then constitute the last element of the OO model, showing communication from sender object to receiver object to get some processing done. In this case the availability service would be used by a Temp Controller object, as it interacts with a vacancy object.

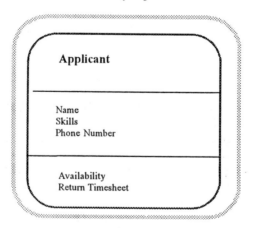

Figure 4.11 The Applicant object with some Attributes and Services

The detail of the algorithm for performing each of the Services needs to be described. To do this we may use the techniques described for minispecs described in the section on structured analysis, including structured English, conventional flow charts or decision tables. Coad and Yourdon propose a particular type of flow chart or Service Chart which recognises the required preconditions for a service to be performed, the trigger that causes it to be performed, and then the actions required to perform the service.

The account of OO analysis given here is necessarily brief and sketchy, and the model developed has been tied quite closely to the structured approach. As such, it could be argued that it fails to fully exploit the power of the OO approach. However, what the above discussion should indicate is that OO analysis can cover similar territory to structured analysis, even if the notations and modelling constructs are rather different. The advantages claimed for the OO approach are based on a number of arguments including being a more natural and comprehensive approach to analysis, and offering greater utility of the analysis output – the model. The resulting model should also have good encapsulation, allowing particular aspects to be isolated and reviewed.

Security analysis

Systems analysis should also include the study of the proposed system's integrity and it should aim to specify the necessary security and integrity aspects that need to be addressed. Security has for long been considered to be a technical matter to be addressed at the design stage by defensive features built into software and hardware and by prescribing good operational practices. Password checks, anti-virus scanning, encryption, control totals, back-up and recovery procedures all contribute to a system's integrity, but they cannot be taken in isolation and in any event only address the technology.

Information systems are hybrids of human and technological components operating in complex organizational settings, and are vulnerable to many diverse threats with equally diverse consequences. Security requirements have to be analyzed and evaluated with care, and actions taken that will in all probability go beyond a few technical arrangements. Fraud for example is often perpetrated by trusted insiders, and no passwords will prevent such acts. Accidents will happen, and no technology is immune to breakdown, and the consequences of such events need to be investigated and their likely impact established. It is important to remember also that tight security measures such as restricted access to information and secrecy may have undesirable effects as they can set barriers between information systems and the organization.

There is little methodological guidance for the integration of analysis with consideration of systems integrity requirements. Baskerville [1988] is a notable exception suggesting including security in the DFD analysis. A more practical and broader focus is given in Angell and Smithson [1991], who provide a list of controls to be considered. A more comprehensive treatment of security issues is given in Caelli *et al.* [1994].

Systems design and programming

Systems design and programming are the next two stages and demand the most technical approach. Together they convert the logical specifications of a new system arrived at in analysis into operational software. Systems design involves the development of detailed technical specifications for programs and database or data files as well as working out detailed security and integrity arrangements, designing new operational procedures and necessary organizational changes to accommodate new computer-based functions. From there, attention proceeds to writing the program code, creating databases or data files, and testing the system as individual parts and as an integrated whole.

Software design is usually seen as forming the core of these activities. It sets out to transform the systems analysis specifications into technical information of sufficient detail for programmers to produce a machine executable system. The fundamental issue in design and programming is how to systematize the transformation of the relevant parts of the systems analysis specifications into a machine executable system and to achieve the following broad qualities:

- *Reliability*. Ideally, the computer system should never fail. The hardware and communication components should not crash and the software should be bug-free.

- *Efficiency*. The software should be built to use the minimum resources and within acceptable times scales.

- *Maintainability*. The system is built with flexibility and generality. The system must be adaptable to meet changing requirements over time.

- *Usability*. The system must be easy to use, easy to learn, and directly serve the needs of people.

There are many different methods for the design, coding and testing of software, each organizing the transformation from logical specifications to a computer executable system with guidelines on prioritizing and systematizing the production of programs and files, and with specific techniques and tools. The most widely used are the 'structured methods', which encourage the systematic use of a small number of basic structures of data and processes. But even among the structured methods there are fundamental differences as to how the design task should be approached. For example, a school of thought based on influential writers and practitioners such as DeMarco, Constantine, Myers, Yourdon follows the principle that a software system should take its shape from the pattern of interactions among functions performed by the system [DeMarco, 1978; Yourdon & Constantine, 1979; Myers, 1978]. Another school of thought, established by the work of Warnier, Orr and Jackson, endorses the principle that a system should take its shape from the structure of the data that drives it [Orr, 1981; Warnier, 1981; Jackson, 1983]. More recently, as one would expect, object oriented design, building on object oriented analysis models has been promoted with a 'seamless' move from an object oriented analysis model to an object oriented design for software and an object oriented programming language for coding [Nerson, 1992].

Software is not the only component requiring technical design. For example, the design of databases requires detailed specification of data organization, access methods, size and controls, and the design of communication networks has to follow its own design techniques taking into consideration such items as traffic volume, peak loads and required performance levels. Such tasks need the skills of professional specialists in these technologies.

Since the mid 1980s considerable efforts have been made to structure and prescribe the transformation of logical specifications into computer executable systems to such an extent that it can be automated. Although this ambition has not been realized, a large number of automated tools, such as code generators which produce computer programs directly from design specifications, have been developed. This technology is another example of CASE tools (Computer Aided Systems Engineering), 'lower CASE' for design into programming as against 'upper CASE' for analysis into design. Indeed, there are computer-based tools available for almost all the various technical design tasks of software development, as well as for organizing and controlling the software development process. The latter are sometimes referred to as Integrated Project Support Environments (IPSE). Nevertheless, even the most detailed technical tasks of the information systems development process require creativity and it has proved difficult to substitute this with automated procedures. In systems analysis, just as in systems design and programming, the enthusiasm and talent of its practitioners have so far proved indispensable.

Exercises and discussion issues

1. It has been suggested in this chapter that analysis may be principally based around concern with the data that a system will contain, the procedures that a system will undertake or the events in the environment that will trigger actions by the system. Consider the approach you think most suitable for each of the following applications:

    an autopilot in an aeroplane;

    a system for a bank to handle the processing of cheque accounts;

    a system that receives large amounts of data from weather stations around the world, and produces weather forecasts.

    Note that there are no right or wrong answers here, just well-argued answers.

2. Prepare a data flow diagram for the following order processing system in a mail order company:

    All orders come on an order form. The form has fields for name, address, items requested (an item code, a description and a quantity). The purchaser is expected to have worked out the overall value of the order and sent a cheque or given credit card details. Orders are received by post. They are then entered in to a computer system by clerks who type in the items ordered, the name of the client and the amount of money sent and the type of payment (cheque or credit card). The system then checks that the correct funds have been sent, checks that the goods are available, and if so produces an acknowledgement letter. If the wrong funds have been sent then a letter is sent back to the customer requesting a new cheque or an amended authorization to debit a credit card. Meanwhile the order is held on file. If any of the goods are not available then the order is also held on file to be reconsidered at a later date. In practice all such orders are reconsidered at the end of the week.

    Once it is ascertained that all the goods ordered are available, then they are allocated to the client, but they will not be sent until the payment has been confirmed. This means waiting 3 days for cheques to clear, or in the case of credit cards doing an on-line check with the credit card company. This takes about 10 seconds. If for any reason the payment is not approved – cheque or credit card – a further letter is dispatched regretting that the company is unable to supply the goods, and all details of the order are removed from the system. When payment is approved, then the details of the orders are passed to the warehouse for dispatch.

3. Prepare mini-specifications for the above system, remembering that there should be one mini-specification for each bubble on the DFD. Try to prepare a data model for the system. Make a note of any further information you would you like to have available in order to do this.

4. Are you happy with the overall logic of the system described above? Are there any ways in which it could be improved? Consider this in the light of the following information: 20% of cheques sent with orders are not good for one reason or another; the average order is for 5 items with an overall probability of 30% that at least one item would be out of stock. Many angry letters have been received complaining about the length of time it takes to receive items ordered. These come particularly from the best customers, those who order many items.

References

Angell, I.O. & Smithson, S. (1991) *Information Systems Management: Opportunities and Risks*, Macmillan Press, Basingstoke.

Baskerville, R. (1988) *Designing Information Systems Security*, Wiley, Chichester.

Beer, S. (1972) *The Brain of the Firm*, Penguin, Harmondsworth.

Bowers, D.S. (1988) *From Data to Database*, Van Nostrand Reinhold, London.

Caelli, W., Longley, D. & Shain, M. (1994) *Information Security Handbook*, Macmillan, London.

DeMarco, T. (1978) *Structured Analysis and Systems Specification*, Prentice Hall, Englewood Cliffs, New Jersey.

Downs, E., Clare, P. & Coe, I. (1992) *Structured Systems Analysis and Design Method*, (2nd edition), Prentice Hall, London.

Flynn, D.J. & Frangos Diaz, O. (1996) *Information Modelling: An International Perspective*, Prentice Hall, London.

Jackson, M.A. (1983) *System Development*, Prentice Hall, London.

Kent, W. (1983) 'A simple guide to five normal forms in relational database theory', *Communications of the ACM*, Vol. 26, No. 2, February, pp. 120-125.

Myers, G.J. (1978) *Composite Structured Design*, Van Nostrand Reinhold, New York.

Nerson, J-M. (1992) 'Applying object-oriented analysis and design' in *Communications of the ACM*, Vol. 35, No. 9, September. pp 63-74.

Rubin, K.S. & Goldberg, A. (1992) 'Object behaviour analysis' in *Communications of the ACM*, Vol. 35, No. 9, September. pp 48-62.

Warnier, J. (1981) *Logical Construction of Systems*, Van Nostrand Reinhold, New York.

Yourdon, E. & Constantine, L.L. (1979) *Structured Design*, Prentice Hall, Englewood Cliffs, New Jersey.

Yourdon, E. (1989) *Modern Structured Analysis*, Prentice Hall, Englewood Cliffs, New Jersey.

Further reading

Corder's is an excellent simple account of the basic methods of systems development and the use of the structured tools described in this chapter. Another source on the basic techniques used in systems analysis is Avison & Fitzgerald. A fuller treatment of a contemporary version of structured methods in systems analysis is contained in Yourdon above. Caelli *et al.* provide a comprehensive review of security issues:

Avison, D.E. & Fitzgerald, G. (1988) *Information Systems Development: Methodologies, Techniques and Tools*, Blackwell, Oxford.

Corder, C. (1989) *Taming your company computer*, McGraw-Hill, London.

5 Information system delivery and operation

- *Implementation*
- *Implementation activities*
- *Systems maintenance and evolution*
- *Evaluation*

An information system may come to be constructed, in the sense that programs are written and tested, databases designed, new forms printed and computers installed, but this is not the end of the systems development process. There are still a number of critical activities that need to be undertaken including the actual setting of a new system to work within its host organization. These activities are in general referred to as implementation. Even when a system has been implemented, and is in use, there will certainly be requirements for some further changes and revisions, and so implementation is followed by a requirement to undertake some adaptation or maintenance activities. Taken together, implementation and maintenance are often the longest lasting and the most resource intensive part of a system's life, and yet they are often the least regarded and planned for.

This chapter also considers a third aspect of the later phases of a systems development project, evaluation. There are, one suspects, many lessons to be learned from any development project; did the techniques deployed work, was the case for undertaking development made at the start of the project born out, or have new factors (positive and negative) emerged that affect the utility and value of this system? These are questions that might be asked when evaluating a systems development, even if they are seldom addressed in any systematic way.

Implementation

Implementation involves the preparations for the beginning of the use of a new information system and encompass a whole set of concerns which take us from a developed system to a system in use. Tasks that may be required as part of implementation include: conversion of existing data files and programs to those suitable for the new system; final tests for the acceptance of the system by the sponsor organization; employees' training for the new tasks and procedures and, finally, the introduction of the new system into operation.

The tasks listed above seem straightforward enough, but they certainly need to be planned for in advance of the day that a system is put to work, and be planned competently. Implementation is a period of great risk. It is at this point that the ideas and expectations of the developers and management sponsors are tested in the real work situation. If those assumptions have been incorrect, or have ignored important aspects of the work context or interests of significant stakeholders, then the outcome is at best unpredictable. Indeed, the manner in which implementation is to be approached should be a significant part of the early phases of a project, since it will have consequences for all the activities within the development project.

One possible solution to some of these problems is to recognise a new and distinct role, that of the implementor – a person who has the specific task of setting a system to work. This may be the systems analyst or project manager, but the qualities needed in such a person, and the particular sensitivities needed to understand the problems and to circumvent them, may suggest that the implementor should be drawn from the user community. Another way to describe such a person or group of people is as 'system champions', people who can enthusiastically speak for the new system and work to convince others of its merits. As noted above, implementation issues need to be addressed early in the life of a project, so to must the implementor. It is not a case of picking such a person or group late in the day, but of allowing them to represent implementation issues throughout the project. In medium sized or large organizations some of the leadership of the implementation activities might come from training departments who have the required skills to convey new skills and work practices.

However implementation roles are understood -and different types of project will call for different balance of roles - we can explore implementation in terms of three distinct aspects. Walsham (1993) suggests that implementation should be understood in terms of content, context and process. Content refers to the particular measures and activities that are undertaken at the time of implementation. In the section below we discuss some of these in terms of preparation of data and files, training, acceptance testing and conversion strategies from old to new systems.

Context refers to the social context within which the implementation will take place, and includes the leadership style used to promote the new system and the balance of responsibilities that are awarded between the technologists, user groups and managers. As discussed above, such leadership may be based on a particular leading role for implementors or system champions, but more generally new systems are understood as needing the explicit support and endorsement of senior managers. If this is not present, then the implied message that the system is not important may easily spread.

The process of implementation refers to the linking themes that relate a particular system to broader directions of change within an organization. In particular, coherent implementation requires that the system itself be understood in terms of broader ambitions of organizational change and business strategy. To put in a new system, as we have explained in earlier chapters and as we explore further in part III of the book, is to promote change. This broader context of change needs to be understood, to some degree at least, if people are to understand how to take up and use the new system.

Implementation activities

Any project will need to explicitly address a number of particular activities that will need to be undertaken at this point in the development process. Responsibility for these activities will in general fall on the development team, though other professional experts may aid them. Thus development of documentation for a new system will be a mainstream activity of systems developers, but the production of training materials may require that others become involved. Similarly acceptance testing may bring in other interested parties, perhaps internal auditors or quality assurance staff.

Preparation of data and files

To begin operations a new information system will often need to be 'filled' with required data. If the new information system is the first computer-based system for the activities of the organization that it is intended to support, the creation of the database or data files will most likely have to be done by time-consuming and labour-intensive data collection and data entry. If, however, the new information system is replacing a previous generation of computer systems, it may well be possible to convert the old data files to the new system's database with a specially written computer tool. However, since a new system might be expected to deliver new functionality, it is seldom as easy as moving one set of data over to the new system. It may also be that there is a requirement to 'recode' data, perhaps mapping it to a new and more elaborate data model. These tasks can represent a very substantial proportion of project effort, particularly in situations in which a software package has been selected. For example, to implement a new accounting package as software may be quite straight forward, but to convert old accounting files to a new systems structures can be very complex, particularly if the aim of the new system is to allow new accounting functions and reports to be used.

Education and training

Training is intended to provide skills and awareness to a variety of categories of people who will be a part of a new system. Those who will operate the new technical system must be taught the technical aspects relevant to their job. For example, those responsible for the running and administration of a computer-based system must know how to start the system up, how to cope with possible system failures, how to maintain the back-up system and how to recover after a failure. Those who will enter data into the system, make enquiries, or use it as a tool for their jobs must learn how the system functions, how to operate it, how to interpret the output or to respond to the various results that it produces, and how to organize their overall job to accommodate the new system.

The change implied by a new system will most probably affect the work of a number of groups of employees who do not have direct access to the new technical system, such as managers of the organization and employees of departments other than those that will accommodate the new system. They too must be informed about the role of the new system and its potential impact on the functioning of other parts of the organization.

For certain systems, training or awareness must also be provided to people outside the organization. Many information systems projects are intended to introduce new means of communication between a company and its customers or its suppliers. For example, a bank introducing a new computer-based service through Internet banking must ensure that its customers have adequate knowledge of what it is and how to use it, and it may be necessary to write letters explaining the new service to customers. There will also be a need to train people to deal with customers' enquiries regarding the new service. A travel company introducing a new system for booking services such as package holidays and accommodation may have to train the staff of the independent travel agencies who will use it, and provide them with an advice service. In short, we need to train everybody, not just the most direct 'users' – train managers, train customers, train operators, train networks staff, train user-support staff, and first of all train the trainers.

Training strategies can be quite elaborate and may require some detailed analysis of the needs of user groups in terms of knowledge and timing. Among the possible strategies to consider are the following:

Incremental – providing training in small doses over a period of time. Each element is small and well focused, but it builds up over time into a comprehensive knowledge of the new system.

Comprehensive – in contrast, is training in big doses. This may be needed for certain new systems, but it runs the risk of putting all the eggs in one basket, and does not allow for learning on the part of trainers and systems managers.

Cascade – training people to train people to train people. For very large systems this is often the only possibility. Perhaps a member of staff in each office can be trained in a new system, and can then in turn train 3 more to train the full office staff. The obvious danger is that the message is lost or distorted as it is passed from person to person. For this reason, such an approach probably also require a strong central user support facility or help desk.

Focused – training on certain key aspects of a systems, and allowing users to self-teach on the rest. With modern user interfaces and higher levels of computer literacy, some systems may not require very much training to appreciate their general functionality. However there may be a limited number of specific parts of a system that do require it.

Training is an expensive activity and directly consumes people's time; this use of time (or waste of time if we are not careful) is often resented and resisted. Dull training will make matters worse. There may be opportunities to improve training by the use of self-paced multimedia and computer based training materials, or even by building training into the help-system of a particular application. When preparing training materials and programmes it is important to consider the time to be taken, the quality of materials used and their level, the sense of purpose and progress that those being trained can feel, as well as building in the opportunity for feedback. This last point can be quite critical. If training is approached as a two way communication, then system developers can tap in to quite a lot of useful knowledge. It may seem too late in the process to be listening to users, but as we explore in the later section of this chapter, systems are adapted and changed after initial implementation, and collecting inform-ation at this point can help to shape this maintenance activity.

Acceptance testing

During implementation the system will often need to be tested to get final approval from the users. We would expect the software and hardware to have been tested already during the programming of the system but, unlike such technical testing, which is aimed at checking whether the computer system's performance is consistent with the design and analysis specifications, acceptance testing aims at making sure that everything is in place for the system to begin operations, that is, acceptable to those who will work with it.

- The system should be tested by those whose work it will support and with real data and under conditions as similar as possible to those of the environ-ment in which it will be embedded.

- A range of documentation must be delivered and approved. This includes the complete set of specification documents produced during the develop-ment project, as well as documentation explaining the features of the new information system to its users and guiding them in how to use it.

- Operating and organizational procedures must be prepared and inspected.

- The readiness of the personnel to work with the new system must be assessed. Employees need to have acquired adequate skills and confidence to begin using the system. They must also accept the new system as a new component of their work and be willing to make an effort to use it effectively.

- Adequate maintenance resources must be in place. A help desk may be required for providing support to the users when they are faced with problems. A team of analysts, designers, and programmers with necessary expertise should be ready to respond to the teething problems of the new system. More generally, maintenance requests will be made throughout the operational life of the system and resources for maintenance work will be needed.

Testing at this stage is the final check of feasibility. Expensive and large projects have been abandoned during implementation when, despite all previous expectations, estimates and efforts, they prove technically, organizationally, socially or economically unsatisfactory. It is never easy to admit the failure of a project when it is nearly completed, but it may be wiser to do so than jeopardize the performance of the organization.

Conversion to the new system's operations

Depending on how confident an organization is about the success of a new information system, and how radical a change it represents, a new system may begin its operations in one of several different ways: running for a period in parallel with the information system that it is intended to replace; introducing modules incrementally in a number of stages; introducing and running the system in pilot sites before implementing it across the whole organization; or starting full operations instantly in the whole organization.

Parallel running is perhaps the safest method. It allows for testing the new information system in a real environment and comparing its performance with the existing system. It is, however, the most expensive method, as the organization will have to bear the cost of running both systems for a certain time. In addition it will need to spend resources for continuous evaluation of the new system against the old one.

Modular implementation is a cautious approach, whereby the change implied by a new system is extended incrementally in manageable steps. This reduces the risk of impairing the functioning of the organization and provides opportunity for gradually learning new information handling procedures. This approach also allows the phased delivery of a system, spreading the work over a longer period with later development benefiting from early feedback.

Pilot implementation provides a way to test the system in practice and to commit the organization gradually to the new system. Pilot sites may be chosen with different criteria. A typical type of environment will demonstrate the capabilities of the system. A site with extreme conditions will give the system a tough test. A favourable environment will facilitate the introduction of the system and give developers the opportunity to update and improve it until it is judged suitable for general use. There could be other criteria used to select initial sites, for example, a site from which users have been involved in system development, or a site in which there is the most urgent need for improved work practices. A pilot implementation may also allow some judgement to be made as to a system's effectiveness, and a matched pairing of sites might be used to contrast the new and the old ways of working.

Cut-over implementation is the most risky way to start operations of a new system, and to choose this approach requires good confidence in the new system or an assesemnt of an acceptable risk of problems in the early days. Nevertheless, it may be the only option, even if it leads to the need to resolve quite unexpected problems in emergency situations. With all the publicity over the introduction of electronic trading of financial securities at the London stock exchange in the 'Big Bang' of 1986, the computer system failed on the very first day, and trading was brought to a halt until it was restored a few hours later.

Critical aspects of implementation

The tasks of implementation are usually technically simple and do not require sophisticated methods. They are, however, crucial for the success of a new information system, and they may represent the most costly single part of an information system project. The cost for training and organizational preparation for information system changes in large organizations such as government departments, banks or retail companies with large numbers of branches may well exceed all other costs for systems development.

However, systems developers need to understand that the most critical aspect of implementation is neither technical nor economic, but is political. It is usually during this stage that people come to terms with the change introduced into their work environment. Their first impression and reaction is significant for meeting the objectives of the change. If the change is not welcome, resistance to it may take various forms, from industrial action, to misuse of the system, or the adoption of informal practices to bypass it. Often managers and information systems developers anticipate resistance to change at implementation, almost as a natural phenomenon of human nature and a general reluctance to accept change, and they prepare their strategy for breaking the resistance and pushing the system through [Keen, 1981].

Keen introduces the idea of implementation and implementors, counter-implementors who try to frustrate the new system, and then a counter-counter implementation strategy to frustrate the counter-implementors. This attitude bears the risk of ignoring genuine signs of dissatisfaction which, unlike the resistance to the new and unknown, will not disappear with time, training, or incentives, but will lead to poor performance or problematic situations if a new system is forced into operation. A more effective strategy is to take into account the opinions and the attitude of employees from the beginning of the inform-ation system project by considering carefully the social and organizational requirements of the proposed information system change. Indeed, this is part of the goal of the SSM approach introduced in chapter 2. Involving the people who will participate in the new information system during the system's development can reduce the element of surprise at the implementation stage and may go a long way towards reducing resistance to the new information system.

Systems maintenance and evolution

Implementation can be understood as a relatively short period of time during which a system is first put to use. Of course, depending on the strategy used this period may become extended, as in a pilot site or incremental approach. We could, in contrast, see implementation as a very drawn out process starting when people first come to hear or become involved in a new systems development, and continuing through the working life of a system as it adapts and changes and as people respond to the new means of information handling. This second per-spective is an interesting one, and one which places implementation at the centre of information systems development proceses. However, in this section we restrict ourselves to a more conventional interpretation of implementation, and thus move on to consider activities to support of a new system as it is used under the heading of maintenance.

Maintenance refers to the period after implementation when a system is in use. Information systems require corrections and, more importantly, enhance-ments to meet the continuous changes occurring in their environment. Maintenance of hardware and systems software is almost always contracted out to the vendor of the system or to specialist firms, but maintenance of software applications requires systems analysis and programming resources similar to those for systems development.

After a system is implemented it will almost certainly require three different types of maintenance: corrective, adaptive and perfective. *Corrective mainten-ance* deals with errors discovered during the system's operations, in particular errors relative to the original specification. In most cases a software application will contain errors of this type, most of which are manifested soon after a system begins operations. Most program testing methods leave some undetected bugs which have to be corrected when they are discovered, often in emergency conditions, to keep the system operational. Program bugs are not the only type of errors in an information system; errors may be in the design or the logic of the system too, and they may require more lengthy efforts to correct.

Adaptive maintenance deals with system changes to satisfy changing organizational requirements and to follow technological advances. Organizational change is often gradual and can be accommodated in existing information systems, without necessarily launching new information systems development projects. Similarly, the continuous change in information technology infrastructure requires gradual system upgrades to keep the system the operational.

Perfective maintenance, sometimes known as enhancements, deals with requests to further improve an operational information system, enhance its functions or performance, or add new features. The experience of working with a system creates new ideas for expanding or refining it. In contrast to adaptive maintenance, it is not about changing demands so much as maintaining the integrity of the system itself.

A fourth type of maintenance is also noted in the literature, *preventative* maintenance. This represents the effort to retain the quality of maintainability in an information system. This might include upgrading documention, forseeing emerging problems and redeveloping parts of the system that are acknowledged as of lower quality. It is, however, a lucky organization that has substantial resources to devote to such activities.

Maintenance is widely acknowldged as accounting for a substantial proportion of the total systems analysis and programming resources of organizations. In the 1970s, research showed that this proportion was about 45% [Lienz *et al.*, 1978]. It was expected then to be reduced as the systems development practices became more methodical and, as a result, systems were built containing fewer errors when they were implemented and fulfilled more effectively the requirements of organizations. Maintainability has been a major concern for systems developers and most methods seek to contribute in some ways to improving the maintainability of the resulting systems. For example, some methods for information requirements determination and systems analysis seek to forecast organizational changes which will necessitate changes of the information system, and they try to provide adequate flexibility to meet them [Fitzgerald, 1990; Land, 1982].

Structured methods such as those described in the last chapter have aimed at producing documentation and software code which is easily understood by the maintenance analysts and programmers, and which permits changes to be made in certain parts as required without interfering with the whole system. Following a more radical approach, some software development methods aim at eliminating the need for corrective maintenance of information systems software by proving the correctness of its code, that is, the equivalence of the code to the specification.

Nevertheless, during the 1980s and 1990s, maintenance costs have remained almost as high as before. Although corrective maintenance has been reduced, the volume of requests for changes to operational systems has grown and the technological environment within which systems run has changed rapidly. In the meantime it has been better understood that in many cases post-implementation systems changes have more to do with the evolving nature of information systems requirements than with the inadequacies of systems analysis and programming techniques. Lehman's [1981] classification scheme for software types, clarifies this point. It identifies three types of software according to their relation with their environment.

S stands for programs determined by their specification. This is software which, once released, operates unaffected by its environment. *S* type software can be got right first time. An example might be a computer program to control a lift in a building.

P stands for programs which have to meet the needs of practice. In this case, the requirements of the application cannot be specified once and for ever, and *P* must be altered to follow the changes occurring in the application area. An example might be a database of names and addresses to be used by a marketing department. An expansion or diversification of business may require alteration of the database.

E stands for programs which evolve. This is software which is embedded in the environment of the problem that it addresses; it has no intrinsic boundary; its operation has an impact on the application area leading to changed requirements. An *E* type program must evolve to meet these changed requirements; the presence of the system itself leads to change in its environment and consequent further changes to the system. An example might be a bank's ATM network which changes customer habits. As customers become familiar with computer-supported services, the bank will have to update its applications to meet their demand for more advanced or different services. This classification shows that for *P* and *E* types of software, maintenance (change) is not an activity which can be eliminated. It must be seen as a necessary part of the context for systems development.

Despite the acknowledged importance of maintenance of computer applications for the uninterrupted functioning of organizations, maintenance tasks are not valued highly by systems professionals and technical experts. Maintenance work requires good understanding of the information system and systematic tracing of its logic, in order to locate the parts of the system that need to be changed and to find the consequences of the change on the performance of the system as a whole. Yet, with the exception of major enhancements, maintenance does not usually involve state-of-the-art, technically sophisticated or challenging work, but rather tedious analysis, design and programming amendments. Most people who work in computing consider maintenance work to be of lower status and less satisfying than working on development projects, and organizations find it difficult to secure the necessary skills for maintaining their systems. Indeed, trying to understand somebody else's ill-documented code, or the implicit logic behind a particular procedure, is not a very rewarding activity.

This points to the critical importance of doing development well in the first place, and leaving behind a sound set of accompanying materials that the maintainer can use.

Maintenance activities can be seen as responding to their own version of the life cycle; identification of needs, evaluation of urgency and priority, specification, testing for user acceptance, amending design and code, testing and finally implementing. Such a perspective can be useful in providing some structure to the maintenance task. In particular most organizations need some procedures to allow maintenance requests to be evaluated and their priority assessed. A great number of requests, possible conflicting, can be generated and some difficult decisions will often need to be made as to which will be rejected, and which will be rapidly accommodated. There is also a need to assess the impact of maintenance changes. A relatively minor change to a systems logic, or one that seems at first to be minor, may have unpredicted consequences on a far larger scale. Ill-informed or casual maintenance work might well introduce into a system flawed logic and substantial systemic errors.

Once again, we have to see that the problem is organizational rather than technical: how to organize information systems development and maintenance work so that analysts and programmers find their work conditions satisfactory and that systems are kept in a form in which they continue to deliver benefit. One solution is to make maintenance the responsibility of a separate group of experts who are not involved in systems development projects and can devote full attention to managing this activity. To overcome the problem of low morale, maintenance staff may be offered special incentives, such as pay raises or opportunities for training in new techniques. Alternatively, staff may be transferred from the maintenance group to development projects periodically, to provide opportunities for enhancing their skills. Another recommended practice is to transfer some members of the development team to the group responsible for a systems maintenance. Such 'maintenance escorts' are valuable for providing continuity from development through implementation and into maintenance, and to transfer skills from development to maintenance groups.

Evaluation

When an information system becomes operational, the organization needs to know how successful the project has been and how good the new information system is. This information is important for a number of reasons. We may wish to know how well the project itself ran, were the techniques and tools used adequate and appropriate, was the budget and time frame appropriate? Building on from here, we may want to use the experience in this project to inform practices in future projects. Informally some learning will almost always take place, but a more formal evaluation or post-project review may be needed to bring out useful information and to pass it on. Also, we may need to examine if the benefits that were expected from a development are actually being delivered. This could be a direct assessment of the initial requirements against what happened, but it probably needs to be a more subtle activity. Evaluation activities will need to recognise that the stated requirement for a project need to be seen as having shifted during the period of development, and that other benefits, or problems, may be discovered and other interested parties identified and consulted.

Evaluation can be seen as the natural final stage of a development project, looking back to see what was achieved and what can be learned. It is also the case that other people, such as auditors, may wish to look at a system and pass some judgement on it. An auditor will ask questions such as does the system have adequate controls to ensure that only valid data goes in. Is there an audit trail of all input data? Are there adequate back-up procedures? These can be seen as sensible general questions to ask, and the kind of issues that should have been addressed in the analysis and design stages.

For the purposes of informing and improving systems development practices four questions need to be addressed:

- efficiency of the development project;
- efficiency of the new information system;
- achievement of initially defined objectives;
- non-intended or non-expected impact of the system on the organization's functioning and performance.

Lessons can be learnt by examining how effective the methods that were applied in a project have been, and how efficient the project management has been. The total cost of the purchase, development and implementation can at this point be calculated and compared with the estimates contained in the feasibility report. The causes of discrepancies between estimated and actual costs can be traced to provide valuable knowledge for making more realistic plans for future projects and for avoiding wasteful mistakes. The experience of using the methods that were applied in the project should also be reviewed, to draw lessons about their appropriateness and to decide how they could be improved for future projects. The effectiveness of the scheduling of the information systems development tasks, of the management of project resources, such as skills, computer capacity, or administrative support, and of the organization of work teams should be evaluated as well, so as to reveal weaknesses that can be avoided in the future.

The first look at the efficiency of a new information system can be assessed shortly after its implementation. Efficiency has to do with the robustness of the operations and the resource utilization of the procedures comprising the new system. Evaluation of the efficiency of the hardware, software, and communication network is a well established practice for the technical experts. However, efficiency assessment should include the manual procedures of an information system as well. Efficiency gains of computer operations may add nothing to the overall efficiency of an organization if the skills necessary to use the system are not available or if the surrounding manual procedures impose their own inefficiencies.

Assessment of the achievement of the initial objectives can be based on the feasibility report which should contain a statement of expected benefits and the costs and risks that the organization was prepared to take for them. This is the evaluation of the effectiveness of the system, i.e. the realization of the intended contribution of the system to the survival and growth of the organization. The feasibility study provides a basis for comparison between intended and achieved changes, particularly with regard to economic, social and organizational benefits and risks.

A new information system may also contribute to changes which were not intended and were not anticipated. Therefore, evaluation would be incomplete without an assessment of the non-intended effects caused by the new system. Information systems may have a wide impact on a variety of aspects of an organization, its employees and its environment. For example, even if not intended, a new information system may have significant impact on the work conditions of certain categories of employees, on the management capacity and political stability of the organization, on the reputation of the organization, and its relations with its suppliers or customers.

Only a few of these aspects can be evaluated with quantitative or other 'objective' techniques. Evaluation involves qualitative assessment of performance and the changes that have occurred. The success of a system will be judged differently by different participants. Only too rarely can an 'objective' measure of success satisfy the various interested groups. An analysis of achieved changes which incorporates the rationale of the various views will provide much more useful information and can be the basis for decisions about the future of the system concerned as well as further information systems developments in the organization.

The evaluation of information systems is, in effect, a negotiation process among various groups of people with different interests in the system (Avgerou, 1995). The most appropriate role of systems developers in evaluation is to support the negotiation process by providing relevant information to the parties involved. The information systems life thus comes full circle and returns to consider issues of conflicting perceptions, alternative understandings and a search for a creative consensus. These are the very same issues that we described in chapter 2 when the development process was initiated.

Exercises and discussion issues

1. An airline consortium is introducing a new reservation system which will put terminals on the desks of numerous travel agents around the world. The

system is designed and ready for operation. Consider the appropriate strategy to be used for implementation. Cover as many aspects as you can and in particular consider the advantages and disadvantages of parallel running, using pilot sites, incremental installation or cut over.

2. A government department dealing with compensation and subsidy claims from farmers has recently installed a new office automation system providing on-line workstations for every clerical officer. This has replaced an old paper-based system which relied on much form filling and which was in part supported by a traditional batch processing system. What broad criteria would you use to undertake a post-implementation evaluation of the system? Who would you ask and what questions would you pose?

3   The task of maintenance of existing computer applications is usually considered to be less challenging, satisfying or important than designing and building new ones. Many organizations maintain two distinct groups of people, one to build new systems, another to maintain old ones. Those in the latter may well be paid less and be seen as less important. Why is this? Is there anything that a concerned information systems managers could or should do about it?

References

Avgerou, C. (1995) 'Evaluating information systems by consultation and negotiation', in International Journal of Information Management, vol. 15, No. 6, pp 427-435.

Fitzgerald, G. (1990) 'Achieving flexible information systems: the case for improved analysis' in *Journal of Information Technology*, Vol. 5, No. 1, March, pp. 5-11.

Hirschheim, R.A., Land, F.F. & Smithson, S. (1984) 'Implementing Computer-based Information Systems in Organizations: Issues and Strategies' Proceedings of INTERACT `84, IFIP Conference on human computer interaction, London.

Keen, P.G.W. (1981) 'Information systems and organizational change' in *Communications of the ACM*, Vol. 24, No.1, January, pp. 24-33.

Land, F.F. (1982) 'Adapting to changing user requirements', in *Information and Management*, Vol. 5, pp. 59-75.

Lehman, M.M., (1981). 'The Environment of Program Development and Maintenance – Programs, Programming and Programming Support'. Reprinted in Wasserman, A.J., (ed) *Software Development Environments*, Computer Society Press, New York.

Lienz, B.P., Swanson, E.D. & Tompkins, G.E. (1978) 'Characteristics of Applications Software Maintenance' in *Communications of the ACM*, Vol. 21, No. 6, June.

Walsham, G. (1993) *Interpreting Information Systems in Organizations*, J.
    Wiley, Chichester.

Further reading

The Powell paper gives a survey of the literature on information systems
evaluation. The Swanson book is a thorough review and exploration of modern
maintenance practices.

Powell, P. (1992) 'Information technology evaluation: Is it different?' in *Journal
    of the Operational Research Society*, Vol. 43, No. 1, January, pp. 29-42.
Swanson, E.B. & Beath, C.M. (1989) *Maintaining Information Systems in
    Organizations*, J. Wiley, Chichester.

Part 2

Concepts, models, approaches and methodologies

In part 1 of this book one account of the cycle of activities required for the development of an information system has been given, together with examples of various methods and tools that practitioners may use to carry them out. The reader must have noticed that nothing in the description given is very precise. It resembles more the guidance that a craftsman might give to an apprentice than the accurate and precise procedures taught to a scientist. In all the tasks presented, there is a great deal of scope for intuition and subjective judgement. This faithfully represents the actual practice in organizations as they set out to develop information systems. There are few if any hard and fast rules about information systems development, nor is there a solid theoretical basis upon which to build such prescriptive structures.

The study and practice of information systems development is a relatively new endeavour. Historically, it is related with the post Second World War efforts of organizations to exploit the potential of new and powerful electronic information handling technologies, and to systematize their management within the framework of new disciplines such as operational research, decision making and business administration. During this period it has become apparent that the application of information and communications technologies affects many aspects of organizations: efficiency and productivity, effectiveness of administration, satisfaction of employees, emergence of new business areas, strategic direction available to organizations, and relations with suppliers and customers. As part of this growing awareness, information has come to be recognized as a valuable resource that organizations must learn to manage prudently.

One result is that information systems has emerged as a new academic field studying the significance of information and information processing in all types of organization, within society and the economy. Central in this new field has been the study of the nature of the information systems development process, the ways information systems development can be practised, and the consequences of the introduction of information technology into organizations. The new field has not, however, been based on a unified 'theory' of information systems which has made it possible to explain or predict with certainty what happens as a result of changes in information handling practices, nor has any strong theory been provided to drive with precision the actions that should be followed in the course of developing information systems. The world of people, organizations and social interaction, which is the context of information systems, seems to defy the discovery of such deterministic laws.

Nevertheless, a body of knowledge and insight has been built up, which gradually improves our capacity to develop information systems with beneficial effects for organizations, for the people who work in them, and for the people they serve. In large part, this has been as a result of turning to contributory disciplines in science, engineering and the social sciences, and exploring what they have to offer. Beyond this, a number of conceptual tools have been developed for understanding various aspects of information systems and their development, in order to provide practitioners with awareness of the many facets of the tasks they undertake and guidance as to how to proceed. This has improved their ability to make judgements and to follow effective courses of action. In the following four chapters the underpinning of this emerging body of knowledge is explored.

Chapter 6 presents an introduction to the theoretical bases upon which four fundamental concepts of information systems rest: information, systems, org-anizations, and technology. The intention in this chapter is to direct attention to relevant work that has influenced perceptions and practices of information systems, rather than to provide a cohesive theoretical basis for information systems development. The chapter must be seen as a point of departure for a journey through many other concepts, such as for example the concepts of 'decision', 'intelligence', 'organizational culture', or 'planning'. The field of information systems is still an eclectic one, requiring continual learning.

While studies aiming at providing a theoretical grounding continue, there are already many analyses of the nature of the information systems development process and generalizations about good information systems development pract-ice. Drawing from work in this field, chapter 7 discusses how the information systems development process may be organized. Specifically, we discuss some abstract *models* of the process of information systems development. These models suggest how the tasks we described in part 1 can be put together in various ways. For example, we can organize them in a linear fashion, as a series of activities; alternatively, we may allow for repetition of some activities, in a trial-and-error fashion, until we reach satisfactory results.

Chapter 8 turns to consider actual *approaches* followed by practitioners. According to their background, training or the nature of the project they are faced with, practitioners tend to be biased in their efforts towards particular approaches. For example, some may pay attention predominantly to the engin-eering aspects of the systems development process, while others tend to handle it as an organizational intervention.

Finally, chapter 9 considers the packages of methods used as instruments of professional practice, the *methodologies*. There has been a great deal of effort expended to create and promote sets of methods in order to establish good professional practice. This chapter discusses the nature and historical development of these methodologies, and explores their value for information systems development practice.

6 Concepts and theories

- *Information*
- *Systems*
- *Organizations*
- *Technology*
- *Theoretical foundations for information systems*

The field of information systems draws concepts and theoretical principles from many other established disciplines in order to understand, explain and guide the development and management of information handling procedures in organizations. Useful knowledge can be found in various fields of the social sciences, including the theory of organizations, psychology, cognitive science, sociology, accounting, economics and anthropology. Equally, since a major concern in the study of information systems is the effective use of information technologies, science and engineering fields, including systems theory, computer science, electrical engineering and telecommunications are also relevant. Rather than treat each of these contributory disciplines in turn this chapter elaborates first on four central concepts: those of information, systems, organizations and technology, which are fundamental for understanding the nature of information systems. The second part of the chapter takes a broader consideration of the basis of studying information systems and introduces some significant contemporary reference theories that researchers and analysts use to 'make sense' of information systems phenomena.

Information

Information is a notion with a key role in understanding many social phenomena. Intuitively we take information for granted; we think of it simply as the way of getting to know about things that matter in the world around us. Information is also a primary constituent of administration and one can recognize a plethora of information seeking and handling activities in all forms of human organizations.

The term information appears as a fundamental concept not only in the study of information systems in organizations, but also in the theory of subjects such as communications, economics, cybernetics and library studies. However, despite the very frequent common sense use of the term, and its fundamental position in many disciplines, we are lacking a single theory capable of explaining information in a unified and comprehensive manner.

The hypothesis that different disciplines should and can share the same concept of information has led many to believe that a general theory is waiting to be developed, and could systematically transfer insight gained in one domain to others. Indeed, there is a widely known mathematical theory of information which was developed by an American communications engineer, Claude Shannon, in the 1940s. It is based on a statistical measure of signal transmission which is named information, and has become the cornerstone for communications engineering. However, this information theory is not concerned with the meaning, truth or effect of messages and, because of this, its relevance to information systems is remote. The mathematical formulae defining that notion of information cannot be meaningfully identified with the intuitive use of the word in a social context and cannot be widely applied in the analysis of information handling in organizations. Indeed the original name of Shannon and Weaver's book was *The Mathematical Theory of Communication* [Shannon & Weaver, 1949], and its authors were aware of the distinction between communication as the transmission of signals and the more general concept of information communication. Shannon and Weaver admitted that the 'semantic' aspects of communication, that part related to meaning, are irrelevant to engineering concerns.

Some still believe that Shannon's theory is a useful starting point for any effort to study the field of information and it should be included in any new theory appropriate for information systems studies. However, most information systems workers make no use of the mathematical theory of information for information systems development and management. The definition of information as a technical term in communications engineering seems to have been unfortunate and has often misdirected people to the belief that the same technical definition is relevant to information when it is used as a fundamental concept in the other domains.

Semiotics

A broader perspective on information, which is much more relevant to information systems, is semiotics [Stamper, 1987; Liebenau & Backhouse, 1990]. This is the study of signs as a means for communication. A sign can be anything, so long as it can be perceived and interpreted, as for example, gestures, pictures or spoken or written words. Communication is then seen as a social phenomenon which involves a sender of signs with intentions to convey, a medium for carrying signs, and a receiver, who has the ability to interpret these signs.

In a semiotic approach communication is studied in terms of four levels: pragmatics, semantics, syntactics and empirics.

Pragmatics considers the broad social context of communication, the assumptions, expectations and beliefs of those involved. The interpretation of signs which are communicated depends on such social characteristics.

Semantics considers the meaning and knowledge of signs. It examines the connections between the signs people use and the interpretation that recipients put on them.

Syntactics is the study of the logic and grammars used for the construction and communication of signs, as for example in the agreed format and sequence in which a postal address is written on an envelope, though this may differ from country to country..

Empirics is the study of the codes and the physical characteristics of signs and the various media of communication, as for example the mechanisms for encoding and decoding a paper document when it is sent from fax machine to fax machine.

Although semiotics has been developed primarily in linguistics, philosophy, and latterly in literary criticism, it offers useful insights for various tasks of information systems development. Each of the above levels is relevant to information systems development, some more to certain groups or styles of practice than others, but overall, semiotics can provide practitioners with a rich set of concepts and techniques in order to understand how information is used and communicated.

Empirics is of particular concern to engineers, for example telecommunication experts. Indeed, this is the field where Shannon and Weaver's work provides an excellent theoretical basis. Syntactics is used extensively by computer scientists. For example, syntactical analysis is applied in the translation of high level programming languages into machine code by compilers. It is more widely appropriate for information systems design tasks when structured data has to be put together or taken apart.

Semantics is also used by computer scientists, in the study of formal and natural languages, but semantic analysis has a wider role too. It is a particularly useful tool for systems analysts when they confront problems of ambiguity as to meaning, as for example in designing a database to hold information on employees. The analyst needs to find out what the various people involved understand *an employee* to be. Is it all workers, or all full-time workers? What constitutes full-time anyway – does it include a person on sick leave, or on maternity leave, or suspended pending disciplinary action? Does it include retired people, or people who are sub-contractors? Can you be an employee and not be paid?

Pragmatics is of particular interest to the information systems analysts. It provides tools for understanding the social environment of an organization, both formal and informal, and for appreciating the culture and the norms which govern behaviour and communication. For example, a study that the authors were involved in found clear differences of culture among the local offices of the social security department in the UK. While in some offices the prevailing culture was one of mission to assist the members of the community in need, others were primarily geared towards serving the interest of the department as an organization, preoccupied with the prevention of fraud against the department, and against overspending. The use of a newly installed computer system to process claims varied accordingly and the interpretation of data on the claimants' forms was undertaken in different ways.

Information and data

Signs which are collected and organized, and which constitute the formal basis for the functioning of organizations are often described as data. A great deal of data can exist in the files of an organization without making much sense to anybody. Also the same data may be meaningful and useful for some users and totally meaningless to others, depending on such conditions as their state of mind, their background knowledge, or their position in the organization. Therefore, while data is a useful, if ill-defined, word for the mass of formal signs collected by the formal information systems of an organization, we should only talk of information with reference to someone who perceives or interprets such signs. One point of difference between data and information according to some authorities is that data become information if they provide surprise. That is if they convey something which in association with what is in the mind, is 'new'. Emery [1971] suggested that it is this attribute of surprise that adds value to data.

Data is not synonymous with information, but the two words are very often used as having identical meaning, and this leads to other confusingly similar terms, such as 'information processing' and 'data processing'. Many authors try to resolve this issue by defining information as data that have been processed and organized for some purpose, but one has to be clear that the output of a data transformation process constitutes information *only* if some person can extract meaning from it. The utility or meaning of an information system's output can only be judged according to the use that is made of it or the effect that it has. The whole objective of developing information systems is to convey meaningful signs to people in organizations, and to satisfy their informational requirements. Applying data to algorithms or computer processing does not necessarily result in information. On the other hand, data stored in the files of an organization, even before they are processed, can be information for those who examine them and understand them. Indeed, users of an information system may on various occasions need to view the 'raw' data to resolve some questions, and if they have the appropriate knowledge of the semantics and syntactics, they will succeed.

Classification of information types

In addition to the theories such as that of semiotics which aim at a comprehensive treatment of the concept of information, there are several less ambitious attempts to classify different types of information. Such classification schemes can guide the analyst to a fuller examination of the information sources and the information processes of a situation that they investigate. In general, people at work make use of all sorts and forms of information: they use written forms of information on events, people and organizations, such as a business or research report; they use administrative records containing data collected from the operations of the organization; they may use statistics or other forms of numerical information; and they can use pictorial and acoustic information too, such as graphs, maps, photographs or videos.

Descriptive Information	*Rules* *States of the world* *Changes in states of the world*
Probablistic Information	*Predictive* *Inferred* *Derived from models*
Qualitative Information	*Explanatory* *Qualifying* *Expressions of patterns and norms* *Appreciations and judgements* *Values, attitudes and power relations*

Figure 6.1 Land's Classification of Information

Different types of information are traditionally stored in different institutions or divisions of an organization: textual documents in libraries and archives, administrative information in the records of organizations, often in computer files, statistics in statistical offices. Each of these institutions has its own ways of processing and administering the information types that it deals with. Recent advances in information technology have made possible the combined processing of different types of information by multimedia or integrated systems. However, to make use of this technical capacity, we need to improve our understanding of the various types of information and the way they contribute to the various cognitive activities. Land [1985] classified information that is used in organizations into three basic types: descriptive information, probabilistic information and qualitative with further elaborations.

Descriptive information

Under this category Land distinguishes three different types of information:

Description of rules that govern or constrain the affairs of the real world. Most organizations of any size function on the basis of a formalized set of rules. Indeed we have a special word for such organizations – bureaucracies. Building on this rule-following behaviour, such organizations developed large-scale data processing systems at an early stage in the history of computing in order to undertake some of the more simple rule-following activities. For example, social security organizations developed batch computer systems which applied the rules for the calculation of the monthly payment of pensions. In such information systems the treatment of rules is highly formalized, almost automated. However, in only a few cases are such rules as inviolate and unchanging as the laws of nature, and the legislation or regulations under which an administration operates will need interpretation from time to time. Thus far computers have been less good at this task. As the line between rule following and discretion is not always clear or easy to draw, computer-based information systems incorporating legislation or regulations run the risk of not allowing interpretation and discretion and thus becoming dysfunctional. It should also be noted that in organizations rules can be felt to exist, be widely and uniformly applied, but are not to be found anywhere in a neat encoded form. Rather they are informal, either as commands from the organizational hierarchy, or as norms which are part of the organizational culture. The systems analyst can find it useful to explore such descriptive information in terms of pragmatics, semantics and syntactics.

Description of the state of the real world. The data files or the accounting record books of an organization contain a great deal of such information, as for example, the records on the stock available in the warehouse, or the employee records in the payroll system. But computer files and databases will often present an incomplete or inaccurate picture of the part of the world that they try to describe. There may be many reasons for this; for example, the data files may not be updated frequently enough, or they may not include accurate descriptions of real but non-legitimate (unrecognized) practices. In any case, the formal data systems in all organizations are always complemented by the informal knowledge, observations and communications of the employees. While the computer records of an airline reservation system may show no availability of seats for a certain flight (number of booked passengers greater than the number of available seats), the airline clerks may *know* that a number of booked customers will not turn up and they may still sell seats to new customers. They are using their informal knowledge ahead of their formally computer-based source. It is quite easy to see how this practice complements the limitations of the computer-based system, but it could get out of hand!

Description of the changes in the state of the world. This refers to the recording of events or transactions taking place as the organization functions. For example, banks record their customers' transactions during the day; and this information is used at the end of the day to update the customers' accounts. In a similar way the computer-based information systems of the stock exchange try to follow with great timeliness and accuracy the changes in traded shares' prices. However, the real information system of the stock market is much more sophisticated, and relies on many professionals observing a great many different events and trends, from the success of crops in various places of the world to changes in the balance of power in the Middle East, all of which eventually result in changes to share prices.

Probabilistic information

Probabilistic information refers to information on the basis of which a description of a part of the world can be inferred or guessed. It includes the following types:

Predictive information. Organizations make use of various types of forecasts and may apply statistical forecasting techniques. Such forecasts may deal with phenomena which are very regular and therefore for which there is a high degree of certainty that the forecast information is correct. Others involve many assumptions and are used to exhibit alternative scenarios rather than to predict a future state. Managers and other professional experts make many predictions without formal statistical support. In fact, in most organizations, strategic decisions depend to a great degree on informal forecasts by expert managers rather than on formal forecasting techniques.

Inferred information. This is information which attempts to describe the world by means of inferences from a limited set of other observations or measurements. This is the case where a statistical sample is used to infer a general pattern, as for example when a sample of customers' opinions is used to make marketing decisions, or when a customers name, age and postcode is used to infer income or social class.

Information derived from a model of the world. Models simulating the behaviour of the world can be built and are used in many decision-making situations. The systems analysis model of a new information systems discussed in chapter 4 is such an example, and it will be used to derive new information about how a proposed system will work. Another example might be computer-based discrete event simulation models, such as may be used in designing a new factory. In these situations models have proved themselves to be powerful and useful for decision makers, allowing hypotheses to be tested, and alternative decisions to be evaluated. Models, however, are always approximations of real world phenomena. They make assumptions, may use statistical techniques on data samples, and can be built to serve particular interests. Consider a supermarket company trying to obtain planning permission from a local council for a new store. What would they put into a scale model of the building that was to go on show in the town hall? A full car-park or an empty one, some mature trees, litterbins full, litterbins empty or no litterbins at all? Apart from such formal models, decision makers will often have their own perceptions of the world which can be thought of as informal models and according to which they make decisions, for example, concerning what formal techniques and models to adopt.

Qualitative information

Qualitative information refers to the explanations that lie behind the description of how the world is now or is expected to be. This category of information is less likely to be found in a formal system; it is conveyed by a great variety of signs. For example, the tone of somebody's voice may convey a message more important than the content of their words. Land distinguishes the following types of qualitative information:

Explanatory information – information that sets out how to interpret other sets of signs.

Qualifying and qualitative information, which moderates descriptive information of a formal system.

Patterns and norms, which determine how things should be done and the values according to which evaluations and judgements are made.

Judgemental information, which is based on subjective or intuitive appreciation of a situation.

Information about values, attitudes and power. This is often important for understanding the motivating forces in organizations.

Land also points to the coexistence of formal and informal information, even of the same type. This is particularly significant for the development of computer-based information systems, which is traditionally a process of developing a formal information system, in terms of data required, their format, their processing and their presentation. The behaviour of a computer-based information system is decided mainly by the analysis and design tasks, and its functioning is in this way fixed to a greater or lesser degree before it starts operations. However, as Land reminds us, any such designed system is only a part of a broader system involving people, who tend to develop informal practices complementing or even overriding the fixed, formally functioning system. Analysts must therefore be able to appreciate the informal aspects of a work environment within which a new information system is intended to operate. They need to be careful not to destroy vital *informal* practices by rigidly formal decision making or other work procedures. They should equally carefully consider how designed rule-following systems can be used in situations in which human intuition and judgement appear to play a significant role. This last point may be considered as controversial and worthy of a bit more debate. Consider the advantages that have stemmed from auto-pilots in commercial airliners, or the improved quality in motor cars that come from an automated factory with welding done by robots.

Systems

Following the discussion of the concept of information it is appropriate that the next concept should be that of a system. In that way it might seem that the combined notion of *information systems* can be firmly established. Unfortunately, this is probably not going to be the case. Just as information is a problematic concept with multiple routes to its understanding, so too is the idea of a system. However, just as with information, there is a common sense idea of what a system is, expressed in terms of a system being a coherent set of interrelated entities and activities. Ackoff [1971] defines a system as: 'an entity which is composed of at least two elements and a relation that holds between each of its elements and at least one other element in the set. Each of a system's elements is connected to every other element, directly or indirectly. Furthermore, no subset of elements is unrelated to any other subset.'

The importance of this general notion of a system – as is explained in a subsequent section of this chapter – is that it suggests a way of perceiving and studying big complex things, without neglecting their components and without treating them as a set of unrelated items. This 'systems thinking', or 'systems approach' has developed a plethora of relevant concepts and models which are widely used. We present here briefly those most relevant to the study of information systems.

The *environment* of a system consists of those elements which are not part of the system but affect the state of the system. A system is separated from its environment by a *boundary*. A system which has only limited, structured or predictable interaction with any element outside its boundary is a *closed* system. Otherwise it is an *open* system. An open system accepts resources, including signs with information value, from its environment, its *inputs*, and returns something to its environment, including signs, its *outputs*.

A system is *goal-seeking* if it is capable of changing its behaviour in order to produce a particular outcome – its goal. A *purposeful* system is one which can select its goals. These latter two concepts are fundamental in systems studies, but they are also controversial. For example, in applying systems thinking, an organization may be considered to be a purposeful system, with the behaviour of its elements geared towards the attainment of a common purpose. Nevertheless, as many sociologists have observed, in few organizations is a clear common purpose discernible. After all, the capacity to display one's will and to select goals is fundamentally a human characteristic, and the purposes of the individuals working in organizations are bound to be different, and to some degree in conflict. An analyst who seeks to determine the purpose for an information system runs the risk of confusing what is really the purpose of a particular individual, or group of individuals, with a supposed common purpose of an organization as a whole, and therefore of imposing it as the system's goal.

In facing such dilemmas it must be remembered that systems models are *not* a full account of the world, they provide only an abstraction of the behaviour of an organization which is a convenient simplification of its functioning. The analyst needs always to be sensitive to the shortcomings of systems methods and use them flexibly to gain insights. An example of this creative use of systems thinking was described in chapter 2, in the account of soft systems methodology. This illustrates the uses of systems models to reveal something about a situation and possible conflicting purposes.

In every system there is some process of *control*, by means of which a whole entity retains its identity and/or performance under changing circumstances. Control requires communication of information. In systems of interacting people such as organizations, communication of information is more than a regulatory factor for the preservation of the system's identity. Communication of information is what makes the setting and selection of goals (decision taking) possible and the quality of such decisions depends crucially on the quality and appropriateness of information available to the decision (or control) process. Organizational growth, transformation, business diversification and other forms of radical change are remarkable results of human communication.

Several authors have crystallized the concept of system into formal systems models which provide a tool for an analyst to delineate the domain of the real world that they attempt to investigate and improve. Notable is the work of Stafford Beer, who applied ideas of cybernetics and modelled organizations through analogies to the human nervous system [1972; 1979].

Do systems exist?

Building on the common sense identification of systems above, we might perhaps agree that there are things in the world that really are systems, sets of connected components, operating together, and giving rise to real effects. On the other hand, closer investigation, and careful scrutiny, will certainly permit a challenge to any *particular* identification of a system. This leads us to shift the location of the concept, to suggest not that there are things called systems, but that collections of things can be *viewed as systems*. The particular configuration of elements of a phenomenon which is viewed as a system is chosen by the observer who studies it. Different observers of the same phenomena may view them in different ways – that is as different systems. For example, the component parts and the activities taking place in an organization can be conceptualized as systems in various ways, according to the particular aspects of the organization that an observer is interested in or sensitive to; a production engineer considers the main elements as the transformations that form the production system, a management expert may see the activities that form the decision-making system, a sociologist may consider the roles and structures of the organization which form a social group and a power system, and an inform-ation analyst would see the elements and transformations of the organization's information flows. In other words, a system is a *model* of an observed situation, not the situation itself. In this way it provides a useful set of tools to perceive and study observed phenomena, but the two should not be confused.

The position stated in the paragraph above is well worth considering in some detail since it has significant implications for information systems design and management. Taken a little further, it suggests that there is no such thing as an information *system*, just information-related activities viewed as a system. The idea of a system is only applied in the conceptions of those who develop, manage, use or are part of such information-related activities. This may come as a shock, given the huge investment that there is in the idea of establishing information systems to support organizations, but it is really a great liberation for those who work in the field. If the notion of a system is a model for perception and thinking, then it can become the key to a richer and more creative understanding.

Organizations

The third concept that we need to explore is that of *organizations*. Organizations, or more precisely formal organizations, such as business firms or government departments, have been studied extensively by a number of related disciplines, particularly sociology, organizational psychology, anthropology, and decision theory. This has not resulted in a unified theory with a single set of well defined concepts and laws about the functioning of organizations, but to a body of knowledge which incorporates various views about what matters in organizations – their structure and management, the employees' motivation for work, the decision-making process, the technology used. Among the most influ-ential perspectives are [Pugh *et al.*, 1983]: Max Weber's study of bureaucracies, which deals with the question of how the activities of organizations can be structured; Frederick Taylor's scientific management, which examines how organizations can be administered and managed efficiently; studies of human relations, such as the so-called Hawthorn Experiment by Elton Mayo's team; Chris Argyris' research on how work in organizations meets the employees' needs for happiness, and which examines the behaviour of employees; and studies of communication and decision making, such as Herbert Simon's analysis of the decision process, which examines how decisions are made and how they might be made more effectively. These perspectives overlap and complement each other, rather than being mutually exclusive. Recent insights of organizational behaviour and management, such as Henry Mintzberg's [1979] study of the structuring of organizations, combine various perspectives into sophisticated schemes which recognize the many different factors that shape organizational life.

Information systems, as a practical discipline, often incorporates or builds on the findings of organizational theorists. They may incorporate decision-making techniques, or new administrative control methods, or they may re-structure the organization's activities. But even if an information system project does not explicitly include such objectives, it is embedded in an organizational context. Any information system project is in effect an intervention in an organization. It affects, even if only indirectly, the organization's structure, the employees' work conditions, or the way decisions are made and management is exercised. For an analyst seeking to improve information communication and decision making, organizational theory is not only a rich source of ideas for innovation, but also necessary source of knowledge for avoiding problems. Unless analysts understand these aspects they risk missing out vital organiz-ational needs and introducing inappropriate artefacts which, instead of providing benefit, may damage organizational performance. Chapter 8 of this book will discuss how the socio-technical approach to the development of information systems has been informed by studies of human motivation and work conditions.

There is one further reason why organizational theory is relevant to inform-ation systems. The success of any innovation in information systems depends on the effectiveness of management within an organization. Paul Strassmann's research [1985; 1990], collecting data from firms that invested in information technology, suggests that managerial effectiveness is the most significant factor predicating the success of information systems innovations. He used the term *return on management* to emphasize that investing large amounts of capital in new technology systems will not bring the expected benefits *unless* the organization first has effective and appropriate management practices in place. This observation has particular significance for information systems developers. Many information systems projects aim at improving the performance of problematic organizations. Inefficient bureaucracies may introduce ambitious computerization projects with the objective of modernizing their functioning and overcoming their inefficiency, but both the development project itself, and the new ways of functioning that the organization has to adjust to, require at the very least competent management of change. The information systems analyst must be able to study carefully not only the information aspects of the organization concerned, but also its capacity to manage the transition to a new way of working and, finally, to accommodate the new organizational function-ing that it introduces. In chapter 11 some of these issues are taken further in the particular context of developing information systems strategies and planning information systems, recognizing these activities as essentially concerned with promoting organizational change.

Technology

The final concept that we will discuss in this chapter is technology, not the bits and bytes of particular computers or networks, but the overall characteristics of the 'new ways of doing things' which we introduce into organizational life, including different ways of thinking about what we do. Technology in this sense is one of the most important factors of any production activity and technological change can have profound consequences.

A good historical example is agriculture. In industrialized countries over the past century, productivity in agriculture has increased at an impressive rate. In the United States, agricultural activities engaged 50% of the country's labour force in the 1860s; now they occupy less than 4%. With the application of science and technology, for example in plant breeding, use of fertilizers, tractors and combines, this small proportion of the labour force not only manages to feed the population of the United States, but produces one of the largest agricultural surpluses in the world. To understand this it is not enough to know that a tractor is equal in power to 15 horses, that a combine can harvest 35 tons of grain per day, or that a certain strain of wheat gives 50% more yield. One must also understand that farmers have changed their ways of thinking, reorganized their farming methods, and the communities in which they live have had to change too.

In a similar way, computers and communications are often seen as being the basis of productivity leaps in modern economies, just as steam power and later electricity formed the basis for the industrial economies that evolved through the 19th and early 20th century. Information processing activities have come to be seen as essential to successful enterprises and information technology provides companies with the potential to put their information resources to more effective use for management purposes and for launching new products or services. Moreover, information itself has acquired a commodity value and new business opportunities have arisen in the emerging information services sector. One classic example is the rise of Reuters as a multi-million pound corporation selling information to the world's financial institutions, as well as news.

Technology does not just bring economic growth opportunities, it introduces social changes too, both at the work place, in the home and society in general. In the early twentieth century, the primary example of technology in the work place has been the mass production factory based on Taylorism, where machines set the pace of the production process and machine operators perform routine tasks endlessly. This style of economic activity, exemplified early in the century by the factories of the Ford Motor Company, has been described as *Fordism*, an economic system based on mass-production of standard goods for mass con-sumption by a population that can earn enough money to pay for them [Jones, 1991]. A balance is therefore needed between the efficiency of the system and its ability to employ its customers. This is the system that has brought us motor cars, refrigerators, radios, televisions and so on, and can certainly be seen as resulting in a profound social and economic change.

There are negative aspects to this style of technology use. Automation of production can be seen as the cause of unemployment and de-skilling, and information technology provides powerful means of control. These means of control fall into the hands of management, corporations, government institutions and rich nations, with workers, customers, citizens, the environment and Third World nations as potential victims. Nevertheless, many look at the social impact of the information technologies more optimistically. They point out the liberating nature of the technology, freeing man from hazardous jobs, as in the cases of robots doing nasty but necessary tasks; they see technology as providing the capability to produce the basic necessities, such as food and shelter, with less human effort, thus allowing free time for creative work and leisure; they see new ways of alleviating poverty in poorer nations by increasing food production and improving health care, education and other social provisions.

To explore the apparent differences between the potential of technology and the actual economic and social changes that are taking place, we need to broaden our perspective to consider the context within which technical change occurs. The capacity of new machines, and new techniques for doing things developed in scientists' laboratories, has only theoretical value. It is the way the new machines and techniques are deployed in the world that makes the difference between economic success or failure, or between emancipation and alienation or oppression. Machines alone, no matter how sophisticated they are, neither perform economic miracles nor determine social change. Their effects depend on economic, organizational and social forces. For example, the elimination of poverty from a Third World country does not come with the acquisition of new machines and the mastering of new techniques. It depends, among other things, on a country's capacity to develop effective administration and to adjust to the dynamics of the global capitalist system. Even in industrialized countries, statistics show that overall productivity did not substantially increase during the 1970s and 1980s, despite the fact that during this period there was heavy investment in the new information and related technologies. This point is taken up further in the introduction to part III, but for the moment we might offer an explanation that organizations have not (yet) managed to fully develop appropriate structures to gain from their technical innovations.

Several theories elaborate on the connections between technology, economic development and social and institutional change. In economics, the theory of 'Kontratiev long waves' links the pervasiveness of certain types of technologies with periods in economic development. A technology is characterized as 'pervasive' if it generates a wide range of new products and services, reduces the costs and improves the performance of the processes, services and products of many sectors of the economy, gains widespread social acceptance, and generates strong industrial interest as a means of raising profitability and securing competitive advantage. Such pervasive technical innovation is accompanied by radical changes in the structure of an economy. It seems clear that information technologies are at the centre of the present wave of change for many countries, but the socio-economic changes that result do not follow neat technological imperatives and, as many researchers have emphasized, to understand the way information technology is taken up or appropriated we need to take into account economic trends and social pressures.

In the microcosm of an organization, the establishment of new information systems is the carrier of the powerful and pervasive information technology. Indeed, very often one of the objectives of information systems projects is technology transfer, that is, the introduction into the organization of the capacity to use certain information technologies. It should be understood that technology transfer does not only mean the acquisition and installation of hardware and software. It includes development of the required skills to make use of the technology, reorganization to accommodate it effectively, and the acceptance of it by employees. The development of an information system extends far beyond the engineering of a computer application. It involves restructuring of the functioning of the organization and the way it relates to its customers and suppliers. Yet many information systems projects aiming at technology transfer are very narrowly and technically defined, and do not envisage, plan or design organizational and social change. It is then uncertain what new structures and work procedures will develop around the new technical arrangements. They may work, if people are motivated to accept them, or be bypassed, subverted, reshaped or rejected if people have reasons to react to them. Technology transfer will succeed or fail accordingly.

Such information systems projects do not only raise expectations for growth and qualitative improvement of services. They can also cause apprehension about deterioration of work conditions and erosion of established rights, and the information system developer is in the middle of this turmoil. Will the advent of yet more office technology turn the office of the future into a place resembling the mass production factory? Will a new management information system introduce stricter control of the various production units of a company, or allow them to develop their business more autonomously? For some questions like these, we can learn from research studies that have related technical systems and technologies with organizational structure, for example linking early mainframe technologies to a move to centralization, and today's network based distributed systems to decentralization. However, very little is predetermined about information technology and organizational change.

Theoretical foundations for information systems

There are many other theoretical works which may provide useful insights for the study and the practices of information handling activities of organizations. Many of them are interesting, even challenging, but rather incomplete (theoretical frameworks rather than theories), such as various attempts in psychology to explain cognitive phenomena, or collective work performed by groups of employees. Some are well defined and comprehensive, such as mathematical theories of decision making and problem solving, but they tend to be of limited applicability to real world situations exhibiting complex combinations of conditions.

Because there is no complete theory of information systems, the field of information systems has been described as 'fragmented adhocracy' [Banville and Landry, 1989]. This fragmentation is problematic in so far as the various approaches do not inform each other. To some extent this has been true, and an antagonistic attitude is often detectable in information systems research and practice, as in the effort to develop competing methods for systems development. However, having multiple theories for a field of study does not need to be alarming. Indeed, although some calls have been made to consolidate different theoretical views into one framework [Falkenberg *et al.*, 1995], it is generally accepted that this is not a good idea, or the time is not yet ripe. A plurality of theoretical approaches seems to be accepted as necessary to make sense of the multi-faceted processes of information systems change.

Closer investigation of the plurality of theories used in information systems research and practice suggests that they can be traced into a few widely influential reference theories. By reference theory we mean an intellectual construct that provides general principles for making sense of the world. For example, Marxism has been a reference theory which has provided fundamental ideas about how human society is structured and how it evolves through history, and has had an impact on many fields of thought, including philosophy, economics, sociology, and history. Reference theories cut across conventional boundaries of academic disciplines; they try to address universal questions about the nature of society and social change, and imply general principles for perceiving social phenomena and for organizing intellectual inquiry. Moreover, they have methodological implications, determining 'valid' ways of conducting research and professional practice.

In the remainder of this chapter we briefly introduce reference theories which have been influential in the information systems field, namely systems theory, organizational rationalism, structuration, critical theory, and post-modernism.

Systems theory

Although the origin of the notion of 'system' is often traced back to the Aristotelian holistic world view and his statement 'the whole is more or less than the sum of its parts', systems theory is a much more recent development, which started taking shape in the late 1920s and grew to become one of the most influential contemporary ways of perceiving the world and thinking about areas of study.

Systems theory was formed as a result of increasing doubts about the ability of classical science to deal with complex phenomena. The basic principles of classical science, as it was established by thinkers such as Galileo and Descartes, are to break down problems into as many separate simple parts as possible and to try to discover one-way causality between the elementary unit or variables of these parts. This approach has worked impressively well in fields such as physics, but was less successful in fields studying complex entities, such as biology. In the study of living organisms, biologists felt that not only did they have to cope with many variables, they had also to understand the order and organization of these variables. Similar problems were faced in social science fields such as psychology and sociology.

Such concerns led to the development of the 'general systems theory', a logico-mathematical field which attempted to formulate principles of 'systems' applicable to all sciences [Bertalanffy, 1972]. General systems theory developed a wealth of models, mathematical techniques and concepts, many of which are applicable across conventional disciplines, addressing issues of interrelations within a 'whole'. These models, techniques, and concepts are general abstractions in the sense that they do not consider the nature of elements and forces in a 'system'. As such it amounts to a conceptual approach for the study of complex phenomena, rather than a specific 'theory'.

The development of general systems theory has had practical and philosophical implications. In the practical realm, it has provided a powerful basis for modern technology. In particular, computer and telecommunication technologies embody systems concepts, models, and techniques, and have themselves contributed to the efforts of advancing the interdisciplinary general theory of systems.

Philosophically, general systems theory contributed to the legitimisation of an epistemology (type of valid knowledge) different from that of positivism or empiricism of classical science, which aims at establishing linear causality between observed parts of the world. General systems theory sought to support the view that perception is not an accurate reflection of 'real things'. Knowledge is not a simple approximation to 'truth' or 'reality', but an interaction between knower and known, and thus dependent on factors of a biological, cultural and linguistic nature.

Yet, the vision of the founders of general systems theory that, with time, common concepts, models, and techniques would provide a cohesive interdisciplinary science, fundamentally different from classical sciences, proved unrealistic. Today the concept of system is widely used in many fields, but often only in its broad meaning of 'interdependent set of elements'. Systems ideas have lost their initial epistemological bite. Without the grandiose intellectual ambition of general systems theory, debate on significant contemporary issues in many fields continues to find useful expression through systems concepts. Such an example is the distinction between 'hard systems thinking' and 'soft systems thinking' which points out a difference of approach for understanding and resolving questions regarding engineering systems and social systems (human activity systems in Checkland's terminology) [Checkland, 1981].

In information systems, elements of systems theory have formed part of the conceptual fundamentals in all of the field's thematic streams. As mentioned above, terms such as system, sub-system, control, boundary, and environment constitute the field's pervasive vocabulary. Systems modelling techniques have been widely influential in designing information technology applications as well as in organizing the design process. Also, systems concepts and models have had an impact on information systems in as much as they are used to conceptualize organizations and society. They have also helped understand that optimizing the behaviour of individual components of an information system does not necessarily result in the most satisfactory behaviour of the ensemble that they are part of. For example, maximizing the production capacity of each machine in a factory does not guarantee maximum production from the factory. It may even have a counter-productive effect on the performance, leading to more frequent breakdowns or over-stretching the people operating the production system, with detrimental results for overall effectiveness. Better results might be achieved by considering the factory's functioning as a whole entity, rather than by working out independent optimizations of its component parts.

Overall, however, the use of systems ideas has not led to a comprehensive theory for the field of information systems. Rather, it has sustained equally well distinct and often conflicting approaches, which reflect more general differences of orientation, such as between perspectives of engineering and of social intervention, that exist in the study and practice of information systems.

Organizational rationalism

With the term organizational rationalism we refer to the stream of thought concerned with the identification of principles for deploying the resources of organizations in order to survive and excel in the capitalist market economy. Unlike systems theory, organizational rationalism is not a theoretical work which can be attributed to a particular person or school of thought. It represents a much more pervasive attitude towards the study and the practice of contemporary organizations, and can be deduced from the shared ideological and epistemological fundamentals of the prevailing 'orthodoxy' of theories and practical rules on how to structure and run organizations. Although more often identified through the work of its critics, rather than the declared intellectual positions of its followers, organizational rationalism can be recognized as a distinct conceptual and epistemological platform for the study of human organizations in contemporary society.

The origins of organizational rationalism can be traced in the work of Max Weber, who at the turn of the last century studied structures of authority in organizations and established the notion of 'bureaucracy' as a mechanism of efficient administration. He defined the 'ideal type of bureaucracy' as an organization functioning according to a formal rationality on impersonal legal and technical rules. The aim was to design the most efficient form of organization possible, working like a machine, with precision, speed, lack of ambiguity, and continuity.

Although the bureaucratic organization was conceived primarily as a way of achieving the goals of political authority, it has been widely adopted as a model of efficient administration for the business firm, and continued to be studied by influential organization theorists, such as Merton, Selznick, Alvin Gouldner, and Peter Blau. Bureaucracy, of course, has had numerous critics and it has revealed many unanticipated dysfunctions, to the extent that the word is now often used as a synonym for inefficiency. Nevertheless, the importance of Max Weber's work lies in being the first attempt to produce systematic categories for organizational analysis, aiming at establishing a universal model of efficient organization. Organizational theory was later developed as a branch of sociology committed to improving organizational efficiency. As such, it is concerned with helping managers and administrators, though it contains a rather mixed bag of general approaches to social phenomena in organizations and a number of specialised research fields, such as decision making theory, management theory, administration science, industrial and organizational psychology. Nevertheless, organisational rationalism has been the dominant approach of inquiry. It aims at deriving the general logic of organizational functioning, applicable to all organizations through the use of 'scientific' method. The first 'successes' of this approach, such as Taylor's scientific management, Fayol's principles of management, or Simon's administrative science, have given rise to ubiquitous practices and underpin up to this day the fundamental knowledge of the professional 'manager'.

From this perspective, a great deal of attention has been given to the structure of organizations and the distribution of decision-making authority. Systems concepts have been widely used, on the assumption that an organization is a complex purposeful entity whose goal is commonly pursued by its participants. However, the use of systems concepts has not, in general, been accompanied by the epistemological wish of the systems theorists mentioned above to overcome the limitations of positivism. Rather, organisational rationalism derives general 'truth' statements through empirical research establishing cause and effect relationship between 'factors', such as technology, and organizational characteristics, such as the structure of management.

Today organizational rationalism continues to be the dominant approach in management research, providing much of the intellectual legitimacy for the mainly normative field of business studies, and has been particularly influential in information systems research. It has provided models of organizational communication and decision making both for the development of applications, such as decision support systems, and the structuring of methodical systems development practice. Moreover, it constitutes the most favoured research approach in the academic establishment regarding issues of information systems management and the value of information technology. The typical research publication in these sub-fields concerns some empirical testing of hypotheses regarding cause and effect relationships between aspects of technology or conditions of its use and organizational characteristics, and is intended to inform professional managers on effective actions.

Organizational rationalism has provided confidence of 'rigorous' social science research to the young field of information systems, and led to the development of theoretical propositions regarding IT and organizational structure and functioning that can inform professional management. But its dominance as 'the right type' of information systems research has restricted both the research questions addressed and the lines of intellectual inquiry pursued by information systems researchers. Increasing criticism of the limitations of organizational rationalism as a reference theory has been accompanied by the use of by alternative research approaches from the social sciences, including structuration theory, critical theory, and ideas of post-modernism, which are outlined below.

Structuration theory

The theory of structuration, developed by the sociologist Anthony Giddens in a series of publications [1979, 1984], provides an epistemological and ontological perspective for sociology, and social sciences more generally. Giddens' theory represents an effort to reconcile a fundamental division between two traditions of thought in the social sciences: one which emphasizes the pre-eminence of the social whole over its constituent actors, the human subjects, and the other which makes the study of subjective experience the foundation of the social or human sciences. The most dominant schools of thought in sociology, functionalism and structuralism, despite their difference of approach, tend to study whole 'structures' of social phenomena, such as patterns of social relations, and they pursue a naturalistic, objectivist perspective. In contrast, the hermeneutic school of thought studies social phenomena by focusing on action and meaning in human conduct.

Giddens' structuration theory retains people as the active, skilled agents who produce, sustain and transform social life. Moreover, he uses the notion of 'structure' to consider the organised sets of rules and resources of social systems. He then links these two ideas and suggests that 'action' and 'structure' are interdependent: structure is produced by actors using it as a resource and at the same time reproducing it as a restraining outcome of their interaction. Social practices are produced and reproduced by knowledgeable human agents, who monitor the ongoing flow of social life. This reflexive monitoring of action constitutes a fundamental idea in structuration theory, and leads to the notion of the 'duality of structure', meaning that 'reflexive monitoring of action both draws upon and reconstitutes the institutional organization of society'. This recursive relationship between structure and action, each iteratively shaping the other, achieves the integration of action and structure conveyed by the name 'structuration'.

The theory of structuration provides a rich perception of social phenomena, which elaborates on the nature and the significance of many fundamental concepts such as communication, power, time and space. Its epistemological and practical implications are relevant to the whole spectrum of social sciences. Structuration theory has provided a powerful perspective for the study of the relationship between social change and technology, and more specifically for the study of the organizational implications of information technology [Walsham, 1993]. Adopting a structuration perspective, 'technology development is a social activity involving a network of actors, such as engineers and users, and structures, such as organizations and markets, that shape the way technology is constructed' [Salzman & Rosenthal, 1994]. A useful overview of structuration theory in the context of information systems is given in Orlikowski & Robey [1991].

Critical theory

Critical theory has its roots in the work of a group of German writers connected to the Institute of Social Research at the University of Frankfurt before World War II, known as the 'Frankfurt School'. Best known among them are Max Horkheimer, Theodor Adorno, and Herbert Markuse. The rise of Nazism forced Horkheimer, Adorno and Markuse to leave Germany. They moved to California, where they wrote most of their work. Horkheimer and Adorno returned to Germany after the war and re-established the Institute of Social Research. Their analysis is concerned with the changing nature of capitalism and the forms of domination emerging from this change [Kincheloe & McLaren, 1994].

Horkheimer, Adorno and Markuse did not produce a unified critical theory. However, their work crystallized particular ways of viewing society, social action, and social science as such, which established the fundamentals of a distinct theoretical thinking and has been adopted by many researchers in all fields of social science. Critical theory pays attention to the construction of social experience and is based on the belief that social sciences have an emancipatory role to play, and can eventually lead to a more egalitarian and democratic social order. Thus, critical theorists in any domain of social science attempt a form of social or cultural criticism based on some fundamental assumptions. They accept that thought cannot be objective and neutral, and practice cannot be impartial, each is mediated by power relations which are historically constituted in society; that contemporary societies tend to reproduce various distinct, although interconnected, forms of oppression, such as on the basis of class, gender, or race; that the inferior social status of unprivileged groups is not inevitable; that social science research should consciously endeavour to assist subordinates to challenge their social status. They also argue that social reality is subjective; values and ideological positions cannot be isolated from the perception and description of facts; and language has a central role in the formation of subjectivity.

Many researchers have built on this line of thinking, and elaborated on critical theory ideas from a variety of perspectives, such as feminism, or Marxism. It is beyond the scope of this book to introduce the variety of critical theory perspectives, such as those found in the voluminous and complex theoretical work of Habermas or Foucault, to mention only the two most influential critical theorists today. Suffice it to say that critical theory, based on the fundamental ideas mentioned above, provides a reference theory for conceptual analysis in many domains of social science.

Critical theory ideas have been used in a number of studies in information systems. Lyytinen [1992] reviewed the use of Habermas' critical social theory – the most explicitly identifiable of the critical theoretical thought in the information systems field. He found that critical social theory has been applied for the following tasks:

To criticize the instrumental rationality underlying information systems research and practice. Authors such as Winograd and Flores [1986], Klein and Hirschheim [1987], and Mowshowitz [1980] use Horkheimer's concept of instrumental reasoning and draw from Habermas' theory on language to discuss critically the assumptions behind the use of computers to support decision making in organizations. The notion of instrumental rationality refers to the application of reason for exploring means and assessing their consequences, without questioning whether the purposes that these means are marshalled to serve are reasonable. The fundamental criticism here is that the use of computer technology without questioning the utilitarian ethos of contemporary industrial society is limiting the exercise of human choice and ultimately endangering human existence.

To criticize the dominant research norms. Such publications, [for example Klein and Lyytinen, 1985; Lyytinen, 1986] create awareness of the prevailing biases of information systems research, and highlight critical theory as a possible alternative research approach. These are based primarily on Habermas' theory of knowledge-constitutive interests, which makes the point that knowledge (including scientific knowledge) is not value free and objective, but serves some peoples' interests. Such interests can be technical (to control and manipulate the physical world), practical (to communicate with other people), or emancipatory (to get free from false ideas).

To classify and criticize systems development approaches. Lyytinen's classification [1986] used Habermas' interest theory and communicative action theory and showed that most information systems development approaches support an interest in technical control. Furthermore, critical social theory has been suggested as a useful basis to develop alternative approaches to overcome the narrowness of vision of currently used methods. For example, Klein and Hirschheim [1985] suggested the use of a hermeneutic forecasting method based on role playing scenarios to overcome the weaknesses of conventional requirements determination methods.

However, Lyytinen admits in the summary of his review, that so far the information systems field has used critical theory mechanistically, by reiterating Habermas' key arguments. Critical theory has not made a major impact on the theoretical grounding of information systems.

Postmodernism

Postmodernism, the debate on the distinction between 'modernity' and 'postmodernity' expresses a variety of criticisms of the industrial societies of the twentieth century and their culture, and expresses a variety of 'different ideals for the present and the future' [Rose, 1991]. There is no general agreement on the nature of the 'postmodern condition', but a number of generally accepted characteristics of modernity are identified and constitute the background for the conceptions of postmodernity. However, it should be clear that postmodernity does not necessarily refer to a state of society following modernity.

Modernity refers to the cultural and economic forms which have been developed during the period from the Renaissance to contemporary time, with more emphasis on the more recent forms in the twentieth century. At the core of modernity lies the belief of the Enlightenment that the development of scientific knowledge can lead to human emancipation from the irrationalities of myth, religion, superstition and arbitrary use of power, and provide people with the capacity to dominate over nature and free themselves from scarcity and catastrophic natural phenomena. The Enlightenment is seen as a revolution that imposed reason as the unquestionable philosophical answer to life and substituted the 'original explanation of life' of different cultural traditions. These ideas imposed also a notion of 'progress' towards a universal truth which is advantageous for all. The process of modernization is seen as one which destroys in order to create, encompasses continuous innovation, and gives rise to the ephemeral and the chaotic in order to lead to the eternal [Harvey, 1989].

The notion of postmodernity, while it can be traced in the early part of this century, is used to refer to certain trends and concerns that have been manifested since the 1960s in advanced industrialised societies. It rests upon the criticism of the fundamental idea of the 'rationalistic' thinking, which is the prevailing philosophy of western culture, aiming at a single correct explanation of phenomena with the implicit assumption that others' views are mistaken. This prevailing philosophy is seen as 'instrumental reasoning' which, as explained above, deals with means but is unable to define the end, and has been repeatedly criticized as catastrophic for humankind [Adorno & Horkheimer, 1979; Weizenbaum, 1976].

Thus, the condition of post-modernity is often perceived in terms of what it is not, rather than what it is. It suggests opposition to all broad interpretative theories which claim to explain and predict individual and social behaviour – the grand narrativee – , and all unified representations of the world. It calls also for abandoning the rationalistic thinking and the seeking of universal and eternal truths. As a result it shows concern with 'otherness', and recognizes that all groups have a right to speak for themselves in their own voice.

The role of information and communication technology and the significance of the intensification of information activities are seen in different ways in relation to modernity and post-modernity. Touraine [1990] points out that information technology has been used to consolidate the triumph of reason, as the machine applies perfectly established rules of operation, usually with a quantitative rationale, and avoids ambiguity and discretionary decision. Thus, he suggests that the 'information revolution' tends to support and strengthen the rationality of modernism.

Other writers, though, discern significant changes. For example, Lash and Urry [1994] present the view that people are becoming increasingly critical and 'reflexive' to the homogenization and abstraction of tradition and history produced by modernism and instrumental reasoning. These authors suggest that, to the extent that such trends gain ground, new information and communication technologies can be significant facilitators of a new socio-economic order.

The ideas of postmodernism can be found in many fields. In organizational theory and management there is increasing interest in the ideas of postmodernism. Clegg [1990], for example, discusses the postmodern organization structures, which can be distinguished from the modernist form of the bureaucracy. An example of postmodern organizational form is flexible specialization, the formation of a network of collaborating firms, which tend to follow a niche-based marketing strategy and have a craft-oriented or multi-skilled workforce. Postmodern organizational theory questions the validity of theories suggesting optimal ways of organizing and managing. Authors on postmodern organizational studies emphasize the significance of culture and point out different perspectives on management, such as a feminist perspective [Boje *et al.*, 1996].

In information systems there has been research into the use of information technology and communications to support the so-called postmodern organizational forms. An example is the Oticon case that we outline in chapter 11. Also, many writers convey the postmodernist rationale and apply postmodern theoretical perspectives and concepts in information systems. Here are some examples: Ciborra [1995], uses postmodern ideas, such as 'deconstruction' and emergent, rather than pre-planned organizational action. Beath and Orlikowski [1994] apply deconstruction as a method to understand the significance (or lack of significance) attributed to participation in professional system development practices. Knights and Murray [1994] study the use and development of information systems in a context of power and politics through detailed and localised studies of management practice, highlighting, in particular, a feminist perspective. Such attempts can be seen as 'experiments' in departing from the dominant positivist research method and intended to develop awareness of the existence and value of interpretative research.

The value of reference theories for information systems studies

Often reference theories are explicitly used as a conceptual vehicle to conduct research and guide practice, for example, to determine questions for investigation or issues to deal with, to present them in conceptual terms, and to determine legitimate tools and methods for their investigation. However, their value is more fundamental than this; it is formative and educational.

The significance of reference theories lies in shaping our perceptive capacity, rather than just providing means for effective inquiry and professional practice. Indeed, no reference theory can provide an efficient and 'failure proof' way of making good use of new technologies, and it is unrealistic to expect that grand theories offer short cuts in the social struggle related with the exploitation of technological potential. Research, as well as professional practice, is to a large extent intuitive, interpretative and judgmental, and exposure to the ideas of reference theories empowers information systems experts with intellectual capacity to grasp significant dimensions of information systems change. As Lyytinen notes, such efforts succeed when they create awareness of the ontological, epistemological and ethical dimensions of information systems research.

Exercises and discussion issues

1. Consider the following letter, written by a marketing director to a colleague in the same firm, and analyze it to discover all the types of information that the writer is discussing using the framework set out in the section on information in this chapter.

   Edith A. Whitley
   Analysis Department

   Dear Edith,
   I am sorry that I lost my temper on the telephone yesterday, I was just very frustrated as I tried to understand the points that you were making.

Now I have received the report and the accompanying graphs the situation is a bit clearer to me.

Your analysis of the market research survey, and the confidential notes you scribbled on it, make it clear that our customers are equally spread over the under 40s and the over 40s, and the projection of population trends makes it clear that potentially the over 40s are going to become our principal customers in the years ahead. I have checked on the computer the raw data on the shape of sales over the last five years and think I can confirm that this is the way the market has moved.

As you might expect, when I then checked on next year's production plans it would seem that nobody has begun to take this on board. The boffins who maintain the mountain of software that produces the production plan are incapable of including this sort of input before the end of the next century!

I will try to put your report on the agenda for the next board meeting, but before that I will have a quiet word with Bill next time I see him at the club. Of course before it goes to the full board it must go to the steering group, but I think we can get round that, everybody else does whatever the correct procedure is!

Now this is just about all done please send me the expense claim form, authorization number, budget account reference and the docket code from the accounting department and I will countersign it and pass it on for their so-called express processing. If there are any further small items of expense that you expect to incur, just put them on the form as if they have already happened, this will simplify matters for both of us.

Yours

Marion Angelides

Marketing Director

2. Analyze the above letter in terms of pragmatics, semantics, syntax and empirics. Consider this in the light of it being sent in an envelope and on headed company notepaper, by fax on plain paper, or by electronic-mail to Edith's mailbox.

3. Is the solar system a system in the terms set out in this chapter? Consider the question from the perspective of a theologian, an astronomer, a physicist and a science-fiction writer.

4. The development of information systems is often organized with a strict demarcation of tasks for analysts, designers, programmers and project managers. Consider how the concept of job enlargement and job enrichment could be applied to each of these jobs. Discuss the benefits and the risks of such reorganizations.

References

Ackoff, R.L. (1971) 'Towards a system of systems concepts', in *Management Science*, Vol. 17, No. 11.

Adorno, T., and Horkheimer, M. (1972) *Dialectic of Enlightenment*, Herder & Herder, New York.

Banville, C. and Landry, M. (1989) 'Can the field of MIS be disciplined?', *Communications of the ACM.*, Vol. 32, No. 1, pp 48-60.

Beath, C.M. & Orlikowski, W.J. (1994) 'The contradictory structure of systems development methodologies: deconstructing the IS-user relationship in information engineering' in *Information Systems Research*, Vol. 5, No. 4, pp 350-377.

Beer, S. (1972) *Brain of the Firm*, Penguin, Harmondsworth.

Beer, S. (1979) *The Heart of Enterprise*, Wiley, Chichester.

Bertalanffy, L. von, (1972) The history and status of general systems theory, in Klir, G.J., (ed.) *Trends in General Systems Theory*, J. Wiley, pp 21-38.

Boje, D.M., Gephart, R.P. Jr & Thatchenkery, T.J. (1996) *Postmodern Management and Organization Theory*, Sage, London.

Checkland, P.B. (1981) *Systems Thinking, Systems Practice*. Wiley , Chichester.

Ciborra, C.U. (1994) 'A platform for surprises: the organization of global technology strategy at Olivetti', in Baskerville, R. Smithson, S. Ngwenyama, O., DeGross J.I. *Transforming organizations with information technology*, North Holland, Amsterdam.

Clegg, S. (1990) *Modern organisations: Organisation studies in the postmodern world*, Sage, London.

Emery, J. (1971) 'Cost/Benefit Analysis of Information Systems', The Society for Management Information Systems, Chicago.

Falkenberg, E.D., Hesse, W. and Olive, A. (1995) *Information Systems Concepts: Towards a consolidation of views (ISCO3)*, Chapman and Hall, London.

Giddens, A. (1979) *Central Problems in Social Theory*, Polity Press, Cambridge.

Giddens, A. (1984) *The Constitution of Society*, Polity Press, Cambridge.

Harvey, D. (1989) *The Condition of Postmodernity*, Blackwell, Oxford.

Jones, M.R. (1991) 'Post-industrial and post-Fordist perspectives on information systems' in *European Journal of Information Systems*, Vol. 1, No. 3, pp 171-182.

Kincheloe, D. and McLaren, P.L. (1994) 'Rethinking critical theory and qualitative research', in Denzin, N.K., Lincoln, Y.S. (eds.) *Handbook of Qualitative Research*, Sage, Thousand Oaks.

Knights, D. & Murray, F. (1994) *Managers Divided, Organisation Politics and Information Technology Management*, J. Wiley, Chichester.

Klein, H., and Hirschheim, R.A. (1985) 'Fundamental issues of decision support systems: a consequentialist perspective', *Decision Support Systems*, Vol. 1, No. 1, pp 5-23.

Klein, H., and Hirschheim, R.A. (1987) 'Social change and the future of information systems development', in Boland, R. and Hirschheim, R.A., (eds.) *Critical Issues in Information Systems Research*, Wiley, New York, pp 275-305.

Klein H., and Lyytinen, K., (1985) 'The poverty of scientism in information systems' in Mumford E., Hirschheim, R.A., Fitzgerald, G. and Wood-Harper, T. (eds.) *Research Methods in Information Systems*, North-Holland, Amsterdam, pp 131-161.

Land, F.F. (1985) 'Is an information theory enough?', in *The Computer Journal*, Vol. 28, No. 3, March.

Lash, S. and Urry, J. (1994) *Economies of Signs & Space*, SAGE Publications, London.

Liebenau, J. & Backhouse, J. (1990) *Understanding Information: An Introduction*, Macmillan Press, Basingstoke.

Lyytinen, K. (1986) 'Information systems development as social action – framework and critical implications', PhD dissertation, Department of Computer Science, University of Jyvaskyla, Finland.

Lyytinen, K. (1992) 'Information systems and critical theory', in Alversson, M., Willmott, H. (eds.), *Critical Management Studies*, Sage, London, pp 159-180.

Mintzberg, H. (1979) *The Structuring of Organizations*, Prentice Hall, Englewood Cliffs.

Mowshowitz, A. (1980) 'Ethics, and cultural integration in a computerized world' in Mowshowitz, A., (ed.) *Human Choice and Computers, 2*. North-Holland, Amsterdam.

Orlikowski, W.J. & Robey, D.. (1991) 'Information technology and the structuring of organizations' in *Information Systems Research*, Vol. 2, No. 2, pp. 143-169.

Pugh, D.S., Hickson, D.J.& Hinings, C.R (1983) *Writers on Organizations*, (3rd edition), Penguin Books, London.

Rose, M. (1991) *The post-modern & the post-industrial – a critical analysis*. Cambridge University Press, Cambridge.

Salzman, H. and Rosenthal S. (1994) *Software by Design*, Oxford University Press, New York.

Shannon, C. & Weaver, W. (1949) *The Mathematical Theory of Communication*, University of Illinois Press.

Stamper, R. (1987) 'Semantics', in Boland, R. and Hirschheim, R.A., (eds.) *Critical Issues in Information Systems Research*, Wiley, New York.

Strassmann, P. (1985) *Information payoff: The transformation of work in the Electronic Age*, Free Press, New York.

Strassmann, P. (1990) *The Business Value of Computers – An executive's guide*, Information Economics Press, Connecticut.

Touraine, A. (1990) 'The idea of revolution' in Featherstone M. (ed.) *Global Culture. Nationalism, Globalization and Modernity. A Theory, Culture & Society Special Issue*, SAGE Publications, London.

Walsham, G. (1993) *Interpreting Information Systems in Organizations*, Wiley, Chichester.

Weizenbaum, J. (1976) *Computer Power and Human Reason*, W.H. Freeman, San Francisco.

Winograd, T., and Flores, F. (1986) *Understanding Computers and Cognition*, Ablex Publishing, Norwood.

Further reading

The book edited by Pugh referenced above provides a rewarding guided tour through the most prominent writers on organizations. Handy provides another accessible and informative view of how organizations work. The Allan & Massey book provides an analysis of the state of the British Economy with a particular focus on how industrial structure has changed and what technology has to do with this. Chapter 3, written by John Allen and entitled *Towards a post-industrial economy* provides an analysis of what the new, information based, service economy really is, while chapter 4, by Richard Meegan and entitled *A Crisis of Mass Production*, discusses the advent of Fordism, its decline, and what is to follow. Ashby's introduction to cybernetics is a classic work on systems concepts, which contains clear description of particularly influential ideas, such as his 'law of requisite variety'. Orlikowski and Baroudi's paper provides a useful overview of alternative research approaches and assumptions in the contemporary field of information systems.

Allen, J. & Massey, D. (editors) (1988) *The Economy in Question*, Sage Publications (in association with the Open University), London.

Ashby, W.R. (1984) *An Introduction to Cybernetics*, Methuen, London.

Handy, C.B. (1981) *Understanding Organizations,* Penguin Books, London.

Orlikowski, W.J. & Baroudi, J.J.. (1991) 'Studying information technology in organizations: research approaches and assumptions' in *Information Systems Research*, Vol. 2, No. 1, pp 1-28.

7 The life cycle model and prototyping

- *The popularity of the life cycle*
- *Shortcomings of the life cycle model*
- *Modifications to the life cycle model*
- *Prototyping within the life cycle*
- *Alternative models of information systems development*
- *What really is prototyping?*

The process of information systems development and use is usually viewed as a broadly linear pattern of tasks similar to that described in part I of this book. This simple model has been extensively used for more than 30 years and has given shape to the practices of systems development. Most methods and techniques used by information system professionals fit one or more of the stages of the life cycle model – with particular emphasis on the analysis and the design stages. Many authors and organizations promoting standards for inform-ation systems development, such as the National Computing Centre (NCC) in Britain, have adopted and spread its use via their training programmes.

The widespread use of the model does not mean that it has always been seen as satisfactory. Often projects that strictly follow the life cycle prove inflexible and unable to cope with the complex information systems development tasks. The life cycle has often been criticized as an inappropriate or over-rigid guide to information systems development, yet the model has not been abandoned. Rather its original rigid form, often referred to as the 'traditional', 'classical', or 'conventional' life cycle has been altered to accommodate flexibility and, over time, the model has become more sophisticated. The result is that the life cycle is still today the fundamental model that underlies most information systems development approaches, but its original linear form has been modified in various ways to overcome its most dysfunctional aspects.

There are, however, some rather different models for systems development, which neither follow a single ordered set of predefined tasks, nor aim at delivering a complete product. These evolutionary or incremental models are the result of more recent efforts to cope with the high degrees of uncertainty, change, and complexity that many organizations face and the need for continuous response. This in turn is reinforced by a desire to exploit the capabilities of modern development tools, in particular packaged software and computer-based tools.

In this chapter we explore the strengths and shortcomings of the life cycle model and describe the most significant modifications that have been proposed and practised. We also examine in detail one widely discussed alternative, the

141

evolutionary model of development. In the discussions of both these fundamental models we will repeatedly refer to the 'prototyping' method for systems
development. Prototyping is often proposed as an effective method to use in
building systems, but different authors mean different things by this term. The
final part of this chapter examines the concept of prototyping and clarifies the
ways it is related both to the life cycle and to alternative evolutionary models for
systems development.

The popularity of the life cycle

The life cycle is a model used to structure the development process as a sequence
of phases each containing a number of specific activities or stages. The names
and the number of phases and stages vary in different authors' descriptions of
the life cycle, but the fundamental characteristics of the model remain the same:
the development project begins with the establishment of clear specifications of
the system to be delivered; the development tasks are ordered as a sequential and
partitioned process of well defined activities intended to deliver specific results
to be handed on to a subsequent phase or stage; the development project ends
with the delivery of a system which is tested against the initial specifications for
correctness and completeness; this system is then expected to be used with
minor alterations for a period of time, possibly a number of years.

The life cycle emerged as the dominant framework to structure the tasks of
computer-based systems development in the 1960s, though the concept of the
life cycle was not first elaborated for the purposes of building computer
applications. It was borrowed from the engineering disciplines where it was
already established. Indeed, in those days computer technology was inflexible
and expensive and the main concern of the professionals who worked with it
was the construction of computer applications, configuring hardware and writing working programs. Their mission resembled that of engineers who construct
complicated artefacts, while the organizational objectives were relatively
straightforward.

Over this period the life cycle has been used to provide a basis for a rigorous
development process such as other engineering domains require. In an abstract
form, a process like this can be seen as a series of transformations: from a
specification containing a description of information processing needs in a
language which is understood by the people involved in and responsible for the
information activity, towards a computer executable system that performs the
functions of the initial specification, understood as it were by the computer. The
challenge is to make this transformation process as efficient and as error free as
possible. This is indeed the abstract ideal of software engineering and, as will be
seen in chapter 8, a great deal of effort has been dedicated to its realization.

However, for the majority of those involved in information systems
development, the life cycle is appealing not so much for its rigour, as for its

simplicity. As development of an information system is nowadays recognized as a much wider process than just the engineering of computer software, and while concern with efficiency of the development practices, and the correctness – or rather the validity – of software systems under development remains a very real concern, it is not engineering rigour which is valued most, but the ability to manage effectively the long and complex development process. In support of this the life cycle provides a simple structure which is easily understood and therefore makes it possible to spread common professional practices, and to generalize from the experience of one project to others.

By following the life cycle it becomes easier to plan and manage the tasks of systems development. The model provides a pattern which helps in planning the resources required: when different activities should take place; the different people who will be needed and when; the amounts of financial and computer resources required. This life cycle model accommodates several project management mechanisms: the project starts with the authorization of specifications and therefore makes clear what system the developers arc undertaking to deliver. At the end of each phase or stage the results can be 'tested' against the initial specifications, and in this way progress towards the goal be monitored. The results of a previous phase – the deliverable – can form the specifications for the next phase. If they are accepted then they can be handed on to another group of specialists to work on. The delivered system should then be able to operate to the satisfaction of the needs captured in the original specification, perhaps with minor changes, for a period of time. Of course, in many cases such project management practices are too simple to cope with all aspects of a development project, but it has been found to be a solid base upon which to build.

Shortcomings of the life cycle model

The main shortcomings of the life cycle model are a consequence of its fundamental principles:

- know your goal before you start;
- proceed along a straight route towards your goal;
- deliver a complete and correct system.

These principles presuppose that clear and accurate specifications of the required system are possible to draw up, that thereafter the development tasks can follow one single direction to realise them, and that the final product which the technical experts deliver will meet the needs of those who requested it for a certain period of time. All these assumptions are to a greater or lesser degree unrealistic.

The fallacy of accurate specification

We saw in chapter 2 that in the beginning of the development process there is
not always a well-defined need or opportunity. For very many reasons those who
are expected to benefit from some change in information handling cannot
describe accurately what system they need, nor can any theory guide the analyst
to form an accurate description of what is required. The expression of
requirements may only be vague, containing unrealistic or conflicting demands.
It is of course a part of the analysts' role to assist in clarifying what is expected
from a new system, and we have seen how the soft systems methodology can aid
them to achieve this. But even if a consensus agreement about a desirable system
is achieved in the problem definition phase, it cannot provide a guaranteed
specification which determines the goal, but only a common understanding
about what directions to take in searching for a satisfactory new system. As there
are no algorithms to describe how information handling occurs in organizations,
the analyst has continuously to consider and reconsider what system might
satisfy the various protagonists.

Many projects aim at assisting an organization to innovate, for example to
organize the distribution of its products in a new way, or to launch new services.
In such cases it is unrealistic to try to specify the new system once and for all in
the first development phase. Neither the analysts nor the other participants in
the process can predict the details of the performance of the substantially
different future organization. They may be able to describe what they believe the
new operations should be, but there is a great danger that any prematurely rigid
version of the new operations may in practice prove inappropriate.

The fallacy of a linear sequence of development tasks

If it is not possible to draw up an accurate specification of the system to be
developed, then it is not going to be possible to organize the development
process as a one-way succession of phases and stages progressing towards the
delivery of the prespecified system. Without clear specifications, the analyst
should continuously seek the co-operation of the participants in the targeted
information handling activity in order to produce a system that they will find
satisfactory. A strict linear set of system development activities is an unrealistic
demand. This linearity of the model has often been depicted with the waterfall
analogy, which implies how much easier it is to go forward (down) than to go
back (up), even when going back is what is required.

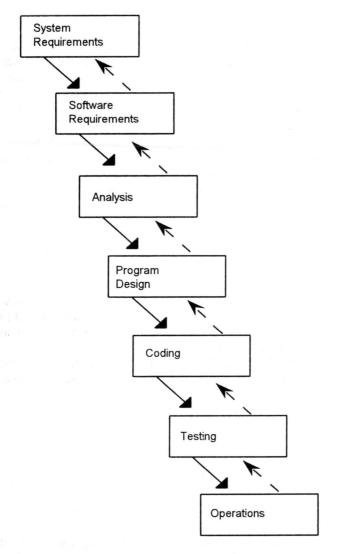

Figure 7.1 The waterfall model of the life cycle [Boehm, 1988]

In this waterfall model, each activity has to be completed in order to provide the input for the next one and there is no easy way to make modifications or incorporate additional insight in previous stages other than by returning to the immediately preceding step – figure 7.1. When the need for such backtracking occurs it is considered as a sign of failure, and often results in confusion and disproportionate increases in the costs of projects. The single-minded focus on using the deliverables produced by each of the individual stages to initiate the next leads to the need to 'freeze' these specifications once they are first approved. No changes are allowed on the output of a stage after it has been authorized and handed on as specifications for the following stage.

Few information systems development projects can successfully follow such a strictly linear structure of activities. For most systems, specifications are inherently fluid and incomplete, and for a variety of reasons the tasks of earlier stages often need to be repeated. As those working on a project proceed into more detailed tasks, they will discover inconsistencies in the specifications of the earlier stages, or they may develop better ideas that they would wish to accommodate. The virtual impossibility of returning and repeating preceding stages poses a particularly severe restriction on large systems projects lasting for many years. In such cases many changes in the organization or its environment are likely to happen after the fundamental requirements of the system are specified and while the system is still under development. If they are ignored the system is obsolete from the very beginning of its operation; if they are accommodated then development starts to take longer and longer.

The dubious role of the 'user'

Another problem with the traditional life cycle is the unrealistic demands it poses on those involved in systems development. Those who will be part of the resulting information systems, who will use its various components, are expected to be able to specify accurately what they want the system to do, confirm that they have been understood, and then authorize the go-ahead for each successive stage if they are satisfied with the previous results produced. On the other hand, they are not expected to be actively involved in the systems development activities themselves. Yet, since in most projects the initial specifications are not accurate and complete, those who have an interest in the outcome of the system under development will be asked to supply information throughout the development process. Without close involvement in the development tasks, these requests are hard to satisfy if they do not provide the context within which the information is being sought and will be used. It is assumed that it is the analyst who understands, who is in control, and who is responsible for the development activities. Most methods applied in projects which follow the traditional life cycle are technical tools assisting principally the analyst, the designer or the programmer, with inadequate consideration for the involvement or understanding of other players.

As information systems development has come to be understood more as a change in an organization's affairs rather than the engineering of a technical product, it has been increasingly recognized that those who will be involved with a new system need to be principal protagonists in the development process. Responsibility for the development of a new system cannot be delegated to technical experts since many decisions throughout the development project concern organizational rather than technical matters.

The inadequacy of a single entity development model

The life cycle, which describes a process for the construction and operation of a single entity, is inadequate as a guide to the multiple technical and organizational changes that comprise the development of an information system. The change implied in the development of a new way of handling information will often be too radical and of too large a scale to be managed as a single project aiming at the development of a single system. Information systems developments can all to often require huge financial and personnel resources, take many years and comprise a great number of component subsystems. The following example of a system in public administration demonstrates just how enormous such projects can be.

The development of a computer-based system for the over 400 local offices of the British Department of Social Security (DSS), called the Local Office Project, was planned to take almost ten years. The proposed new information system was more than a system of computer applications for the local offices. It was part of an ambitious effort to integrate the operations of the local offices with central data processing facilities. The DSS provides a complex set of social security services to British citizens, such as unemployment benefit, housing benefit, income support and old age pensions. Because these services have been introduced gradually over the years, the operations performed in the department had become fragmented. Essentially the data needed for each service was collected, stored and processed separately. People claiming more than one benefit had to supply information about their circumstances more than once, and the department stored and processed the duplicate data, with the obvious waste of resources and frustration to the claimants. In the early 1980s, the DSS (it was then called the Department of Health and Social Security – DHSS) developed a strategy to change its operations, to develop new procedures for processing claims to benefits, and to build new information systems that collected and stored all the details on individual claimants once only. This was known as the 'whole person concept'. The implementation of this strategy – appropriately called the 'operational strategy' of the department – comprised a series of information systems development projects, one of which was the local office project. This was intended to reform the operations for the administration of one class of benefits largely administered by the local offices.

The local office project became a huge and immensely complicated undertaking. It had to develop a new pattern of operations in the offices; to develop and introduce new computer applications; to develop and install telecommunications links between the local offices and the computer centres where the claimants' data is stored; to prepare the local offices staff for performing the new operations and for using the new information system effectively; and to develop the necessary management and security mechanisms. Undoubtedly such a project requires careful planning and management, and a great deal of discipline and co-ordination for the many tasks. It would be impossible to organize as a strictly linear process from drawing up the specifications to the delivery of a system that embodies them. Indeed, in 1985, while the project was underway, the government decided to reform social security benefits. This changed radically the nature of the benefits that the new system was supposed to support. The specifications for the project had to be redrawn.

Of course, not all organizations change equally rapidly or dramatically; some operate in more stable environments, and therefore a time span of many years of systems development may be reasonable to plan and relatively easy to manage. Other organizations operate in dynamic and turbulent environments, and face considerable uncertainty, and therefore their systems may need to be delivered rapidly and to change rapidly. In any event, the organization of information systems projects is a much more sophisticated business than following strict procedures for the delivery of a prespecified entity.

The fallacy of the complete system and the maintenance burden

Practical experience tells us that most systems need to be changed significantly after implementation in order to continue to be useful. But the life cycle is not primarily intended to lead to systems that can be changed easily, and 'maintenance' can become a very problematic task. As already described, most organizations separate the activities of the development of new systems from the maintenance of systems in operation. Maintenance is considered a burden and staff find the work unrewarding and often frustrating. To have to change a system after implementation is considered tedious and inappropriate by those trained in the rationale of the life cycle model. If systems have not been designed to accommodate change, even simple modifications can become cumbersome tasks, which may carry the risk of destroying the fabric of the system, and of introducing more problems than they solve.

Many organizations are quite sensibly keen to prolong the life of the information systems that support their main operations, by upgrades and gradual changes, rather than having periodically to enter a comprehensive redesign process. They would prefer their systems to evolve rather than be redeveloped, but the maintenance stage of the life cycle model does not provide for such a positive attitude to gradual change or evolution.

Modifications of the life cycle model

During the period of thirty or so years since the life cycle was first used to structure the development of computer-based information systems projects, the model has been expanded and modified in many different ways. A number of factors have led to changes in the original life cycle model: the technology has become more flexible and allows an almost unlimited variety of systems that potentially could be constructed or acquired with different degrees of effort; the perception of information systems has become increasingly sophisticated; and development projects have become more ambitious.

Sophisticated management context

Many organizations have by now a complicated mixture of information systems using several generations of information technology. They have an infrastructure of databases and a variety of applications supporting their primary operations as well as various management and control functions and other specialized tasks. They have also developed sophisticated information systems management procedures. The management of information systems is discussed elsewhere in this book; here we only need to point out that the management of development projects is often part of a larger, overall effort to sustain, improve and exploit information resources. Management and planning of information systems is not then organized as a number of independent projects, but as a co-ordinated endeavour, part of a continuous and sustained effort.

Organizations make long-term plans for information systems, and have developed a view of information systems as complex entities consisting of various subsystems. This facilitates the split of overall development into manageable sub-projects which can perhaps be seen as following separate life cycles and that can indeed be organized as phased sequences of development tasks. This provides a framework within which individual projects of manageable proportions and with clearer objectives can be conceived and undertaken. Within this framework the life cycle can continue to guide development activities of well-delineated and modest proportions.

The development of systems using software packages

The advent of powerful microcomputers and high quality packaged software for almost all organizational functions has brought another great change. The development process, in so far as it is about producing useful software components, has to a degree been split into two separate endeavours: the development of software packages by specialist software houses, and the development of information systems by their clients choosing and implementing ready-made software.

A larger and larger proportion of software development is now done by specialist software houses and is aimed at capturing common generic information processing requirements. The producers of such packaged software strive to achieve a number of qualities: reliable software, efficient software, user-friendly software and comprehensive documentation or independence from specific hardware. To that end, such organizations place particular emphasis on achieving the most productive and efficient software engineering practices.

The development of information systems which make use of such off-the-shelf software concentrates on the tasks of understanding the requirements for information systems change, choosing a combination of software, hardware and communications that satisfies the organizational requirements, and implementing the new arrangements. It does not require extensive programming efforts.

A typical case is the development of office information systems. There are a plethora of office products (hardware and software) on the market, such as word processors, spreadsheets, or electronic mail systems. It would be foolish to start to reinvent these items. The development of an office system then has to accomplish the following tasks: a careful study of how office work can be effectively reorganized to make use of the new possibilities offered by office technologies, the choice of viable technologies which can support the new information procedures, and the reorganization of work, learning to use the new component technologies and transferring operations from the old to the new system of work procedures and equipment. Such projects can still be effectively organized within the broad phases of the life cycle, and can be supported by methods devised to support tasks of the life cycle. For example, a structured analysis study of the information flows of the office may be a useful way to describe and understand the information processes that the office performs, and to specify the software and hardware that should be sought for purchasing. It is not however the case that the project will progress to the same type of activities in, for example, the construction phases.

Introducing flexibility into development practices

As the difficulty of drawing the initial specifications has come to be recognized, the life cycle has been extended to give more emphasis to the tasks of problem identification and information requirements specification. The early systems development practices enriched the life cycle with efforts to elicit the requirements, and totally new methodologies have emerged, such as SSM, approaching the question of systems specifications from more context-sensitive perspectives.

The problem of the linearity of the life cycle has also been addressed, and various ways have been devised to allow iterations in the development process. Most modern systems analysis and design methods include ways for systematic backtracking if needed. We have seen, for example, that the DeMarco structured systems analysis method acknowledges that the analysts will most probably need to redo some parts of the analysis and tries to facilitate such revision of the structured specification. A major advantage of this method is that it makes the task of drawing the specification simple enough to encourage revisions. DFDs are easy to draw, and redraw if they are not satisfactory. The levelled and partitioned DFDs provide a structure, which helps the analyst to locate a part of the system to be revised and to make changes in one part without jeopardizing other parts. DeMarco's emphasis on redundancy-free specifications aims at the same effect: to be able to preserve the integrity of the system when the specification is revised.

As the significance of the involvement of multiple players in the development of new systems has been recognized, several methods have emerged to assist the collaboration of technical experts and users, and graphical representations of systems specifications, which it is said can be better understood by non-technically trained people, have gained ground.

Introducing the computer into development practices

To improve the ease of revising analysis and design work, and to break out of the document driven waterfall, it is now often advocated that a project should have a single design database, rather than a sequence of individual transformations of the specification. Within such a database various forms of cross-checking and tracing can be supported, allowing the impact of any given revision to be traced through to all affected parts. Of course, in the age of the computer, any description such as that just given immediately suggests maintaining the database on the computer, and letting the computer do the tedious cross-checking. This is indeed part of the ambition of the movement to introduce computer aided software engineering (CASE) tools into systems development work, based around a common database (usually called a repository) [Gane, 1990]. It is perhaps more appropriate that the acronym CASE should be taken as referring to computer aided *systems* engineering in the context of this book, and it is generally seen as an approach that has more to contribute than just some better form of software production.

The development of CASE tools started out in attempts to provide computer support for systems developers and drew on the more general use of computer aided design (CAD) in other engineering disciplines. CASE tools are largely based on providing help in performing the analysis and design elements of an information systems project, such as drawing DFDs, managing a data dictionary and storing data models. As such they mirror the methods that are currently in use. Many authors, and many software development companies, are very enthusiastic about the benefits of CASE and offer comprehensive and integrated CASE tools that can support an organization and its analysts all the way from problem definition, or even business planning, through to the generation of computer code.

It is not easy to generalize about the impact of this approach. Available CASE tools range from the small and simple individual application, for example a program to draw data flow diagrams, to large and ambitious products that

attempt to implement the repository concept, and to support systems development from problem definition to post-implementation review. There are a
number of hopes that are attached to such developments. Some emphasize their
potential for improving the productivity of analysts and designers, others
emphasize their ability to allow close control and management of projects, while
yet others expect improvements in the quality of developed systems and their
ability to be modified and maintained.

Prototyping within the life cycle

One way to overcome some of the rigidities of the conventional life cycle model
– namely the prerequisite of getting the initial specification right, and the
difficulty of making iterations and to accommodate wider involvement
effectively – is to employ prototyping – figure 7.2 [Dearnley & Mayhew, 1983].

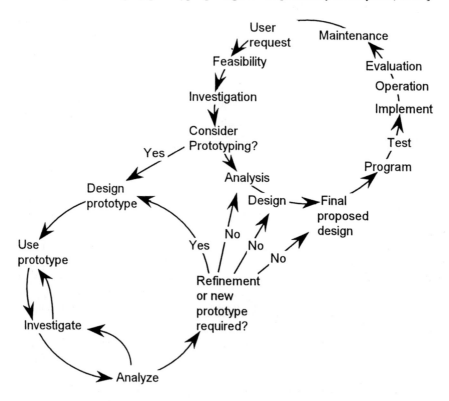

Figure 7.2 The revised system life cycle with prototyping [Dearnley &
Mayhew, 1983]

A static description of a proposed information system, on paper or in a computer database, however formally specified or rigorously defined, is far from adequate for communicating the real characteristics and dynamics of a system in use. How much better it would be to be able to illustrate this using a 'working model' of the system. It is this working model, albeit crude and incomplete, but always speedily constructed, that is a prototype. Analysts can acquire an initial understanding of requirements, and proceed to develop a prototype using appropriate tools. The prototyping approach is usually based on the ability to undertake extremely rapid construction and revision of systems. Speed is achieved by the use of appropriate materials, databases, 4GLs, very high level languages, microcomputers, screen generators, expert system shells and so on.

A prototype in this case is not a 'real' system, it may not have full versions of all data files or support all the procedures and functionality of the desired system, but it should be able to perform in a way that demonstrates the most pertinent characteristics. Prototyping is often found useful for exploring particular parts of a system that have the most direct relationship with the operating environment, for example interactive user interfaces or report formats. The idea is often extended well beyond specification as such, to try different design options. Nonetheless, at some point it is discarded. For example, a prototype of aspects of an accounting system may be built to demonstrate the data input screens, to produce output screens for typical categories of data or to demonstrate the reports that the system produces. The analysts can then demonstrate the prototype and invite comments and suggestions for further refinements and extensions. The working model can be revised accordingly and the cycle repeated. In this way many interested parties can participate in an iterative process to clarify the requirements that the new system must fulfil. When everybody is satisfied with the characteristics of the working model, the life cycle systems development tasks can be resumed. The exact point of return to the life cycle depends on how refined the prototype is. If the prototype has communication value only, the life cycle continues from the systems analysis stage; if the prototype has incorporated the logical structure of the users' needs, the development process can continue from the design stage; if the prototype has involved the design of the system as well, the stage to follow is the further refinement of the prototype to produce the final operational system or to rewrite the programs. Alternatively, the prototype might be used as the specification of requirements for the purchasing of a package.

As the above shows, the reasons to build working models of aspects of a system can be quite varied, including requirements elicitation and validation, software or hardware evaluation, or the facilitation of broader involvement in development. The prototype might also be kept to be used for the maintenance of the system; it may be useful to do experiments on requested improvements to the prototype before implementing them. Even medium and large-scale systems may be built in this manner, first using the tools appropriate for rapid construction and rapid feedback, and subsequently re-implemented in a traditional manner.

Hekmatpour and Ince [1986] call this 'throw it away' prototyping. Such a throw-away prototype can still be useful even if built with different technology to the final system, and operating with a minimal loading of data.

Advantages and disadvantages of prototyping within the life cycle

The use of prototyping within the life cycle, as described above, promises several gains: the distance between developers and other participants is reduced; with a working version of a system in front of them, those who will use a computer system are less likely to be alienated by technical jargon and technical tools. They are able to express requirements in terms of tangible features and the functions of the working model. Those who will work with a new system have an opportunity to understand and learn the system from the early stages of its development, and they acquire confidence and are better prepared for the changes to come.

Requirements specified through a prototype may capture more needs and preferences of those involved in information handling. If this is the case then implementation and maintenance costs will be lower. Developers too have reasons to adopt a prototyping approach. It can provide them with an opportunity to test alternative designs before committing to a single development route, and in this way uncertainty can be reduced.

Nevertheless, the practice of prototyping has revealed a number of difficulties. One difficulty is that prototypes may have poor performance both in response time and effective use of computer resources. The performance of a prototype may degrade rapidly as the number of users or amounts of data increases.

The initial and up-front costs of prototyping can be large, if it means acquiring and establishing new software systems appropriate to rapid construction. These may be recovered by overall life cycle savings resulting from better understanding of requirements, but the expense of installing the prototyping environment and the perceived delay while building and revising the prototype are often seen as unjustifiable.

The co-operation between analysts and other participants may be strained in the effort to improve the prototype further. Not everybody responds favourably to the prototyping experience and even enthusiastic users will have to learn a system at the same time as providing feedback on its characteristics. Sometimes this enthusiasm may be lost after the first few rounds as the analyst demonstrates endless revised versions of a system and asks for comments. Others find it difficult to understand the significant additional effort and time it takes to move from the prototype to produce and deliver the final operational system. The working model may seem so close to the real thing that the long time for the development and implementation of the 'proper' system appears unjustifiable, even if the provision of such facilities as full security and back-up procedures is essential in the final delivered system. There is no obvious point where the iterative process of revision stops and the development or delivery of the production system begins.

Prototyping also requires an enhanced ability to evaluate what has been done and re-target or re-establish objectives. It is easy perhaps to build the first prototype, but capturing the feedback from those who see it, or use it, is a sophisticated task in its own right, and one that analysts may not be trained to perform. The wish-list produced can be very large and unrealistic, setting up hopes that can never be fulfilled.

Finally, with prototyping the life cycle becomes more difficult to manage, particularly for large systems where many interested parties may be involved. The number of iterations, and hence the cost and time scale, slip out of the direct control of the project managers.

For all these reasons, project sponsors and information system managers have to weigh carefully the risks of the more rigid life cycle using more conventional methods against the risks introduced through prototyping. While the idea of prototyping appears to put an end to many of the shortcomings of traditional systems development, and many claim that it is not so widely used as it ought to be, it needs to be used with caution. It is not just because of the inertia of professionals to go beyond their cumbersome established practices that prototyping is less common. Professional development requires not only effective methods but also confidence that the whole process is controllable and manageable.

Alternative models of information systems development

The discussion of prototyping in the section above has described it as a complementary technique to the life cycle. The idea that some aspects of systems requirements are incrementally developed, can be taken further to the position where a system is under continuous development throughout its life. Such an evolutionary process is in clear contradiction to the traditional model of the life cycle. Development is intended neither to specify accurately and fully the needs that the system under development aims at satisfying, nor to produce and deliver a complete system. Rather it is founded on the perception that information systems are inherently incomplete, 'organic' and continually changing. Instead of being entities having a life span that is clearly delineated in time with a beginning, a middle and an end, information systems are seen as following a continuous evolutionary pattern.

Systems developers and users alike have become very aware of the uncertainty of information systems requirements statements and the certainty of continuing change. A system is developed today to face an uncertain world of tomorrow. However excellent our understanding of today's situation, it will be of little use if tomorrow is very different and our system is incapable of adaptation to the new circumstances. The very introduction of computers into organizations, taking over aspects of tasks previously done by humans enhances this effect. People are adaptable, intelligent and resourceful, and can easily amend or develop their activities in response to changing conditions. Computers on the other hand need to be configured and programmed, and programs or program changes need to be designed, tested, debugged and installed. Changes in computer-based systems have to be explicit, and if changed circumstances are to be met, then it will be that much easier if change has been anticipated.

Therefore, the evolutionary systems development model suggests that systems should be constructed and implemented in their environment with the intention to change them repeatedly as circumstances change and new ideas emerge about how they can be improved. This is, as explained above, the basic principle of the method of prototyping, but in the evolutionary case the prototype is the system itself. The prototype is not only for experimentation and demonstration purposes, and it is not intended to be discarded in favour of the development of a 'proper' and durable system. If a system is developed in this manner the organization can incrementally adapt to the presence of the new system, and on the basis of experience, the system can be refined and further functionality be added. The system continues to operate as alterations are made, with the direction of evolution being determined by experience.

While evolutionary prototyping is clearly challenging for medium-sized and large projects, it is followed by default in most small projects. Thus, using a database package, a simple single user system to aid a distribution manager could be built in a few days. Changes and extensions could be made at any time and in response to experience or urgent unanticipated need. This also illustrates another aspect of evolutionary systems development. Systems need to 'belong' to their immediate users since these are the people who will identify required change, and should be able to initiate and even make it. For example, a distribution manager with a modest level of training could design a new report format or alter a database to record further relevant data.

What evolutionary development cannot easily provide is the management controls of the life cycle. It requires analysts and other players to act together. In this scenario those who work with information cannot expect the 'experts' to deliver them systems by anticipating their needs. They must appreciate the ever-changing and elusive nature of information requirements, tolerate 'imperfect' systems, and be prepared to be actively involved in improving them.

Evolutionary development is often considered suitable for small systems, involving small groups of motivated users. Nevertheless, evolutionary development can with care be effectively organized as an incremental process that is appropriate for controlling the development of large-scale systems, because it avoids change in one radical discontinuous step. Such a development process may then start with a broad architecture of a set of desired systems, the various components of which will be developed gradually. This architecture can be implemented initially with limited functional components, but retaining assigned slots and interfaces for further components. The concept of 'core' systems (networks, corporate databases, key operating systems) may give the shape to an architecture, and allow the various groups in an organization considerable flexibility as to how and at what pace they develop their own systems. This is a topic returned to, from a management perspective, in part III.

What really is prototyping?

We have suggested in this chapter two different ways to use prototyping. Indeed, prototyping seems to mean something different to every person who uses the word. Authors have given various definitions and classified them in many different ways, for example: *explanatory*, if used to clarify some ideas or some of the features of the system; *experimental*, if it is used to test new aspects of a system about which users or developers have not much experience; *incremental* if it used as a strategy leading from a rudimentary core system towards more complicated versions of it; or *evolutionary*, if it is used as a strategy to cope effectively with a changing context .

Many authors emphasize speed and speak of rapid prototyping, and advocate it, among other reasons, for the speed with which a system can be built and made operational. Speed of itself is seen as an important way of improving development outcomes. A pilot system may also be seen as a prototype, meaning the first of many similar systems. It is tested in its environment with the expectation of changes being specified for subsequent revisions. The development of popular software packages is often undertaken in this way, with trial 'beta' release versions going to trusted customers for evaluation and feedback.

One fundamental idea, which permeates all these notions of prototyping, is the development of a working system – or some part of a system – using facilities to speed up its construction and facilitate subsequent change and refinement. However, the purposes that the prototype may serve differ significantly, and prototyping cannot be said to define one specific way of systems development. It should rather be thought of as the method of quick systems component construction, which is adopted within the framework of a broader systems development approach or methodology to solve contentions between analysts, users, software and hardware [Mayhew & Dearnley, 1987].

Prototypes for the determination of systems requirements can be thought of as laboratory systems, and are used in the early phases of a project. People interact with a system to understand its features, and to form a better sense of the kind of system they would like to work with, to specify more completely and correctly. System builders accept more costly technology and continual change in order to match changing user perceptions of need. Such a prototype is built out of its environment, and evaluated out of its environment. The prototype in this case is discarded at some stage (perhaps after many iterations), and a full specification is derived from it for conventional system building – though this derivation may be automated to some degree. In contrast, evolutionary prototyping takes place in its real environment. Its key distinction from the requirements specification prototyping is that the prototype is not just an intermediate step, it is the system that is used by people as they perform information handling activities.

It must also be understood that prototyping is not only applicable at the beginning of a systems development process. It may be used to experiment with alternative software designs and hardware configurations. It may also be used as a method for systems implementation, as in the case of pilot prototyping. It may be used as a method in the 'top down' systems development practices of the life cycle, or it may be chosen as a 'bottom up' effort for building systems gradually as users develop confidence and can express more sophisticated information handling requirements.

The various different ways that prototyping is used at present suggest that systems development practices, far from forming a neat process governed by sound theoretical models, are organized according to context, available skill and individual judgement. The role of the life cycle in establishing various phases and professional practices, and the confidence it once gave to project sponsors and leaders has broken down as the notion of information systems development has become more sophisticated, embracing more than software development. The result has been a proliferation of methods that can be employed according to the developer's judgement of the situation. To be able to understand their judgement, and therefore to assess the effectiveness of the systems development problems, we need to investigate underlying views of information systems change. We should be aware that information systems development is a process driven by many different concerns, technical, organizational, managerial and social, and not by some ideal description of the necessary and sufficient tasks to be undertaken in every project.

Exercises and discussion issues

1. Consult 4 or more text books on information systems development and compare their versions of the systems life cycle. Do they use the same words to describe the various tasks? Prepare a table showing the equivalencies and discrepancies among the various versions.
2. Would you envisage that a strict life cycle, a revised life cycle or an evolutionary approach would be most appropriate for the following systems:

    a system to control the signals on a new high speed railway line;
    a command and control system to be used by the London fire brigade to dispatch fire engines in response to emergency calls;

a system for a university to handle student applications for courses, including central administration and departmental selection procedures.

3. A common criticism of prototyping, both for requirements determination and in evolutionary development is the lack of opportunity it gives for management control of projects. How serious do you believe this to be?

4. Most organizations introduced their first computer-based information systems for various administrative tasks such as payroll, accounting, invoicing and payments, in the 1970s. These applications had to be changed for various reasons, e.g. when the technology – hardware, software or telecommunications – was updated, or if the company changed its business.

    Talk to a manager responsible for such systems in a company, asking him to tell you their history. Ask how the systems were changed over the years, how the major developments were organized, what were the main 'phases' of development and operations. Then try to see if there is a pattern similar to that of the life cycle model in the 'story' you heard. Write a description of the history of one of the systems using terms from the life cycle model.

5. Undertake some research into how a mechanical or civil engineer and an architect would use prototypes – consider how a new model of a motor car is developed, or a new suspension bridge. Is there a direct relationship between how these professions use the concept and its use in information systems design?

References

Boehm, B.W. (1988) 'A Spiral Model of Software Development and Enhancement' in *IEEE Computer*, May, pp. 61-72.

Dearnley, P.A. and Mayhew, P.J. (1983) 'In favour of system prototypes and their integration into the systems development cycle', *The Computer Journal*, Vol. 26, No. 1, February, pp. 36-42.

Gane, C.(1990) *Computer-aided software engineering: The Methodologies, the Products and the Future*, Prentice Hall, Englewood Cliffs, New Jersey.

Hekmatpour, S. & Ince, D.C. (1986) 'Rapid Software Prototyping' in *Oxford Surveys in Information Technology*, Vol. 3, pp. 37-76.

Mayhew, P.J. & Dearnley, P.A. (1987) 'An Alternative Prototyping Classification', in *The Computer Journal*, Vol. 30, No. 6, January, pp. 481-484.

Further reading

The Friedman & Cornford book provides a review of the history of information systems development practices. Chapter 7 of the book contains a number of versions of the life cycle. The Boehm paper listed above provides a critique of various life cycle versions and synthesizes them into a risk driven and contingent model. Yourdon provides a thoughtful discussion of issues of the life cycle within structured systems analysis.

Friedman, A.L. & Cornford, D.S. (1989) *Computer Systems Development: History, Organization and Implementation*, Wiley, Chichester.
Yourdon, E. (1989) *Modern Structured Analysis*, Prentice Hall, Englewood Cliffs, New Jersey

8 Approaches to information systems development

- *Engineering approaches*
- *Socio-technical approaches*
- *The ad hoc approach*

We have seen in the previous chapters that the development process that is undertaken to achieve new means of information handling is driven by a combination of technical and organizational concerns. Developers try to achieve:

- technical sophistication;
- organizational objectives;
- desirable changes in people's work conditions;
- development project completion within budget and time restrictions.

While all of these concerns are discernible to some degree in most projects, some subset of them tends to prevail in any particular development effort. The dominant concerns determine the way the development task is approached, that is, which aspects receive more attention and which are neglected, what methods are applied and how they are organized. It is essential to be aware of such biases in approach, in order to understand the way project sponsors and analysts set up the development process and the underlying perspective of any proposed methodologies.

In this respect the literature is often confusing. Most books and research articles argue for particular development methodologies and project management models, or suggest deterministic trends towards some 'best' development approach. Specialist training programmes, which similarly tend to focus exclusively on a particular set of techniques reinforce this attitude. It is the contention of this book that there is no single best way to develop information systems, nor is it sensible to try to establish one. We should not hide the biases of an approach we adopt, rather we should strive to be aware of the bias, make our perspective explicit, and be able to defend it. At the same time we need to understand alternative perspectives, and be able to enrich our approaches by incorporating elements from others.

Being biased in this sense does not mean being rigid and inflexible. Indeed, as is explained below, in practice initially distinct approaches tend to converge under real world pressures as a necessary response to address the multi-faceted concerns that surround information systems development. In this book we made clear from the beginning our own bias in favour of a socio-technical or people-

161

centred perspective. This does not prevent us from presenting the rationale of other, different perspectives. On the contrary, it leads us to explore them.

Because there is no single best way to approach systems development, we need to acquire the capacity to tailor-make the development process for the particular circumstances addressed in each and every project. To do this we need:

- to be well informed about the range of technological options available, and to understand their organizational implications;
- to understand well the nature of systems development as an organizational intervention, the prerequisites and the implications of the various technical and organizational options chosen;
- to be able to assess the circumstances facing a project, and to judge the feasibility of alternative approaches.

Developing information systems is a creative endeavour, requiring skills of insight and judgement. Creativity, however – as well as judgement – is not an idiosyncratic or mysteriously intuitive process. Rather it is sustained and cultivated by continual enquiry and reflective consideration of experience. In that spirit, this chapter explores some of the most widespread approaches used as a basis for systems development. It examines their fundamental principles and theoretical underpinnings, and the various forms that they may take.

Engineering approaches

If technology is understood as being at the heart of the discipline of information systems, with a concomitant requirement for understanding materials, design and construction, then it is not surprising that engineering has been extremely influential in establishing a fundamental approach for information systems development.

The driving concern of the engineering approach is the development of a complex technical system. Information systems projects are often immensely complex, they require substantial investment, and they are expected to deliver systems with a key role in an organization's existence. Too often, the development process is inefficient and the resulting systems, as technical systems, are problematic. This can be expressed in two main ways: that the ability to control development processes is low, or that the items produced are of poor quality. We may be concerned with a deficiency of process or a deficiency in the product.

The overall productivity of many systems development projects is acknowledged to be unacceptably low, and projects easily get out of control with escalating costs. An example which illustrates this problem is the well publicized increase in cost of the implementation of the operational strategy of the DSS in Britain, which was described in chapter 7. In 1982, the cost of the strategy was estimated to be £700 million, while in the late 1980s an investigation by the National Audit Office found that the strategy was in fact costing £2000 million. The administrative savings that the Department was expected to achieve – savings being a major objective of the strategy – fell by 55%, with fears that they might never be realized at all.

The second problem is that the quality of information systems, in technical terms, is often very poor, and software and hardware faults come to jeopardize the operations of organizations. Dramatic cases, such as of factories whose operations have been brought to a halt, or banks that have mislaid millions because of systems failures, are reported in the press. Less dramatic problems of systems crashes and faulty operations are so frequent that they are taken as a normal hurdle of information systems' use and do not make news. They are, however, damaging, expensive and demoralizing.

These two problems, the productivity and controllability of systems development practices and the reliability and robustness of the resulting systems, are therefore primary concerns. Computer manufacturers, software houses and computer services companies, as well as users of information technology, are all to some degree involved in attempts to improve on the situation, and have been keen to develop efficient professional practices and raise the quality of the systems produced. Efforts to overcome these problems have drawn mainly on systems theory and the general principles of engineering. The emphasis has been on mastering complexity, achieving efficiency, and producing error-free systems. The realization of these goals is sought through project activities that are well planned and disciplined, taking a top-down, reductionist, approach to decompose the inherent complexity of information handling into smaller achievable and verifiable tasks.

Systems engineering and systems analysis

Information systems development is not unique in terms of the undertaking of complex projects which involve sophisticated technology. The study of complex systems development activities emerged as a general scientific field after the end of the Second World War. The war saw the limits of technology broadened significantly and a great deal of experience was gained in marshalling human effort towards the construction of complex artefacts and the achievement of strategic goals. Two disciplines emerged from this experience which have been particularly influential on information systems, namely systems engineering and systems analysis.

Systems engineering emerged in the post-war period as a theory to guide the building of complex human–machine systems. It emphasizes conceiving and studying total systems and not their isolated components. This is how the sequence of steps that it comprises has been described by Hall, one of its major proponents [1962].

- *Problem definition*: transform an indeterminate situation into the data required for setting objectives and for systems analysis.
- *Choosing objectives*: make a formal definition of wanted outputs and inputs and all other boundary conditions and the needs which the system aims to satisfy.
- *Systems synthesis*: on this basis synthesize alternative systems.
- *Systems analysis*: in the light of the objectives, assumptions, and boundary conditions deduce the relevant consequences of the hypothetical systems.
- *Systems selection:* select the optimum system, i.e. the 'alternative that shows the most promise'.
- *System development*: work towards the development of the system and its delivery to a customer together with instructions on the way it should be used.
- *Current engineering*: monitor, extend, correct, adapt, or provide special assistance to the customer after a system's installation.

The systems engineering strategy outlined above makes mention of a task of systems analysis. It is appropriate to point out here that this phrase has two rather distinct meanings. In Britain today, and increasingly in North America too, systems analysis is a synonym for the analysis phase of information systems development. A job advertisement for a systems analyst would imply that these were the skills required. This was not always the common meaning of the phrase, particularly in North America. There, in the 1950s and 1960s, another meaning was attached to the phrase where systems analysis was an effort oriented towards the analysis of strategic and policy questions, first in the military context, and later in a more general context. In this respect it is similar to operational research. Compared with systems engineering, systems analysis shifted the emphasis to cost and to strategic considerations. The elements of systems analysis when it first began to be applied, during the 1950s, have been described by Hitch and McKean [1960] as follows:

- an objective or objectives we desire to accomplish;
- alternative techniques or instrumentalities (or 'systems') by which the objective may be accomplished;
- the 'costs' or resources required by each system;
- a mathematical model or models; i.e. the mathematical or logical framework or set of equations showing the interdependence of the objectives, the techniques and instrumentalities, the environment, and the resources;
- a criterion, relating objectives and costs or resources for choosing the preferred or optimal alternative.

Both systems engineering and systems analysis are rooted in systems theory. They proceed systematically for the completion of a complex task. They aim at optimal solutions or the construction of the best system and, to do that, they need to use appropriate mathematical or 'logical' techniques. It is easy to recognize the parallels of the traditional life cycle as discussed in the last chapter to both systems engineering and systems analysis. This way of problem solving, as the life cycle, has often been criticized as inappropriate for dealing with the vague requirements for improving problematic situations that occur as organizations consider changing their information handling activities. The systems engineering and systems analysis approaches require the objective to be attained to be clearly defined and modelled at the beginning of the problem solving process.

As a result, systems analysis as a problem solving and systems development approach has evolved to put greater emphasis onto efforts for exploring the problem area and reaching agreement on requirements for a satisfactory rather than optimal solution. Systems analysis has become an approach aimed not at finding an optimum, but at helping a decision-maker to choose a better course of action in a particular problem situation than he might otherwise be able to select. Quade and Miser [1985] describe the activities that comprise this more recent systems analysis approach in the following terms.

- It marshals the evidence relating to the problem and the experience and scientific knowledge bearing on it (when necessary the analysis gathers new evidence and develops new knowledge).
- It examines the social purposes relating to the problem, and helps persons and institutions to reconsider these purposes.
- It explores alternative ways of achieving these purposes, which often include designing or inventing new possibilities.
- It reconsiders the problem – and its possible reformulation – in the light of the knowledge accumulating during the analysis.
- It estimates the impacts of various possible courses of action, taking into consideration both the uncertain future and the organizational structures that must carry forward these courses of action;
- It compares the alternatives by applying a variety of criteria to their consequences.
- It presents the results of the study in a framework suitable for choice.
- It assists in following up the actions chosen.
- It evaluates the results of implementing the chosen courses of action.

Here, again, we can recognize the more recent practices of information systems development, which attempt to overcome the rigid rationale of the life cycle, and to address organizational and social concerns in addition to project management and technical problem solving.

Software engineering

More recently the engineering approach in information systems development has grown stronger, taking the form of various specialised disciplines, the best known of which is software engineering. Software engineering has emerged as the discipline of organizing and controlling the production of software. Its aim is to replace *ad hoc* or semi-structured software development practices with a systematic process which is efficient, controllable, and improves the quality of software produced.

The essence of software engineering is the formalization of software development and evolution. Its most extreme version is manifested in the efforts to realize the software technology of the 'software factory' and to introduce formal, that is to say mathematically based, methods into the specification and design of software. Ideally, the engineering of software in this way starts with an abstract model, which is the specification of the system to be developed and which can be validated with a formal theory. This is decomposed through a process of transformations towards more detailed specifications until a computer-executable system is produced. Each transformation step is formally verifiable for equivalence between the initial specification and the resulting transformed specification. In addition, the output specification of a transformation step is horizontally verified for consistency and completeness in relation to the features that were to have been added, or the problems that were to have been resolved in the current step. The search for software development notations and methods with a sound mathematical basis has produced various tools to support the formalization of software production, as for example the formal specification languages Vienna Development Method (VDM) and Z. Great emphasis has been put into proving mathematically the correctness of the software produced, something which is of great significance for safety critical systems, such as aeroplane flight systems or the control of nuclear power stations. The notion of the 'software factory' implies the application of a formal software engineering process within a specialised production facility. Some see this as the most efficient means to organize an industry capable of producing high quality software.

Despite the significance that formal software engineering holds in the eyes of many academics, it has had limited applicability to information systems development. Undoubtedly it provides a promising approach for a category of safety critical and mathematically driven applications. However, a fully formal development process is seen by most as neither practical nor desirable for the development of information systems. It is not practical because there are no formal models which capture the richness of the application domains; there are no formal theories describing organizational behaviour. Without a formal specification neither formal decomposition nor systems proving are possible. It is also undesirable because it alienates non-specialists from the systems development process and stifles the creativity of systems developers. For many technical components of information systems the only notion of 'correctness' appropriate is that their performance satisfies their users. In such cases, the use of formalisms which inhibit participation is counter productive, because it blocks the most crucial mechanism for monitoring whether the system proposed is valid or not. Also, the formal organization of systems production in a factory mode is not necessarily cost effective, because it ignores the significance of human creativity and the need for interaction with the informal world of human behaviour.

Despite these limitations in realizing the ideal software engineering process, software engineering in its more modest form, of a discipline studying how to organize and support the efficient production of reliable software, has been very influential on information system development practices. It has led to the development of a plethora of facilities and project support tools, including higher level computer languages, automated tools for various systems analysis and design methods, libraries with reusable software components, and sophisticated project management techniques.

In general, three tendencies are discernible in the advances of software engineering: towards formalization of specification; towards formalization of project management; and towards accommodating human interaction. One route from *ad hoc* methods and specification languages to a more formally organized development process can be seen in the efforts to develop various styles of the CASE and IPSE approaches discussed in chapter 7.

A well publicized strategy for research and development of IPSEs was that undertaken under the Alvey research programme of the British government during the 1980s. This strategy envisaged advancing from IPSEs integrating widely practised methods and tools, such as structured methods and COBOL programming, towards fully integrated environments which apply formal methods, support the reuse of components, and carry out many of the development activities automatically [Dowson, 1987]. However, in the 1990s the flexible use of a variety of smaller scale software engineering tools is more prevalent than formally integrated environments. A great deal of effort has been made to incorporate methods which allow for user participation and human creativity and to reconcile them with the efforts for improving technical discipline and project control. Characteristically, methods which employ flexible graphical notations which can be understood by users, such as DFDs, continue to be used extensively, although they are not adequately formal to be amenable to automatic and provable transformation to computer-executable notation. Similarly, prototyping has become a more popular technique within software engineering, allowing the possibility to involve other participants, while keeping the technical systems development tasks in the hands of software developers. Nevertheless, even though software engineering has been responsive to the needs of a human dimension to systems development, its perspective is still that of the efficient development of a technical product.

Other forms of the engineering approach

The engineering approach has been enriched with special endeavours to improve particular categories or aspects of systems development. We will mention here only two examples, knowledge engineering and human–computer interaction (HCI), to demonstrate how different specialisms are carriers of the same approach.

Knowledge engineering involves the application of a number of techniques to capture and imitate the decision-making behaviour of human experts in certain domains of knowledge. It has grown out of the artificial intelligence (AI) discipline, with its roots in psychology and models of mental processes. The knowledge engineering field has become a distinct specialism with major concerns to elicit human knowledge and to represent it in computers. The systems built by this approach, called 'expert systems' of 'knowledge-based systems', seek to make inferences which resemble those made by skilled humans. Nevertheless, knowledge-based systems are only a special case of information systems. Once again, knowledge engineering puts emphasis on the systematic application of special techniques for the construction of a complex technical product.

Human–computer interaction has emerged as a special effort to develop systems which are pleasant, and easy to use. It applies knowledge from disciplines such as ergonomics and psychology to design the interface between a computer system and the human environment within which it is used. This has so far involved mainly the design of screens, hardware, and keyboards, as well as the design of menus and dialogues. More recently efforts are directed also towards the design of job procedures to accommodate the use of a computer-based system. As the objective is to achieve usability, the development process pays attention to 'human factors', and follows what is often called 'human-centred' design. Nevertheless, HCI usually follows the engineering approach, in that it aims primarily at improving the quality of a technical system. The objective of developing usable systems requires attention to human behaviour, but does not necessarily change the principles of the development process. In most cases, systems developers try to accommodate user friendliness by specifying usability aspects according to their understanding of the users' profile, but their approach remains, primarily, that of engineering a technical system.

Data modelling

The starting point and the driving rationale of systems development is often the structuring or restructuring of an organization's data. There is a philosophical view of reality which lies behind this approach: that the information categories expressed by an organization's data describe objects and states of the real world which are less ephemeral than the organization's procedures for handling them. A customer is a customer, even if there are twenty ways to process their orders. The organization may change the way it does business, but it will still need to refer to the same categories of information, for example customers, suppliers, products. Modelling the information categories in a general form or as a database, it is argued, provides a stable basis for the development and evolution of other aspects of an organization's information systems. Subsequent developments and changes become easier and less distracting because they deal with procedures which are by their nature changeable, while the vital information resources of the organization remain intact.

This ontological principle has been reinforced by the significance that organizations started to attach to their data resources during the 1980s. In the 'information age' the data that an organization collects and uses are perceived to have a value similar to that of its capital assets. In some cases information has a direct financial value and is transacted in the market in the form of some service. More generally, organizations have come to realize that to create and maintain the data files which are so vital to their functioning requires considerable investment. In many cases, the survival and growth of a company is directly related to its capacity to structure and use its information resources. Such terms as 'information management' and 'information policy' became common phrases, catching some of the main concerns of the modern manager.

In this climate, the creation of an adequate data infrastructure acquired great significance. It is interesting to note that in the early 1970s the main, and very influential, voice from management regarding the creation of a general data infrastructure to serve management purposes was a rather negative and certainly very cautious one. Ackoff, in his widely read article *'Management misinformation systems'*, warned against the dangers of burdening managers with the output of management information systems [Ackoff, 1967]. Twenty-five years later, managers seem to feel confident that a general data infrastructure can be built and effectively managed.

One of the most influential factors which has given rise to the data modelling approach is purely technical, the development of database technology and the software of database management systems. In the 1970s this technology acquired sound theoretical foundations and significant practical experience was gained in its use. The debate over the three basic models of relational, hierarchical and network database models began to settle, with the recognition of the merits of the relational model, but also the acceptance that in some cases one of the other models may be more appropriate. This is an interesting area to study in so far as it is one of the few areas of information systems development where 'theory', in particular Codd's concept of normalization, has had direct influence on practice. More generally software manufacturers have been keen to promote their database software, and data modelling approaches have been popularized by a plethora of 4GL database management software packages.

Object oriented approach

Data modelling has achieved a widespread acceptance in information systems development. Even if it may not be given the leading role, it is often seen as an important contributing perspective to a broader approach. There remains however a problem with a pure data modelling approach in that it is essentially static. A data model describes relevant aspects of the world that a system will function in, and this can provide solid foundations for systems development and evolution, but describing what is in the world, and hence should be in the database, is not the same as describing what happens or should happen in the world and how this should be mirrored in an information system. There is therefore a parallel requirement for some description of this other aspect, the procedures and actions that are to be undertaken with data.

The usual solution to this in systems development, building on established programming practice, has been to analyze and describe data and procedure separately, and in so far as possible, independently. This practice has however been increasingly challenged by the emergence of the object-oriented ideas. This is a way of thinking about information and systems that has emerged out of developments in programming practice and languages as well as out of extensions to the data modelling approach. The influence of object-oriented thinking is now very widespread in both design and analysis activities. As described in chapter 4, the basic principle behind object-oriented thinking is to set out to understand and model the world in terms of the items found therein, their attributes, relationships and the actions that they undertake. It is this latter point, considering the actions that objects undertake, that sets the approach apart from data modelling and gives it a dynamic and procedural dimension. Object-oriented approaches focus on modelling the world in terms of hierarchies of objects sharing or inheriting general characteristics, but accommodating the particular.

As presented in Chapter 4, object oriented approaches to systems development can provide a cleaner and well integrated model of system behaviour, and can smooth some of the transitions between analysis, design and programming activities. The proponents of the approach go further, and often argue for the more natural fit of object concepts to human means of understanding complex situations. However, in terms of the discussion in this chapter, object oriented ideas represent a development within the engineering tradition, rather than a new point of departure.

Socio-technical approaches

Unlike the engineering approaches described so far in this chapter, the basic principle of the socio-technical approach is that the information systems development process is an intervention in an organization, intended to improve the way people communicate with each other and do their jobs. Information systems are not seen as isolated technical constructs or repositories of data; they are seen as systems involving people and being embedded in human organizations. They are, therefore, primarily social systems which rely to a greater or lesser degree on technology, and development is seen as a multidimensional process of social change. While this may involve the design and implementation of a technology-based system, the main focus of effort in this approach is to lead to a new organizational environment for information handling in which social actors can effectively perform their roles. The goal of socio-technical development is a system which promotes a work environment in which people can perform effectively their organizational role and can achieve personal development and satisfaction.

The socio-technical approach is well established in organizational theory. It first emerged after the Second World War in the work done by E. Trist, K.W. Bamforth and F.E. Emery at the Tavistock Institute in London. Trist and his colleagues studied how the performance of workers in the coal industry changed when mechanized mining was introduced in various collieries. They observed that mechanization drove a process of work specialization which in turn imposed an impersonal work organization which put an end to the self-regulating social groups that had carried out the previous manual methods. The mechanized mining conditions bred interpersonal and intergroup conflicts, and workers exhibited various forms of alienation. These observations led Trist to reconsider the way technology should be understood as effecting work processes in organizations. In particular, he proposed that the technology allowed choices as to the social framework within which it was deployed. These choices needed to be carefully made in a manner that built a viable social group and satisfied the various needs of those involved. In the case of coal mining, this was represented by a more flexible division of tasks between workers, and the development of teams. A further discussion of the work of Trist and his colleagues is included in Pugh *et al.* [1983].

In information systems development, this approach conveys a mixture of practical, ethical and theoretical concerns. The major practical concern is that information technology-based systems, even if they are well designed, often fail to bring the desirable benefits that they are intended to produce. The social dynamics of the organization within which a technical system is embedded may override the intended performance of the technical system as it was determined during the development process. We have already discussed the significance of the informal aspects of organizational performance and how a new technical system may be undermined by unforeseen behaviour.

A great deal has been written about the problem of 'resistance to change', meaning (as explained in chapter 5) that the employees of an organization often oppose a new information system [Keen, 1981]. Opposition may take various forms, some directly offensive such as boycott, strike or even sabotage. More often, however, more subtle and indirect methods are used, although they are probably equally destructive, such as working to rule, non-use or misuse of the system, lack of commitment to work, or low morale. Many developers and managers explain employees' resistance to new systems as a general character- istic of human nature, and therefore set out to circumvent it with such tactics as training and familiarization sessions, or with strong management action. The socio-technical approach addresses such dysfunctional phenomena in organiz- ations by shifting attention to the social dynamics and human needs throughout the development process. Avoidance of discontent through positive action to structure change processes is a primary objective of the socio-technical approach.

The basis of the ethical concern of the socio-technical approach embodies a fundamental value of industrial democracies, that workers should have a share of the benefits brought by new technology in their workplace. Progress is viewed not only as an increase of wealth, but as the betterment of human conditions. It is therefore ethically desirable to use an approach that can develop systems which promote a satisfactory work environment. In Scandinavian countries and certain other north European countries this ethical value is embodied in their legislation, the so-called 'co-determination' acts, and companies are obliged by law to seek the involvement of their employees in deciding and working out changes to information systems.

This conception of information systems as social systems builds on valuable insights offered by several theories of the social sciences. The socio-technical approach is influenced by theories of social change and human communication, even though the theoretical underpinnings of particular methods are rarely made explicit. As an intervention for social change, the socio-technical approach conveys awareness that information systems development is a political process which may redistribute organizational power. Information is a key element of power. The development of a new way of handling information may introduce new means of control, may alter the decision making scope of particular organizational actors, may empower certain parts of the organization, while disempowering others. For example, the first twenty years of computer applications tended to centralize information handling in large data processing departments. Many managers were concerned that control of information resources was transferred to the technical experts of these centres. It has also been observed that the traditional struggle of power between management and workers is often accentuated by information systems developments. Trade unions are particularly concerned that new technology may put more power in the hands of management or lead to worse working conditions. The socio-technical approach recognizes the political nature of the development process, although it has so far offered little guidance as to how developers should deal with this fundamental aspect of projects.

Another important consequence that leads on from considering the social dimension of information systems is that the process of their development and use is often treated as a non-deterministic process of interpersonal dialogue. As such it is influenced by the hermeneutic tradition of the social sciences [Boland, 1985], which considers social interaction as based on subjective interpretation of phenomena that social actors experience. From within such a perspective the development of a new information system is attempted by paying attention to the study of how particular user groups may interpret information, and semantic and pragmatic aspects of the information system become the central focus of analysis.

In practice, emphasis on the social aspects varies from guiding systems analysts to consult the system's participants and pay attention on their needs, to allowing the participants full control and responsibility for the change of their information systems and the development of new technological components. It is not possible to present here all the manifestations of the socio-technical approach; we will only outline the two most widely known ones, participation and job design.

On participation

Some form of participation by interested parties other than technical analysts occurs in most systems development projects. We have already seen that users are expected to contribute to the formulation of specifications which capture the requirements that the technical parts of a new system must satisfy. However, proponents of participation believe that the role of the user of the technical system should not be restricted to being a source of information on requirements, and suggest various reasons why they should be encouraged and facilitated to become more deeply involved in the development process. The main arguments put forward for participation are:

- On moral, and often legal, grounds those who will work within an information system should have the opportunity actively to shape it; indeed sharing such values is almost a precondition for achieving success with participation.

- Such participants are a valuable source of information for systems development. They are the people who have full knowledge of the circumstances of their environment; only they can validate those features of the new system that are likely to be effective.

- They also come to learn the new systems by participating in their development. Implementation becomes easier, as understanding leads to more positive results, people feel less threatened by the change and will not react to its introduction in their work place. It is also more likely that they will make more effective use of it.

- For those invited to participate it is a way that they can acquire valuable knowledge about a new information system which is crucial to retain control of the means of their jobs.

- From the perspective of the analyst, this is a process that also enhances the quality of their jobs, providing the opportunity to be more creative and to be involved in developing information systems that are not only technically good, but liked by those who work in them.

Despite these arguments in favour of a participative systems development model, achieving effective participation has proved a non-trivial matter in practice, and several reservations as to the effectiveness of participation have been raised. There are a number of issues facing the organization of a participative information systems project: who exactly are the people who should participate; what form can participation take; and what methods can support it?

Land and Hirschheim [1983] identify five categories of users:

- Those who request the new system, authorize the development project, and probably pay for it. They may not be the people who will use the system in their everyday jobs. Nevertheless, they expect the system to produce certain benefits for their organization. Usually these are the people that developers consider as their clients and try to satisfy.

- Those managers who supervise the part of the organization that the new system is intended to support. Again, they may not directly use the system in their jobs, but most likely they will be responsible for its effectiveness;

- Those people whose jobs the new system is going to support. They are going to have the most direct contact with the system, either by operating it or by relying on its information output to perform their work.

- Customers of the organization, whose services are going to be delivered with the support of the new system. These are people beyond the boundary of the organization concerned, but they may have a direct influence on the organization as they may opt to withdraw their custom if they are not satisfied with the organization's products or services.

- Groups of people from the broader society that may be affected by the organization's new information systems. Many organizations use information technology to collect information about large parts of the population for market research purposes, or other pro-active research regarding their potential clients and their environment. Although they may have no contact with the new system, they may be affected in significant ways by a new system.

How could all these groups of people participate in a development project? Land and Hirschheim distinguish between two different types of participation: participation in *decision making about the project*, and participation in the actual *analysis and design*.

Participation in decision making can be *consultative* only, in which case participants are invited to express their views and provide evidence to support decisions about the requirements of a new system and its features. Nevertheless, the systems developers are not obliged to conform to the views expressed by the various participants. In contrast, participation in decision making may be *democratic*, in which case all participants have an equal voice in the decision-making process, for example by vote, and the project leaders are obliged to comply with the final decision. This may be the case when management and trade unions enter negotiations about a new way of working. Even stronger is the case of *responsible* participation in decision making. In this kind of participation, participants are given full authority to decide on their systems, if necessary by involving their own professional advisers. This is often the case when particular departments of an organization are given authority to acquire their own systems.

Participation in the development process may similarly be of three different kinds. It may be *consultative*, with various interest groups contributing their opinion about the desirable features to be included in the specification of the system. Alternatively, participation may be *representative*, with the formation of teams of user groups representatives to support the analysis and design tasks. Representatives may be elected from various grades of personnel and various departments concerned, or they may be chosen on the basis of some criteria, perhaps technical knowledge and broad business experience. Finally, the third kind of participation in a system's development is *consensus* participation. This is the case of systems analysis and design with active involvement of the staff concerned. Alternative design strategies are discussed at staff meetings and consensus decisions are made.

Effective participation is very difficult to organize, and does not happen as extensively as one would perhaps expect. It is not enough to invite representatives from other groups to participate, it is also necessary to facilitate their participation so that they can follow the development process and contribute genuinely. Participative processes require strong and confident management – even if that management is self-imposed by the participating group. Participative methods cannot be seen as an alternative to methods of project control. Another problem is that representatives, despite their interest in a project, can find themselves overwhelmed with technical aspects and unable to contribute to the decisions. Several solutions have been tried to this problem, not all with great success. We have already written about prototyping. Users of a computer do not have to master the developers' jargon to communicate their views if they can respond by referring to the performance features of a prototype. As we discussed, however, prototyping is seen as rather inappropriate for large-scale systems. Another effort to make participation effective has been to train representatives of other interest groups to understand the developer's techniques. In this way representatives can work closely with technical experts. Unexpectedly, in some cases where this kind of participation has been organized, the results have not been very positive. The trained representatives may become too involved in the technicalities of the project, gradually losing contact with the groups that they represented and thereby inadequately serving their interests.

The choice of representatives is another difficult issue. For example, what kind of participative procedures could be organized for a project intended to introduce some new technology-based information system in hundreds of branches of a bank or of a government department? It is impossible to expect each branch to be represented by an individual, and even if possible, one individual may not be in a position to provide opinions for all aspects of the work in the branch. Alternatively, a representative branch may be chosen for close collaboration with the technical developers. The major risk here is to overlook the differences among branches. Even if the functioning of an organization is heavily regulated, as in government organizations and in many large corporations, differences among regions and branches do exist. Different offices have different cultures, they may have different informal procedures, different styles of management. If these cannot be taken into account it is unlikely that the new system is going to be found satisfactory by the various branches.

Once again, the example of the DSS systems may illustrate this problem. The first system that the DSS introduced in its local offices was designed in close collaboration with the staff of three local offices. Yet, a survey conducted during the period this system was being installed in all the department's local offices reported staff complaints that their particular requirements were ignored. There were differences in the ways individual branches organized their work and the new uniform system could not easily fit into any of them. In most offices visited by the researchers, staff were not even aware that some colleagues from other offices were involved in the analysis and design of the system.

In summary, the main difficulties facing user participation are:

- Participation tends to lead to confused responsibility. After all, responsibility for making decisions lies with management, and managers reserve the right to manage.

- Participation is a time-consuming and expensive process which tends to lead to compromises regarding systems design. Developers are often concerned that, with participation, the resulting systems are technically poor.

- Participation can become a process of manipulation, and hostage taking rather than a genuine opportunity for people to influence the development process to their benefit. Participants may be invited to take part and yet realize that for various reasons they are not equal partners in the development process, either because systems developers and project managers do not give them decision making authority, or because they cannot cope with the technical aspects. Their participation, however, is seen as legitimizing the new information system, and they are expected to be committed to its effective use.

Despite all these problems identified in the literature, most practitioners give some recognition to the idea that participation is likely to lead to more effective systems, and many methodologies provide some guidelines for organizing it successfully. The difficulties presented above are obstacles to be overcome, rather than arguments against wider involvement in information systems development.

Job design in the development process

One form of the socio-technical approach directs the development process towards redesigning the work environment within which a new information system is going to be used. Information systems development is aimed at using the technology flexibly to provide satisfactory work conditions for the employees of the organization. The basic belief is that systems developers should be informed by the lessons that organizational theory can offer on the detrimental effects of scientific management and the use of technology on strictly efficiency grounds, and actively try to promote work conditions which satisfy human needs. The most influential writer on this approach is Enid Mumford of the Manchester Business School. Her research team worked out a framework for examining job satisfaction [Mumford & Weir, 1979; Mumford, 1983, 1995], and a methodology for incorporating job design in IS development called ETHICS (an acronym for Effective Technical and Human Implementation of Computer Systems).

Job satisfaction is defined as a good 'fit' between the employee's job expectations and the particular job requirements defined by the organization in which he or she works. The literature suggests that a number of factors contribute to people's job satisfaction:

- An individual's *psychological needs*. Psychologists find that the satisfaction of needs such as achievement, recognition, responsibility or status provides motivation for work.

- *Leadership style*. The kind of supervision that employees receive influences their attitudes to their job.

- *Wages*. The way wages and salaries are constructed, overtime pay and the conditions of the labour market are also related to employees' attitude to their work.

- *Management ideology and values*. The way an organization manages its business – whether for example it follows an impersonal bureaucratic mode, or a decentralized responsible problem solving mode – influences employees' job satisfaction. The values and moral philosophy adopted by the management of a company is another factor of job satisfaction. It is necessary that employees perceive the functions of their organization as legitimate.

- Finally, the *content of the work* that somebody does, and the *way it is structured*. These are factors intrinsic to the job of an employee and yet they can be controlled by careful design.

Taking into account these factors, Mumford suggests that the following 'fits' must exist in an employee's job:

- The *knowledge fit*. Employees must find that they have adequate opportunities to use and further extend their skills and knowledge.

- The *psychological fit*. Employees must find that their job offers them recognition, achievement, responsibility, advancement and status.

- The *efficiency fit*. Employees must find that they are financially well rewarded for their work. In addition, they must feel that they receive adequate support for their job, such as information and supervision, and that the control exerted is acceptable.

- The *task structure fit*. The job must have adequate task differentiation built in, to meet the employees' needs for variety. The employees must find the job interesting, and must feel satisfied with the degree of feedback and autonomy allowed.

- The *ethical fit*. Employees must find that the values and the philosophy of their employer do not contradict their own.

These factors provide a guiding framework for monitoring work conditions when developing new information systems, identifying the areas that need improvement, and setting objectives to that end. Mumford proposes a diagnostic tool, a questionnaire based on the above concept of job satisfaction. It can be flexibly used for identifying human needs and for evaluating how well an information system caters for them. It is important to note that, although Mumford's method is based in some fundamental beliefs about what conditions contribute to an individual's satisfaction at work, the design of a work environment should not deterministically target one 'best' set of work conditions. People with different aspirations and personal background require different values for the combination of the above factors, some perhaps putting more emphasis on receiving good support and supervision, others liking more autonomy and working more effectively in a more anarchic work environment. The questionnaire prompts employees to express how well their job caters for the above factors and whether they would like them to be different. In this way it exposes areas of dissatisfaction that the new system should try to put right, and areas that are satisfactory and should be preserved or built upon.

The discussion in chapter 6 suggested that organizational theory provides several principles for job design. In particular, it referred to job enlargement, allowing for job rotation to perform the fragmented tasks of a work environment, and job enrichment, reorganizing the fragmented work tasks in a way which allows an employee to have more control of his or her job and to use a number of different skills. Many authors, including Mumford, suggest another idea for designing jobs to satisfy human needs; work can be organized in multi-skilled, self-managing groups. Each group can organize its own activities and be given responsibility and even a budget to do so. The group is more likely to be responsive to the needs of its individual members and be efficient as well. The support of such work teams by information technology-based systems has recently become a strong research theme.

The essence of the ETHICS approach is the pursuit of the objective of a satisfactory work environment simultaneously with that of constructing an efficient technical information system. It therefore follows a dual process of social and organizational change paralleled by the technical system development. Figure 8.1 shows this dual process in a schematic form.

ETHICS does not propose any particular methods for the technical tasks of information systems development. However, this process requires heavy involvement of the many interested parties and the methods have to be accessible to non-technical people. Indeed, Mumford has argued consistently for her views on job design, that information systems should be designed by their members, organized in self-managing, multi-skilled groups. It is those who will be a part of the new system, its members, who should drive the development process, and their work group needs which should determine what is the most effective information system. The role of the technical experts is to facilitate the members' effort to employ new technology for achieving a more effective work environment. It is the people who are involved every day in handling information who should drive the process of change, and the technical expert who should support it by informing and advising on technical options.

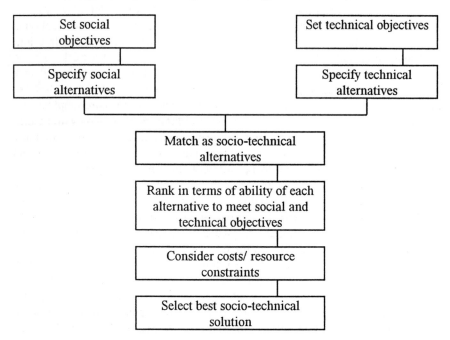

Figure 8.1 Socio-technical systems development [Mumford & Weir, 1979]

Some comments on the socio-technical approach

The humanitarian predisposition and the democratic industrial values of the socio-technical approach easily attract the interest of students. Yet, this approach is not so widely followed as one would expect. We discussed above some of the difficulties of participation. Other problems stem from the relatively inadequate methodical support for the activities of the approach, and the unfavourable management culture which prevails in many organizations.

Analysts undertaking systems development projects, and business managers who authorize them, tend to seek the security of prescriptive professional methods. Few analysts feel confident with the vague suggestions of organization theorists and social scientists more generally. In contradiction to engineering methods, they provide neither a clear pattern of actions nor the certainty of specific outcome. Dealing with people and the social aspects of information handling is far more difficult to organize. Besides, most professional analysts have not been trained in how to work with people and intervene in political, messy and unpredictable organizational problems. Understandably, they are concerned about losing control of the project, its cost and its deliverables. Humanitarian aspects may be respectable, as is the argument about increasing the effectiveness of new systems and averting the threat of industrial disputes, but project control and tangible deliverables are usually more pressing concerns and the only ones that project leaders feel professionally qualified to handle.

Many organizations cannot easily accommodate socio-technical principles. Authoritarian management and bureaucratic structures are to certain degrees incompatible with the socio-technical principles. For example, it is very unlikely that a management will allow a survey of their employees' job satisfaction if the organization is not committed to reorganizing according to social requirements. The employees themselves may be suspicious of the motives of those asking them. If an organization in general does not encourage employees' initiative, they may be unmotivated and perhaps unable to take an active role in a creative activity such as information systems development.

Because of all these problems, the socio-technical approach, while in principle desirable, is in practice seldom applied. Yet, it presents systems developers with a challenge which they cannot easily ignore. Indeed, over the years information systems development has become more sensitive to the notion that information systems are not purely technical, but socio-technical systems. Although few professionals are committed to a pure form of socio-technical approach, most projects try to accommodate some level of involvement, perhaps only of a consultative form, and care about the human context of the technical system, if only in the form of the human–machine interface.

Ad hoc approach

It would be misleading to give the impression that information systems are always developed by systematically following a clear and theoretically based approach. Perhaps most systems are developed in what we shall call here an *ad hoc* approach: by people who, technically qualified or not, address whatever concerns they may be faced with according to their judgement of the circumstances, and within the limits posed by their personal biases and skills. Such systems developers may have some technical knowledge, they may be systems members themselves, or a team of both. They may stick to a particular limited set of systems analysis and design methods and techniques, or they may use little more formalism than paper and pencil descriptions and a high level computer language or a 4GL language. Almost certainly, however, they use a great deal of judgement, creativity, and informal means for making decisions.

There are many reasons for the continuation and perhaps proliferation of such practices today, despite the fact that they are in general considered unprofessional. Many information systems changes are too small and technically obvious to require a sophisticated effort to implement them. They can be handled with inexpensive stand-alone microcomputers and user friendly packages, and they fit without any significant disturbance into an organization. For example, it may be superfluous to think of a 'theoretical approach' in order to introduce a spreadsheet application into a small administrative office. The hardware and software are widely available, and plenty of advice is available from colleagues, people in other similar offices, or magazines. The people involved will need to take adequate training and to work out how this application will effectively combine with other tasks that they perform. If the office, and perhaps the system too, is shared with other groups, more consideration may need to be given to organizing the use of the system in an acceptable way. The physical position of the system and the noise of the printer may be a problem to be discussed. Such changes as these can be undertaken by following common sense, and do not need an elaborate and systematic approach.

An important factor which leads to *ad hoc* systems development is the spread of computer literacy, again in combination with the availability of flexible and widely available technology and technical facilities. Many employees in a company, in industrialized countries at least, are likely to feel quite confident with computers and in developing their own applications. It is, however, much less likely that they have any significant knowledge of systems development methods. They may seek advice and make special efforts to update their technical knowledge before they undertake the system development tasks, but in most cases only limited and very often simplistic knowledge of methods is gained as a result of last moment self-teaching efforts. Usually, internal understanding and informal discussions provide the new system's requirements, and then either a packaged solution is sought in the market, or somebody sits with a crude first design in front of a microcomputer with a database package or a 4GL and writes some code. Perhaps the only other tools used by such amateur developers are DFDs and flow charts. It is mainly the commitment and enthusiasm of those undertaking such efforts which makes all the difference between a success and a failure.

The growth of a market in freelance systems development services has also fostered *ad hoc* systems development practices. In the 1980s, in most countries, demand for relevant skills outweighed the capacity of data processing centres. The business of software houses and small consultancies prospered and indeed, a great deal of methodical professional practice originated in, and spread from, such companies. This still left substantial opportunities for individuals and very small groups, many of them with very few methodical skills other than common sense and a knowledge of programming. Freelance systems developers often work in support of established information systems departments on contracts for parts of systems which have been systematically analyzed at some high level of requirements. Nevertheless, a significant part of systems development is delegated to practitioners who approach their tasks with limited ability in terms of methodical technical practice, let alone sophisticated ideas of social or organizational intervention.

From an organizational perspective, it has been significant that with the advent of 'end-user computing', initiatives such as the above have been accepted as legitimate, and indeed desirable. Centralized information systems departments, unable to cope with the load of requests for enhancements and developments, and despised for the restrictive service they often provided, lost full control of systems development practices. Other departments were given permission to acquire their own computer systems, and variety of applications is not necessarily considered problematic any more. In chapter 10 we discuss end-user computing in more detail and we describe there efforts to promote methodical practices within this community of empowered customers for new information systems.

Finally, the justification of the *ad hoc* approach stems partly from the failures of formal approaches in dealing with the complexity of information systems development. As in all domains, where systematic theory and formal practices fail, informal practices, and human serendipity come to the rescue. In a sense information systems development has proved too complicated an activity to be adequately directed by either engineering or social science based formal disciplines. Many methodically organized approaches stifle creativity and judgement, which have to play a crucial role in achieving improved information handling. Thus, the *ad hoc* approach should not always be seen as an undesirable lack of professionalism which should be stopped, but as a natural expression of human creativity. This is perhaps the approach that has produced the greatest results so far and is the most legitimate practice.

Exercises and discussion issues

1. Make a list of the benefits that you would expect to accrue from using a computer-based tool as the basis for undertaking a major part of information systems development activities. Are there any disadvantages that you could foresee?

2. Consider the role of the analyst in the engineering approach and in the socio-technical approach. What kind of skills do each of these approaches require from such professionals?

3. Explore the fundamental characteristics of engineering as a human endeavour. It would be useful to interview an engineer in another field to find out what he or she feels is the essence of the engineering approach. Does this relate closely to the tasks that information systems developers face? Architects are not in general considered as engineers, though they work alongside them. Why is this?

4. Does the phrase, *information systems are social systems* tell us anything useful about the appropriate way to approach systems development?

References

Ackoff, R.L. (1967) 'Management misinformation systems', in *Management Science,* Vol. 14, No.4, pp. 147-156.

Boland, J.R., Jr (1985) 'Phenomenology: A Preferred Approach to Research on Information Systems', in Mumford, E. *et al.* (editors), *Research Methods in Information Systems,* North-Holland.

Coad, P. & Yourdon, E. (1990) *Object-oriented Analysis,* Prentice-Hall, Englewood Cliffs, New Jersey.

Dowson, M. (1987) 'Integrated Project Support with IStar', *IEEE Software,* November, pp. 6-15.

Hall, A.D. (1962) *A Methodology for Systems Engineering,* Van Nostrand, Princeton N.J.

Hitch, C.J. & McKean, R.N. (1960) *The Economics of Defence in the Nuclear Age,* Harvard University Press, Cambridge, Massachusetts.

Keen, P.G.W. (1981) 'Information systems and organizational change', in *Communications of the ACM,* Vol. 24, No. 1, pp. 24-33.

Land, F.F. & Hirschheim, R. (1983) 'Participative systems design: rationale, tools and techniques', in *Journal of Applied Systems Analysis,* Vol. 10.

Quade, E.S. & Miser, H.J. (1985) 'The Context, Nature and Use of Systems Analysis', in Miser, H.J. & Quade, E.S. (editors) *Handbook of Systems Analysis,* Wiley, Chichester.

Mumford, E. & Weir, M. (1979) *Computer Systems in work design – the ETHICS method,* Associated Business Press, London.

Mumford, E. (1995*) Effective Systems Design and Requirements Analysis: The ETHICS Approach,* Macmillan Press, Basingstoke.

Pugh, D.S., Hickson, D.J. & Hinings, C.R. (1983) *Writers on Organizations,* (Third edition), Penguin Books, London.

Further reading

There are many books elaborating on each of the engineering approaches discussed in this chapter. Churchman's book provides a general analysis of the theoretical underpinnings of systems approaches. The Graham book provides further insight into the object-oriented approach. Zuboff's book provides further interesting reading within the socio-technical tradition.

Churchman, C.W. (1968) *The Systems Approach,* Dell Publishing Company, New York.

Graham, I. (1991) *Object-oriented Methods,* Addison-Wesley, Wokingham.

Zuboff, S. (1988) *In the Age of the Smart Machine: The Future of Work and Power,* Basic Books, New York.

9 Methodologies for information systems development

- *The ambition of the methodology movement*
- *A historical perspective on methodologies*
- *Methodologies today*
- *The future for methodologies*

However persuasive the materials presented thus far in this book, and however well developed the conceptual underpinning of systems development is, this is a field that is characterized by a clear feeling of anxiety about the quality and appropriateness of its *practice*. Even if we are convinced of the merits of a certain approach, we need to know how to translate it into actual day-to-day working practices in the thousands of organizations across the country that need to develop computer-based information systems. Translating theories and models into detailed prescriptions and sequences of actions for the employees of these organizations to follow is a non-trivial task. In the last decade the most common answer to this question has been a widespread acceptance of the need for more or less comprehensive and detailed descriptions of how to develop information systems, in general described as *information systems development methodologies*. The word methodology would seem to imply a prescription of how to get something done, and thus methodologies for information systems development are expected to describe how the overall task is to be achieved. Following that sense, methodologies are in general normative and prescriptive, providing detailed guidelines for systems development activities; but we need also to recognize their analytical characteristic too. In stating *what* should be done, a methodology also implies how a problem area will be investigated and understood. We should also note here the usual caveat that writers in this field offer.

The word *methodology* should perhaps be reserved for the *study* of method, not for a description of method. In any event the word is by now so well embedded in the field that we cannot seek to change the established usa

Since almost every organization of any size has to develop systems, it is not surprising that there has arisen a strong mark guidance on how it should be done. This ranges from the gentl to the commercial marketing of comprehensive framework courses and consultancy services. Many methodologies a with brand names and are marketed as sets of ma courses. Some are documented in widely avail described in internal documents of organizations that have established their own 'house style' of methodology. Indicatively, the book by Olle *et al.* [1991] lists over 30 commercial or academic methodologies together with their sponsors.

The main stream of ideas in methodologies in the past decade has been based around the concept of structured systems analysis, the so-called structured methodologies. One of the earliest and most influential of these, the methodology proposed by DeMarco, has already been partially described in chapter 4, and the tools described there are a component of many of the subsequent variations on this theme. A more recent, and more complex, methodology in this vein is Structured Systems Analysis and Design Method (SSADM), a methodology developed for and by the British Government for use in the public sector, though with a far wider influence in Britain [Downs *et al.*, 1992]. It soon becomes clear in studying methodologies that there is a great deal more in common between most structured methodologies than there is distinctive or different.

Apart from the structured methodologies other and more distinctive methodologies have developed around a number of other perspectives. The problems of programming and software engineering have long influenced information systems developers, and Jackson's Structured Development (JSD), for example, is a direct outgrowth of an approach to programming and program design [Jackson, 1983]. The participation of the people who will be involved in a new information system in analysis and design and the establishment of an appropriate mix of social and technical considerations is the basis of the methodology ETHICS that was mentioned in chapter 8.

Strategic information systems planning, taking an organization-wide perspective to information systems has been guided by methodologies too, and the various methodologies in the Information Engineering school are examples [Finkelstein, 1989]. Yet another example comes from the domain of developing knowledge-based systems where a methodology known as KADS has been developed as part of joint European project [Hickman *et al.*, 1990]. Finally, in chapter 2 of this book, the use of Checkland's Soft Systems Methodology (SSM) has been introduced, and this methodology has had considerable influence on information systems developers, even if it is some way from being normative and prescriptive

The adoption of methodologies has taken national dimensions, and different countries have tended to develop and use their own types and styles of methodology. Thus in Scandinavia a methodology called ISAC has been influential, just as SSADM has been in the United Kingdom; France has its MERISE, while the United States has developed a looser adherence to Yourdon's and DeMarco's works as well as to Gane and Sarson's STRADIS [Lundeberg *et al.*, 1981; Pham & Chartier-Kastler, 1991; Gane & Sarson, 1979; Yourdon, 1989].

It is not the purpose of this book to describe all of these methodologies, nor to choose one to consider in detail. A number of other books provide such an overview, and all the methodologies mentioned above have their own detailed mentation in text books and training materials. This chapter rather explores what methodologies attempt to achieve, and looks at the essential problems that all methodologies face in providing concrete and applicable advice to systems developers.

The ambition of the methodology movement

Establishing widely applicable rules or guidelines for good practice in systems development has proved to be a challenging and controversial endeavour. By now we certainly know some things about how *not* to develop information handling activities based on computers, and we may have some specific principles and theoretical views about the nature of information systems changes. We also have examples of good and bad outcomes that can be studied for clues, but there is nonetheless still a feeling that the essence of good practice in bringing technology to bear on information handling problems in organizations still eludes us.

As the previous chapters indicated, many fundamental issues of information systems development are still debated, as for example, the extent to which it is a concern about developing technological ensembles of high quality or, alternatively, about achieving successful intervention in a host organization, exploring and improving information handling activities. Against the background of such debates, the development of methodologies aims at providing specific, shareable and communicable knowledge about the required practices of systems development. To that end, the questions which are addressed – whether explicitly or implicitly – by setting down a methodology, include the following:

- Why is an information system being developed?
- How should an information system be developed – the process?
- How can this process be managed – the project?
- What is the best way to set down this knowledge?
- What is the best way to teach or pass on this knowledge?

Methodologies usually assume, and sometimes explicitly explore, the objectives that the development of a new information system is intended to achieve. They then go on to provide an approach to systems development by recommending a particular sequence of development tasks and methods for executing them. In this way they provide a structure for organizing systems development tasks, usually based on some variation of the life cycle model, with the addition of mechanisms for monitoring progress. Techniques and tools are generally specified which facilitate both learning and practice of the systems development process as advocated by the particular methodology.

The last two points in the above list are less often directly addressed. Nonetheless, the question of whether we have enough understanding to be able to set down and communicate the essence of good practice is highly relevant, since if the answer is 'no' then what hope do those who adopt methodologies have of obtaining any benefit from their efforts? The elements of a methodology are generally presented and packaged so as to be easily disseminated in the form of work standards and supporting training materials. This aspect of methodologies is crucial in real organizations, because it is only through a capacity to disseminate and pass on understanding to those who work in information systems development that real improvements in the quality and return on system development activities can be achieved. A theoretically sound methodology that cannot be successfully communicated to and adopted by ordinary organizations and businesses is of little practical value.

In the effort to address the points enumerated in the list above, the establishment of methodologies confronts fundamental problems of systems development work. Here we enumerate four specific problems, each of which suggests some requirements for a successful methodology.

The problem of perception and description

As is emphasized repeatedly in this book, information handling activities in organizations are undertaken by and for people and in support of the tasks they set out to achieve. To develop an information system we must be able to see and understand this world and be able to detect and describe the relevant parts. This leads to many problems in fully understanding the world into which a system will fit, and hence in fully establishing and setting down the requirements for any new system. It will almost always be the case that a number of different and contrasting views of this world will need to be taken into account order to gain sufficient insight. For example, we may use a perspective that concentrates on the information flows, one that concentrates on the information stocks, one that concentrates on the tasks and transformations undertaken, or one that concentrates on the information needs of the people involved.

Within different methodologies different weights are given to these contrasting perspectives. In the mainstream of structured methodologies two principal perspectives have been used. The first concentrates on the information handling processes and transformations undertaken – referred to as the process oriented approach. This can be seen as a direct outgrowth of computer programming and a concern with establishing algorithms. The second perspective is concerned with modelling the world in terms of the items (entities) about which data is stored – referred to as the data modelling approach. The establishment of this perspective, as discussed in chapter 8, can be seen as resulting in part from the take-up of database technology and the need to understand and specify carefully what is to be in a database. Some blend of these two perspectives is used in most current mainstream methodologies, and is seen as appropriate in the context of what we might loosely call *data processing* type applications which involve the establishment of a database and the description of how specific types of incoming transaction are to be handled. For other types of application it may be more appropriate to adopt alternative perspectives. In an office situation a concentration on understanding and satisfying the needs of the people who will use a system may be appropriate – a participative or human-centred perspective, while development of a real-time control system for a power station would perhaps be better approached through a perspective that looked at the events that could happen and their priority – an event-based perspective.

The problem of perception and description is not just a problem that relates to the world today, but it also relates to being able to describe the world as it will be tomorrow, with the new system we wish to build in place. Just as we need to see the world today in multiple ways in order to *analyze* an information handling situation, so too the *design* of any proposed new information system will need to be expressed in multiple ways, building up to both a specification of how the system is to be built and a description of how it will operate. As we discussed in the introduction to part II, specifications are used as a design blueprint for the construction of a new system, but the description also serves other purposes such as allowing workers or managers to understand the system that is proposed and comment on it, as well as allowing the new system to be maintained throughout its life. The aim is, then, to develop and populate easily understandable and shareable models of both today's situation and tomorrow's.

We might express this problem of perception and description in more theoretical terms. We need to establish both a clear *ontology* and a clear *epistemology* for systems development efforts. We need to be aware of the assumption that we make about the character of the world we are working in, and these ontological assumptions will provide the frame through which we see the world and will consequentially constrain the aspects of the world that we see. The epistemology that we use will inform us about how to set about exploring this world, how to acquire knowledge about it [Hirschheim & Klein, 1989].

The problem of hard and soft

Each information systems development methodology implies a certain balance of attention between objective and subjective, structured and unstructured, measurable and intangible. Information systems are composed of complex and ill-specifiable human behaviours as well as hard or programmed behaviours of designed parts of the system and man-made artefacts. Unlike a physical product or artefact, information systems are largely diffuse and abstract in terms of their realization and their highest level characteristics. Systems development practice has therefore to encompass both a hard and reasonably deterministic world, as well as one that is soft and relative.

The development process has similarly to encompass, and to some degree integrate, both the hard and the soft. Either taken in isolation is not sufficient.

Alternative boundaries around a systems development, based on alternative ontological assumptions, may change dramatically the balance of hard and soft, and alternative approaches or methodologies will alter the sequence in which they are considered.

The problem of confidence

A further purpose of methodologies is to build confidence that the information systems development tasks will lead successfully to desirable results. There are two aspects of development in which confidence is required: in the validity of the information systems changes which are proposed and undertaken, and in the manageability or controllability of the development process itself. When development proposals are made we need to be able to express some confidence in them as effective and achievable. In so far as a system's components are to run on computers, this is a problem of attaining quite specific confidence in the consistency, correctness and completeness of a design. But, building on the problem of hard and soft, there is much more beyond these 'programmed' components. Just knowing that the programs meet the specifications, will not crash or contain few or even zero errors, or that the technology is correctly specified and configured, says nothing about the way in which a system will fit into and affect the world. This leads back to the problem of perception, since it is only possible to predict or specify with confidence the effect of an open system if one has an appropriate understanding of the environment within which it will operate.

The other aspect of confidence that exercises the minds of information systems developers is achieving assurance that the actual development project itself will be able to go forward, that it is manageable, with appropriate checkpoints and controls, including controls on elapsed time and on the utilization of resources. This is essentially the same problem which the life cycle model addresses. In chapter 7 we discussed how this general model of organizing the information systems development process has not been able to capture the true complexity and multi-dimensional character of real systems development. Increasingly, it is seen that information systems development projects run into problems not because of technical concerns or even poor specifications, but because the project is literally out of control and is not being managed. One of the concerns of methodologies is therefore to help make projects more manageable by providing the right kind of work-breakdown and the right kind of information on the progress of work. If this can be achieved, it is argued, then control can be re-established and rational management decisions made.

This ambition of methodologies, to help establish control over projects, is not always welcomed by all, and in particular by those who actually do the development work. For example, being expected to provide an accurate estimate of how long a programming task will take, or how many 'staff-months', is irksome enough. Being expected then to report progress regularly, to stick by the estimate and to be held responsible for any delay, is worse.

The problem of generality versus context

Information systems and information technology are ubiquitous and pervasive; they turn up everywhere and anywhere. Methodologies seek to provide at the same time appropriate general guidance on development, but also to capture the particular characteristics of individual situations so that they can be approached in particular ways. How far any one model of context can be stretched is a recurring problem. For example, can the context of transaction processing in large organizations be stretched to the context of decision support systems in small non-profit organizations, or knowledge-based systems in medical domains, or avionics, or hospital patient records? While methodologies seek to offer comprehensive advice on how to develop information systems, we need to be aware that every situation is unique, yet a unique approach every time is equally unhelpful even if any approach tailored to the situation can share some tools and techniques.

In practice, as described in the introductory section to this chapter, methodologies do tend to focus on particular types of situation and the development of different classes of system, be it transaction processing systems, real-time control systems, clerical and office automation systems, decision support or expert systems.

A historical perspective on methodologies

It is not surprising that the early computer applications in organizations were undertaken with no clearly predefined approach and only limited understanding of systems development issues related to the technology. At that time, of necessity, the technical specialist ('the programmer') was largely informally or self taught, and acted as analyst, designer and implementor. The result was (and to some degree still is) that systems were idiosyncratic, based on one person's *ad hoc* interpretation of requirements, ill-documented and produced by a process that defied management. Furthermore, the overall process was difficult to understand and evaluate and hence to learn from.

The history of today's methodologies can be traced directly back to the 1960s and the coming of the mass produced and widely marketed third generation computers, such as the IBM 360 range. This era saw systems development projects beginning to be undertaken on a larger and wider scale. This provided a rich environment for the uptake of new ideas that would set systems development activity on a more solid foundation. In Britain the National

Computing Centre (NCC) course in Basic Systems Analysis was established and provided a firm and widely adopted set of guidelines for systems work [Daniels & Yeates, 1969]. In a revised form it is still taught today. The NCC recommendations, sometimes referred to as 'the classic approach', emphasized a number of key features:

- establishment of the job of systems analyst as both investigator and as designer;

- a stage-based model of systems development based on a notion of the life cycle;

- development of standard paper and pencil tool sets to aid in analysis and design;

- establishment of clear documentation standards to leave behind a trace of development work and to provide a basis for the maintenance activity needed for the lifetime support of a system;

- a focus on the design practices needed to make the best of the restrictive characteristics of the available technology, for example magnetic tapes as filestore.

It is from this beginning in the 1960s that our current level of expertise and understanding of the problem of information systems development has grown, and methodologies have for the last decade been one of the primary fields for debate in the information systems world. A fascinating insight into this debate can be obtained by studying the various reports of the Comparative Review of Information System Design Methodologies (CRIS) conferences of the 1980s [Olle *et al.*, 1982, 1983, 1986, 1991]. Over this time information systems developers have become aware that a range of other issues exist for the users of methodologies, issues that are not necessarily adequately addressed by the classic approach. New concerns, as discussed in chapter 8, have come to be added to the simple bringing of order to technical chaos, and the 1970s and 1980s have seen methodologies turn their attention to a number of further aspects of the information systems development process.

Perhaps the primary identified problem has been the lack of satisfaction that those outside the technical specialisms feel with their contribution to development effort and with the systems that are produced. Guidance and insight has been sought as to the appropriate roles for the multiple stakeholders who are involved in the process of providing information about requirements and in checking and approving them along the way. A part of this dissatisfaction is attributable to problems of maintenance. Information systems are not just built and thereafter operate without any intervention. A system needs to be capable of being easily altered and changed throughout its life. Documentation of design is important here, but the characteristics of good maintenance documentation are somewhat different from those of good implementation specifications.

There has also been a consistent perception of low productivity and low productivity growth in systems development. It has been widely observed that, despite the introduction of the structured methodologies, the productivity of systems development staff has not increased as rapidly as might have been expected. One result has been that most organizations still have a large backlog of systems to be developed and maintenance activities to be undertaken. This has exerted great pressure on information systems departments and often helped to sour their relationships with the rest of the organization.

With the advent of database and communications technology, it is less and less the case that individual systems are developed in isolation. Rather they need to be developed as part of more comprehensive and integrated approach to information handling. This has required the linking of information systems development to the broader context of an organization and its future plans. This is not just a reflection of the fact that individual information systems are technically interlinked, but that the whole activity of information systems development and management is linked to the overall objectives and goals of an organization. As part of this, the successful use of the technological power of software and hardware has become an issue that methodologies need to address. In the 1960s and 1970s technology, particularly data storage technology, was a significant constraint on systems development. Today the reverse is perhaps true, and the task is rather to find ways to exploit the power of today's machines and to achieve greater creativity in systems development, discovering new solutions and innovative applications. The result is that methodologies that assume the automation of an existing set of procedures are increasingly inappropriate and most now offer some element of strategic planning for information systems.

Finally, methodologies should be able to provide concrete support for understanding and accommodating the political and social dimension of information systems development within organizations. Information systems development activities need to provide a route for the expression of the various legitimate interests of those who are affected by systems development work. One possible route to achieve this has been through incorporating a socio-technical approach into methodologies.

In the 1990s, a methodology has potentially to offer a lot more than a simple set of guidelines and tools for the technical tasks of systems analysts as they work on isolated projects. From the earliest days of the use of computers within organizations it was realized that this was a problematical process. A good deal of experience and understanding has been acquired over the years and been transformed into practice with various routes being taken. In general three main areas of development can be identified, each of which can be traced through the history of organizational computing up to present-day developments, with different periods, national traditions and user groups concentrating on different areas.

A focus on professionalism and skill

Methodologies can be seen as serving a defining role in developing the distinctive job of the *systems analyst*, a person to stand between the world of users or clients, and the technical world of computers with its own specialists. The establishment of this new role has led to much debate over the years as to which side the systems analyst owes ultimate allegiance, the technical world or the organization and its problems. While the ideal is of course perfect balance and harmony, the reality is that most commentators seem to think that the technical pull has been too strong and ultimately dysfunctional. If the systems analyst is more committed to computers than to solving the problems of the information systems participants, then this will inevitably lead to tensions within a project and a poor climate for collaboration in the future.

In recent years one response to this dilemma has been a growing interest in a new kind of professional, the so-called *hybrid manager*, a deliberate mix of business and technical skills. The argument is put that if such a role can be created, filled by an individual with both a solid understanding of computers and a knowledge of the particular business, administration and management, then greater success will be achieved in the development and use of information systems. This new hybrid manager will bridge any gulf and be able to combine real user understanding with judgement on how new systems are to be constructed. Taking either the traditional model of the systems analyst or the new model of the hybrid manager, it is clear that to achieve that particular status there will be certain things that need to be known, and certain ways of achieving ends that are expected to be a part of good practice. In so far as methodologies set down these things, then they can be seen as representing a move towards establishing the professional credentials of those who develop information systems. It has thus become common for people in Britain to hold certificates in systems analysis such as that offered by the National Computing Centre (NCC), or in the methodology SSADM.

A focus on procedure and sequence

The second theme detectable in the rise of methodologies has been concerned with setting down the necessary and sufficient steps to be taken to develop an information system. This entailed formalizing the process of systems development into a discrete number of stages, and prescribing a full set of necessary and sufficient activities within each stage. In this way development work is broken down into achievable sub-units of work each intended to produce carefully specified results – the deliverables. Using this breakdown it is then possible both to ensure that all necessary work is done and to improve the management and control of projects.

The description given in part I of this book of the essential tasks of systems development within a life-cycle model has illustrated the basic understanding that has developed of the appropriate sequence of these stages. Nonetheless, as explained in chapter 7, there has proved to be great scope for refinement and reinterpretation of the life cycle within a concrete set of guidelines. One such debate, relevant to methodologies, revolves around the question of whether and to what depth it is appropriate to study an existing information system prior to developing a replacement. The classic position is that the current system should be studied in its physical (actual) form and abstracted to a current logical model prior to developing a future logical model. It is then from this future logical model that a future physical model can be developed, and construction begins. When information systems based on computers are intended to replicate or replace existing manual or computer-based procedures this makes some sense. Even so, the effort and anguish in modelling a system that is to be superseded, needs careful justification. When new or novel applications are being developed, undertaking a study of the existing situation in great detail is rather less easy to justify.

This concern with physical and logical models is a more general theme worth exploring. Physical models are about the actual way a system operates, with all the constraints imposed by the implementation environment, constraints of computers, buildings, people and so on. Logical models are the pure unconstrained image of a system, ignoring all these dreary details. How should these two ways of working with a system's design data be related? Should a new system be developed in totally logical terms before being mapped onto an actual implementation, or is this just going to lead to an impossible design that has no hope of achieving implementation?

A focus on tools and techniques

While concern with procedure and sequence has occupied the academic end of the methodology debate, much of the refinement of information systems develop-ment *practice* has been concerned less with revising this overall sequence than with developing a stronger notion of the techniques and tools to be employed within each step or stage, and the form that the deliverables which they produce should take.

When specific tasks can be identified within systems development, then ways of doing them are sought that will facilitate or possibly 'automate' aspects of development work. The oldest example is perhaps the development through the 1960s and into the 1970s of so-called high level or third generation programming languages, such as COBOL, FORTRAN or PL/1, but also includes methods of describing the design of a system, for example program logic in a flow chart, data structures in a database schema or a program's interface in a state transition diagram. These tools have been in general manual, based on paper and pencil methods, including a plethora of diagramming techniques. More recently, a great deal of interest has been expressed in transferring these design tools and techniques onto computers and to providing software support for systems analysts in their job. The general term used today for such efforts is Computer Aided Systems Engineering or CASE. Most CASE software available mirrors to some degree established methodologies, and presupposes that the user is familiar with the basic techniques.

Methodologies today

The section above has outlined three main themes in the emergence of methodologies. It is now time to set out in more detail what a methodology is today. What is it that organizations are asked to put their faith in? This section reviews a number of aspects of today's methodologies.

Prescriptive character

All methodologies have something of a 'cookbook' character. They describe how some tasks of systems development are to be achieved by following steps and stages, the intermediate and final products that result, and the roles and responsibilities of the people who participate. In other words, methodologies provide a very useful distinction between what is to be done next, who is to do it, and how. The usual way of describing the distinctive character of particular methodologies is by determining these three features. Almost all methodologies that you will find described in books such as those listed at the end of this chapter can be seen as a mixture of these three features. They tend to contain an overall description of the phases or stages of systems development and identify those that they particularly relate to. They contain descriptions of tools and techniques to be used in each of these stages, for example data flow diagrams, entity relationship models, or the technique of normalization. They describe the linkage between stages, and how the results of one stage are passed on and used in subsequent stages. There is also usually some description of who is to be involved, and where, in the overall process.

Most methodologies quite naturally put the skilled analyst at the centre of the stage, and most of the detailed description of the what and the how will be aimed at such a person. Nevertheless, other actors are also given roles. Consultation with the people who will be involved in the information system may be described, preparation of materials for senior management and project sponsors specified, and the substance of the interaction with the programming and software specialists may be sketched.

Prevalence of structured life cycle

Most widely practised methodologies adopt some version of the life cycle. Structured methodologies follow a top-down development strategy, supported by structured analysis and design methods. In this approach the higher level functionality is first analyzed, designed or coded, and the details filled in later. Thus, for example in an on-line office system, design of the main menu system can overlap with analysis of the individual operations on that menu, and all design does not need to be completed before any implementation activities commence. Top-down implementation also encourages the analyst to talk to the user *after* specifications have been established – they may even get to be changed! DeMarco [1978] expresses more generally what top-down structured methodologies attempt, couched in terms of their role in developing a structured specification that has these characteristics:

- it is *graphic*, made up mostly of diagrams;
- it is *partitioned*, not a single specification, but a network of connected mini-specifications;
- it is *top down*, presented in a hierarchical fashion with a smooth progression from the most abstract to the most detailed;
- it is *concise*, the 5000-page Victorian novel specification is out;
- it is *iterative*, elements of the specification stand on their own; they can be moved back and forth between analyst and user until they are right ;
- it is *maintainable*, a specification that can be updated to reflect changes in the requirement;
- it is a *paper model of the system-to-be*, the user can work with the model to perfect a vision of the new system.

DeMarco wrote the above in 1978, and since then the basic ideas of the structured methodologies have been developed further. In particular, modern methodologies seek to develop a variety of distinct project activities, to be done in parallel, rather than just mirror the stages of the life cycle with its implications of strict sequence. There has also been attention to adding more structured methods to the analysis phases, such as data analysis, and to setting out explicit and richer roles for management and users too. Such modern methodologies acknowledge far more the environment within which a project takes place, and the cognisance that needs to be taken thereof. As a result methodologies have a more contingent character, with choices as to how the overall guidance in a methodology is interpreted in a particular situation.

Completeness and concreteness

Another distinctive feature is the degree to which a particular methodology is complete in itself and gives a fool-proof and complete method – of course none does. Different methodologies set out to cover different parts of the overall problem space of systems development. Some are restricted to essentially design and programming areas, others aim to start in the earliest problem structuring stages, while others are more concerned with the intermediate tasks of analysis and design, accepting a broad problem definition and producing a set of deliverables that can feed into implementation. Even within their own defined scope most methodologies provide extremely varied levels of detail on what exactly to do, and how. An obvious example of this is in user interface design, which is universally agreed to be vital to successful systems, but is very poorly supported or integrated in most popular methodologies.

Another aspect of this question is the extent to which a methodology consists of concrete guidelines for action, 'do it this way', or alternatively a more general recommendation to 'consider these issues, base your approach on these ideas'. Many studies of the actual experience of the use of methodologies in real world information systems development reveal that the detailed guidance contained in the methodology text book or imparted on the training course is quickly violated as analysts come to make their own decisions on what is important and what is not in a given context. This may be seen as a problem, or a problem waiting to happen, or it can be taken as a correct and appropriate response to varied contexts. In most walks of life 'doing things by the book' or 'working to rule' is a way of slowing down and degrading performance. On the other hand, being backed up with a firm model of how things should be done, for reference, support or to stimulate thinking, can be very useful.

In this vein Checkland describes his notion of methodology as, 'A set of principles of method which in any particular situation has to be reduced to a method uniquely suited to that particular situation.' [Checkland, 1981]. Checkland poses methodology as lying between a philosophy – broad non-specific guidelines for actions – and a technique – a specific programme for action which will produce a standard result. To use a methodology demands that a particular context be addressed in reducing this meta-model (principles of method) to a particular method suitable for the task in hand. It should be noted that the kind of methodology that Checkland is associated with is one that is essentially about understanding and changing the world, not technical considerations of setting up computer-based systems.

Approach

Finally, there is a broad split between methodologies that are concerned to build a computer-based information handling apparatus, and those that are concerned to intervene and alter some state of affairs in the world. It should be possible in this way to discern within any methodology a fundamental adherence to one of the approaches to systems development described in chapter 8.

Several methodologies attempt to address both the technical and the social aspects of information systems development. For example, the authors of the Multiview methodology attempt to co-ordinate a variety of perspectives on systems design and they propose in a contingent manner the following sequence [Avison & Wood-Harper, 1990]:

- analysis of human activity systems;
- analysis of entities and functions;
- analysis and design of socio-technical systems;
- design of human–computer interface;
- technical design.

It is, however, important to be able to recognize that a systems development methodology provides only a partial way for analysts to see the world, and a partial way for them to capture and describe the things that they see either as a static image or perhaps as a dynamic model. It is also probably fair to say that in most of the methodologies used today engineering concerns are much more prevalent than the social and organizational ones, and that most methodologies make the assumptions that technology is good, that more information is better than less, and that efficiency is the most desirable benefit to be achieved by a new information system.

The future for methodologies

In the 1980s the choice of a methodology was a prominent issue of academic debate and organizational policy, not only in business organizations but in the public sector too. During the period, the debate on methodologies took many forms. There was the practical question of what were the features of a 'good' methodology. There were also some more challenging questions about the nature of the products which are called 'methodologies' and the promise that they offered to improve information systems development practices. Is a methodology a cookbook, a tool-box, or a philosophical basis for intervention in human organizations? Is the term 'methodology' a misuse of language, a pompous name for what is really a collection of simple methods, or is it truly a different concept, able to capture effectively the essence of good practice in systems development?

This debate appears to have eased in the 1990s, not because very satisfactory answers have been reached, but rather because the limitations of a movement to spread standardized professional practices for activities whose nature is so little understood have been accepted. Yet the development and spread of methodologies has brought and continues to provide several real benefits to the mass of organizations that have to develop information systems. It has, for example, proved to be very useful for purposes of education and training and has helped to create a critical mass of skilled practitioners speaking a common language. The facilitating of communication among practitioners has, among other benefits, significantly improved information systems maintenance activities. Indeed, the area of information systems development which has been most improved with the adoption of methodologies is perhaps documentation. The existence of adequate documentation of the analysis and design tasks, in a standard form and in a notation which is understandable by other analysts and designers in an organization has reduced the problems of idiosyncratic 'black-box' systems whose design was only understood by the person who wrote them. Such benefits are particularly significant for large organizations with many separately developed information systems. A methodology provides them with a common way of creating and grading professional roles; it makes possible continuity of practice and mobility of practitioners.

Even so, while the prescriptive nature of methodologies can be of help in introducing a novice into effective systems development work, it is not necessarily so useful for the experts. The development of information systems does not have the precision of a science or an engineering discipline, and general guidelines are necessarily incomplete. The development process involves many decisions which are sensibly made by judgement and creative thinking. A rigid, structured, prespecified approach to development activities may prove restrictive to those who command a deep understanding of the complex process of information systems changes in organizations and are capable of making the crucial decisions which are not prescribed by a methodology.

Methodologies which are more permissive, which avoid imposing rigid guidelines but, instead, make explicit arguments for and support a particular approach, allow more space for practitioners to make their own decisions. Even so, as has been argued in chapter 8 as well as in this chapter, methodologies are inevitably biased. Training in and adoption of a methodology involves indoctrination in the worldview to which the authors of the methodology aspire. In this way methodologies act as instruments of conformity, and perhaps put obstacles in way of reaching valuable insights into the distinct features of particular information systems development projects.

The ultimate statement of good practice, the ultimate methodology, has not and perhaps never will be discovered. As this chapter has sought to show, the complex and contrasting pressures that are felt as experts attempt to understand and set down the rules of system building will ensure that the debate on methodologies will continue.

Exercises and discussion issues

1. Consult a few text books on information systems design and try to locate the definition of methodology that they offer. Contrast the definitions and try to spot the differences of substance or emphasis that they offer. Most of the books contained in the references below contain such a definition.

2. Can a gourmet cookery book, written by a world famous chef, make you into an equivalent expert? In so far as such a book can improve your ability as a cook, what features of the book would be most important – the sample menus, the lists of ingredients, the recipes themselves, the tips on how to do the various tasks, or what to do when things go wrong. If the cookery book is aimed at professional caterers in large factory canteens or hospital kitchens, rather than the ordinary family cook, how should the approach be altered?

3. What is the relevance of question 2 to the problems of information systems development methodologies?

4. Why have different countries developed an adherence to different methodologies? Try to set down the various important considerations that you believe would need to be considered if a methodology were to be successfully adopted in large banks in Sweden, Britain, Greece or the United States.

5. You are asked to do analysis work prior to the development of a new information system to support foreign exchange dealers in a large bank in London. Which *two* of the following perspectives would you consider most important in analyzing the current system?

   - one that concentrates of the information flows;
   - one that concentrates on the information stocks;
   - one that concentrates on the tasks and transformations undertaken;
   - one that concentrates on the people who do the work.

   Would you change your recommendation if the system under discussion was one to support social workers in an inner city local authority?

6. What are the desired benefits that lead organizations to mandate a single comprehensive development methodology for all systems development work? Are there any costs associated with such a decision?

References

Avison, D.E. & Wood-Harper, A.T. (1990) *Multiview: An Exploration in Information Systems Development*, Blackwell, Oxford.

Checkland, P. (1981) *Soft Systems Methodology*, Wiley, Chichester.

Daniels, A. & Yeates, D. (1968) *Basic Training in Systems Analysis*, Pitman, London.

Downs, E., Clare, P. & Coe, I.(1991) *Structured Systems Analysis and Design Method: Application and Context*, (2nd edition), Prentice Hall, London.

Finkelstein, C. (1989) *An Introduction to Information Engineering: From Strategic Planning to Information Systems*, Addison-Wesley, Sydney.

Gane, C. & Sarson, T. (1979) *Structured Systems Analysis: Tools and Techniques*, Prentice Hall, Englewood Cliffs, New Jersey.

Gane, C. (1990) *Computer Aided Software Engineering: The Methodologies, The Products and The Future*, Prentice Hall International, Englewood Cliffs, New Jersey.

Hirschheim, R.A. & Klein, H. (1989) 'Four Paradigms of Information Systems Development', in *Communications of the ACM*, Vol. 32, No. 10, October.

Jackson, M.A. (1983) *System Development*, Prentice Hall International, Englewood Cliffs, New Jersey.

Lundeberg, M., Goldkuhl, G. & Nilsson, A. (1981) *Information Systems Development: A Systematic Approach*, Prentice Hall International, Englewood Cliffs, New Jersey.

Olle, T.W., Sol, H.G. & Verrijn-Stuart, A.A. (editors) (1982) *Information Systems Design Methodologies: A Comparative Review*, North Holland, Amsterdam.

Olle, T.W., Sol, H.G. & Tully, C.J. (editors) (1983) *Information Systems Design Methodologies: A Feature Analysis*, North Holland, Amsterdam.

Olle, T.W., Sol, H.G. & Verrijn-Stuart, A.A. (editors) (1986) *Information Systems Design Methodologies: Improving the Practice*, North Holland, Amsterdam.

Olle, T.W. *et al.* (1991) *Information Systems Methodology* (2nd edition), Addison-Wesley, Wokingham.

Pham, T.Q. & Chartier-Kastler, C. (1991) *Merise in Practice*, Macmillan Press, Basingstoke. (Translated by Avison, D.E. & Avison, M.A. from the French *Merise Appliquée*, Eyrolles, Paris.)

Yourdon, E. (1989) *Modern Structured Analysis*, Prentice Hall International, Englewood Cliffs, New Jersey.

Further reading

The references for this chapter provide many sources for study. A useful review of methodologies is given in Avison & Fitzgerald. Olle (1991) above gives a very detailed framework within which individual methodologies can be placed.

Avison, D.E. & Fitzgerald, G. (1995) *Information Systems Development: Methodologies, Techniques and Tools*, Blackwell, Oxford.

Part 3

The organizational and management context

Parts 1 and 2 of this book have addressed themselves to issues of how information systems are developed and how we might think about and undertake that development process. In the third part of the book we turn to the effort that organizations make to get value from information systems. It seems so natural that information technology brings benefits to organizations, that questions about the value expected to be gained from information systems using computers – and more recently telecommunications – sound naïve or rhetorical, aimed at informing those few who are not yet aware of the tremendous potential of these new technologies. Isn't it obvious that computers with their enormous processing speed increase substantially the efficiency of routine clerical tasks in organizations? Does it need explaining that computers facilitate communications and provide accurate information to decision makers? Don't they obviously open scope for organizations to create wealth by offering all kinds of new services to consumers? There is no shortage of such clear needs and opportunities. If information systems professionals get the requirements right, surely organizations only stand to gain from their continuous efforts to introduce successive generations of IT applications?

Nevertheless, even such obvious benefits are often doubted by experienced managers. It is not that they do not understand the potential capacity of information and communications technologies to 'enable' substantial benefits, it is that they are not confident that their organizations will be able to achieve them. For each impressive success reported in the business press or analyzed in the academic literature there are many stories of frustration, 'problems' and 'failure' whispered at golf club encounters.

The productivity paradox

It is also the case that the so obvious benefits we came to expect have been difficult to confirm through research. For example, it became apparent towards the end of the 1980s that those banks which had been investing in the most extensive computerization efforts were not necessarily among the leaders in the banking sector. Most shockingly for the community of information systems academics and practitioners, research conducted by economists in the USA challenged the widespread expectation that the diffusion of these technologies contributes to the growth of productivity as a whole. Such unexpected research findings became known as the 'productivity paradox' and puzzled the research community, created scepticism among business executives, and initiated an on-going debate about the 'real' economic value of IT. Let us examine briefly the productivity paradox challenge.

At a period of rapid increase in the use of these technologies in the USA there was a slowing down of overall productivity growth [Landauer, 1995]. The problem was particularly acute in the services sector, which had the highest investment in IT – representing about 85% of total US computer hardware investments – but its productivity remained stagnant. Specifically, the service sector made a $750 billion investment on IT in the 1980s and had an average productivity growth of 0.7%. This was a rate significantly lower than that of the 1970s, and much below that of the manufacturing sector, which did not invest as much in IT [Ives, 1994].

Even after accounting for other factors that affected the economy during that period, such as increased oil prices, the negative correlation between productivity growth and diffusion of computers was surprising. Information systems research-ers found the economists' claims that IT investment is not accompanied by expected productivity increases threatening to shaken executives' faith in the economic value of IT, and set out to explain and disprove the productivity paradox. Several explanations were put forward. The first was methodological, suggesting that the measures used to account for the economic effects of IT are inadequate. The second explanation was that there may be lags between invest-ment in IT and the occurrence of productivity results. Third, it was suggested that the expected productivity did not materialize because of mismanagement and misuse of IT in organizations. Finally, it was pointed out that at a macro economic level, IT may not create new wealth, but only contribute to wealth redistribution among competing firms.

More recent studies indicate positive productivity findings [Brynjolfsson, 1994; Brynjolfsson and Hitt, 1993], although these studies have also been criticized for methodological bias, because they draw general conclusions from a selective set of business organizations. While the debate continues, the most interesting 'findings' from an information systems perspective are not proving or disproving the productivity paradox, but pointing out that the diffusion of IT is associated with various fundamental business changes beyond effects on productivity and efficiency, such as quality and variety of products and services produced, and organizational restructuring. In other words, when embarking on IT innovation, business organizations do not merely expect to increase the efficiency of their operations, but are consciously pursuing complex strategies to improve their competitive position in their economic sector. Increase of production efficiency is one of the ways for a business firm to stay competitive, but it is by no means the only one. Within a context of changing economies, organizations are obliged to innovate in terms of what they produce and how they capture and retain their markets.

Indeed, since the mid-1980s a great deal of the effort of information systems professionals, and the main literature of the information systems as an academic field, have concentrated largely on two areas: how can information systems innovation enable the competitiveness of the business firm, and how can it support organizational change? It is on these two topics that this part elaborates within a framework of concern for the management of information systems activities.

Information Systems Management

As with the management of all other areas of an organization, the management of information systems is concerned with securing, allocating and utilizing resources to achieve desired ends. If a broader focus is applied then information systems management may be seen as also concerned with discovering what those ends should be and with exploiting the possibilities provided by new information technologies and the consequent alteration in the shape, structure and the overall direction of an organization. There are then three basic aspects to the management of information systems:

- Working through projects for the development of new information systems. This has been the topic that the earlier parts of this book have dwelt upon.

- Support of on-going information handling practices and resources. As has been discussed earlier, information systems do not cease to require attention when they are put into use. Establishing the right management frameworks for systems in use, the technology they incorporate and the various groups of people who support and work with them, are vital.

- Working out improvements and changes in the organization consequent on or driven by changes in information handling. The increasing importance of information, and its effective and carefully considered use, leads to the requirement for methods of planning information systems that gets beyond individual tasks or projects. Information handling activities need to be linked to the more general goals of organizations, and organizations need to devote careful attention to understanding how information handling contributes to their overall performance.

The management of information systems in modern organizations, whatever their size, is a complicated and dynamic subject and there is a diverse literature about it. In essence, this literature shows a fundamental uncertainty as to what the advent of new information technologies really mean for organizations and hence how they should set out to respond.

A study of a medium-sized commercial organization in the early 1980s would probably have indicated a clear answers to these questions. A central department, named perhaps the Data Processing Department, would have existed to develop and manage data processing based around the computer. It would have been headed by a data processing manager two or more steps down the hierarchy, and reporting to a senior manager with a wider brief, probably in finance. The technology in use would have been based on a mainframe or powerful minicomputers running the various applications of the organization, most of which would have been of a transaction processing character. The older applications would perhaps have been run in a batch mode – that is one job at a time on the basis of data prepared off-line by data entry staff. There would probably also have been some newer on-line applications, working through terminals and accessing on-line data, but this would still have been considered an expensive option that needed to be carefully justified. Requests for new computer-based information systems would have been directed towards the Data Processing Department, and the analysts and programmers of the department would have been responsible for the design and development almost all new systems. Once systems had been developed the department would then go on to run the computer processing on behalf of the other departments.

In the 1990s such a simple picture is much less probable. A single data processing department may well no longer exist, but if it does it will undoubtedly have developed a more complex role, and quite possibly will have changed its name. The various managers who once brought all their computing requirements to the department may now undertake much of their own development work, and take responsibility for their own computer systems. Important areas of organizational computing, such as office automation, desktop publishing or decision support for middle managers, may be handled either by the various units of the organization or by separate specialist support groups. The Data Processing Manager, who once was the highest placed information systems professional in the company, may still be in place and still be responsible for some of the same systems, but there are probably other professionals involved with equally significant responsibilities. Such responsibilities may include data administration – looking after the databases of the organization, network administration – managing the communications infrastructure used by the organization, or decision support – looking after the information handling needs of the various managers and professional staff within the organization. Most important of all, it is very likely that a senior or even board level executive has an active responsibility for overall co-ordination of information systems activities. Other managers will also be directly involved, managing changes in work processes within their areas of responsibility, and they may have far more power to shape the ways in which technologies are adopted.

This part of the book explores recent changes in the way information and communication technologies and information systems are managed, and outlines current understanding of the way information systems contribute to organizational change and business strategy. In chapter 10 the organizational and technical pressures on organizations are explored and the question of how an organization can establish and develop management structures for information systems is investigated. Chapter 11 explores how we can think about the kind of organizational change associated with information systems and the rationale for treating information handling as an issue of strategic importance for organizations, and discusses the limits of methodical practices for planning information systems.

References

Brynjolfsson, E. (1993) 'The Productivity Paradox of Information Technology', *Communications of the ACM*, Vol 35, pp. 66-77.

Brynjolfsson, E., & Hitt, L. (1993) 'Is Information Systems Spending Productive? New Evidence and New Results' *Proceedings of the 14th International Conference on Information Systems*, Orlando.

Hitt, L.M., & Brynjolfsson, E. (1996) 'Productivity, Business Profitability, and Consumer Surplus: Three Different Measures of Information Technology Value' *MIS Quarterly*, Vol 20, No 2, pp. 121-142.

Ives, B. (1994) 'Probing the productivity paradox', *MIS Quarterly*, Vol. 18, No 2.

Landauer, T.K, (1996) *The Trouble with Computers*, MIT Press, Cambridge.

10 Information systems management

- *Technology explosion, technology convergence*
- *Organizational pressures*
- *The outsourcing debate*
- *The context for information systems management*

As has been argued throughout this book, the nature of information systems is such that they demand a consideration from a variety of perspectives – a subtle mix of the social, the organizational and the technological. Exploring management ideas while maintaining this subtle balance is not easy, yet each of the main management tasks listed in the introduction of part 3 needs to be approached with this mix in mind. Earl [1989] has provided a framework for studying information systems management that encompasses to some degree the social, organizational and technological dimensions – figure 10.1. In this he proposes three main domains of responsibility, each of which will require its own management – in Earl's terms, a management strategy.

The first domain of *information systems* is concerned with securing adequate information handling to support the various tasks of the organization. In commercial organizations this probably implies that the primary driving force behind the establishment and development of individual information systems is understanding how they contribute to achieving business objectives. This further suggests that the lead needs to be taken by the managers of the various functional activities that are supported, and it is appropriate that information systems themselves should be managed on the basis of *demand* from those with responsibility for such task achievement.

The second domain of *information technology* is concerned with ensuring that the technology itself works and that it is made available to those who wish to use it. The growth of networks as a key component of organizational information handling has also led to the identification of their management as another key task. Of course, this must not become a question of technology for technology's sake; it needs to be combined with a clear service orientation to ensure that information technology is delivered and supported across the organization and in the forms that are required. Hence it is appropriate that information technology should be managed on a service or *supply* basis, and the leading role be taken by those with technical expertise.

Domain	Primary question	Management basis	Focus and responsibility
Information Systems	*What to do?* Information handling to support organizational activities.	Demand driven with a business focus.	Information handling applications. Concern of managers of business units.
Information Technology	*How to do it?* Providing the mechanisms to implement desired information handling.	Supply of technology and support services.	Maintenance of infrastructure. Concern of technical specialists.
Information Management	*Why do it?* Overall development of the organization.	Strategic direction of the organization.	Planning, regulation and co-ordination. Concern of senior management.

Figure 10.1 Three domains of information systems management
(after Earl [1989])

The third domain of *information management* is concerned with managing the use of information resources across and throughout the organization. It is not about technology *per se*, nor about establishing or developing individual systems. Rather it represents the requirement for organizations to understand and manage the interrelationships of individual systems and technologies, and to co-ordinate these with overall organizational concerns. It is usually seen as appropriate that senior managers with a broad organization-wide perspective should take responsibility for this level of management. The analogy often used is with the role of the manager or director who is head of the finance department, and who manages and is accountable for the financial resources of an organization. In the era of the database and network this is not a far-fetched analogy. Another way to look at this is to observe that information systems, as an ensemble of technology and information, provide the *infrastructure* that establishes and enables the shape of an organization. The quality of such infrastructure comes to define the ability of an organization to adapt and respond to its environment.

The mix of management concerns described above is the result of two interlinked trends. The first trend is of a family of technologies which have become ever more powerful, more diverse and more complex. The second trend is the recognition of what can be achieved by enhanced methods of handling information across and throughout the organization, and equally the possibility of inadequate performance or even disasters if the technology is poorly used or necessary systems are not developed. This has made information systems too important to be left in the control of a technology-based (or technology-biased) service, and information systems management has become a regular concern of the various departments of an organization and of the senior managers.

We must recognize that there is an important contradiction implied here. The technology is more complex and sophisticated, demanding knowledgeable specialists with appropriate skills. At the same time the potential and risk associated with information systems demands that the users of technology and business managers become intimately involved in steering its use. Finding a route through this apparent contradiction has been the main focus of information systems management in the last decade.

Technology explosion, technology convergence

The spreading of powerful microcomputers

Foremost among the new technologies that have shaped the information management agenda is the development of the ever more powerful micro-computer linked to networks and available to any and perhaps every desktop. In a very short period of time in the 1980s the 'customer' for computing within the organization rose, from a limited number of business functions that dealt with large volumes of regular data or specific 'number crunching' tasks, to include almost everybody and every task that an organization undertakes. Managing this explosive growth in demand, just at the level of technology, has been a particular trial for information systems departments, and they have struggled to establish solid guidelines for their organization to follow and to be able to support a huge diversity of hardware and software.

By the mid 1990s the dominance of one accepted standard for micro-computers (the Windows-based, IBM-type microcomputer), and the pre-eminence of a few million-seller programs such as Lotus 123, Microsoft Word and Excel, has made this a somewhat easier task, but the rate of technology development has not slowed and neither has the appetite for experimentation. In the 1980s 'managing the micro' was about managing *personal* computing, small systems that helped individuals to do their jobs rather better. Today the microcomputer, or its more powerful successor the workstation, is being built into the main information systems of organizations, replacing or supplementing the traditional centralized systems based on minicomputers or mainframes. The result is a new architecture of distributed information systems, based on a complex web of communicating computers, databases and software applications. This new architecture is often referred to as client-server computing, a reference to the concept of desk-top machines as clients accessing information resources located on shared server machines. Servers may be themselves microcomputers, but they equally can be minicomputers or powerful mainframes. Indeed, the advent of client-server computing has given a new life to the mainframe (or its successor) as a part of a distributed approach to computing. In management terms, the consequence has been that while information systems departments in the 1980s had to learn how to support microcomputers as personal computing, they have had to reorient their expertise towards supporting microcomputers and their networks as a primary technology for essential and mainstream information handling.

The development of data communications

Microcomputers can put computer power on the individual desktop. As part of a client-server architecture using networks, these isolated computers can be connected together to share and exchange data and provide access to other resources such as printers, databases or electronic mail. The technology of communications has developed very substantially over the last decade, moving from a technology in the early 1980s that relied on links back to substantial central computers (a star-shaped approach), to the local area network (LAN) technology of today. Local area networks permit the fluid interlinking of individual computer systems and the sharing of data and other resources among them. At the same time the availability and cost of long distance communications via telephone connections or dedicated wide area networks (WANs) has improved. A more recent phenomenon has been the development of intranets, internal communication and information sharing facilities modelled on Internet and World Wide Web technologies, and providing an open and multi-function communications capability. It is now common practice for organizations to establish and maintain extensive communications links across the country and around the world. These are links that operate both within an organization and between organizations.

Electronic Data Interchange (EDI) is an example of a communications technology that extends beyond individual organizations. It is used to allow independent parties (say customers and suppliers) to exchange information such as orders, invoices and delivery information, replacing a large and complex flow of paper by electronic messages [Krcmar *et al.*, 1995]. The motor industry is just one example of a heavy user of EDI. This enables motor manufacturers to maintain communications with their many component suppliers, exchanging such information as orders, delivery schedules or invoices. It is an efficient way to handle the flows of information, but more importantly, it enables a motor manufacturer and component suppliers to share more information and more timely information, and to absorb it smoothly into their internal information systems. This is in turn a requirement for running more efficient manufacturing operations and using approaches such as just-in-time inventory control. We should also note that the overall result has been a subtle shift in the way that this industry operates with a transfer of power to the manufacturers at the centre of this network, and away from their suppliers.

Adding communications to the technology portfolio that the information systems department is expected to manage is one example of where the scope of the department has extended into a domain that has traditionally been outside their responsibilities. In most organizations the earlier communications technologies, such as telex and telephone systems, were the responsibility of some other unit, perhaps a management services department. The process of convergence and the ability to mix various types of data within a single network now makes it sensible for organizations, particularly large ones, to combine all electronic communications functions and to manage their networks as a single entity.

Sharing of data

Another key technology to influence information systems management structures has been the use of databases. While once it was usual for each individual computer application to have its own distinct files, it is now more common for data stored on computer to be recorded as part of a larger database. In this way information can be kept more up-to-date and be shared among different applications. But once information is brought together and pooled in a database it is essential to consider who is responsible for its management.

As an example, consider the recording of the name and address of a customer. It can be used by the accounting systems to send out invoices and statements, by the service department to arrange maintenance of products already sold, by the marketing department to send advertising materials and by the distribution department to arrange a delivery. Recording the address just once makes a great deal of sense so long as it is really the same address for each of the tasks. Four users of a customer's address are described above, but who is responsible for keeping the record of the address up-to-date, and who controls access to the address record? One possibility may be that a separate and distinct role of *database administrator* has to be created to undertake the task.

Once a database approach is adopted, then attention may turn to finding means to exploit further this informational resource. In the 1990s new ideas have emerged, including data warehousing and data mining. These require not just new technologies (though they do), but also the fostering of new attitudes to the value of data [Inmon,1992].

The diffusion of office and decision support applications

The focus of the largest growth area in organizational computing in the last decade has been on the provision of computer power in the office [Hirschheim, 1985]. This started with the introduction of wordprocessors but has expanded rapidly with a range of associated technologies including simple database packages, desktop publishing systems for document preparation, electronic mail systems for inter- and intra-organizational communications and the extremely rapid take-up of the fax machine. Nor do office technologies stop arriving. Organizations are now just starting to work through the implications of document image processing – laser scanning technology which allows paper documents to be scanned, stored on disk, transmitted and printed. Alongside this array of office technologies has come a requirement for extensive and continual training and day-to-day support, as well as the need to consider carefully how the new working environment of the office can best be shaped and exploited.

Another class of computer applications with significant implications for the management of information systems resources is decision support systems [Keen & Scott Morton, 1978]. While computers and terminals linked to databases can provide access to data, the real benefit of such systems comes when a manager is able not only to access such data but also to manipulate it and to use it to explore and inform decisions. The growth in the use of spreadsheets has familiarized many with the basic idea of manipulating numerical models, and the possibility of supporting the decision making tasks of middle and senior managers with carefully constructed and sophisticated modelling software has become widely appreciated.

In the 1990s another broad class of systems have come into use, going by the name of Groupware or Computer Supported Cooperative Work (CSCW) [Ciborra, 1996]. The best known software in this area is perhaps Lotus Notes. Such systems aim to support the organization by fostering interaction between people through some computer mediated means. Groupware perhaps started with email, group decision support and information sharing, but today it is usually seen as a distinctive type of application, posing distinctive problems for information systems management. For example, the implication of many such systems is that information can and will be pooled and shared, in particular some of the less formal information which an organization contains and which is located with individual people. As many case studies show, this basic assumption is not always valid. People indeed hold relevant information, but do they wish to share it? A case study that we were involved with in a financial services organization showed that, despite management's aims, individual sales staff were very reluctant to share their knowledge of clients and potential clients. Among the many reasons for the lack of success with this system was the perhaps obvious reason that sales staff worked on an individual commission basis and guarded their knowledge of potential sales opportunities. Another well known case study with similar findings is Orlikowski's (1992) study of the consulting firm Alpha.

Development and management of such applications cannot be accommodated easily within the established procedures of data processing departments. The building and validation of the models that underlie decision support applications may call for specific modelling skills and knowledge of statistical and quantitative techniques which are not found in the average systems analyst. Furthermore, the use and adaptation of such applications is more likely to be the responsibility of their users rather than a central department of information systems experts.

Information convergence

The explosive growth in available information handling technologies has been paralleled by a convergence in the handling of traditionally distinct forms of information. For example, where once there were islands of technology dealing separately with voice, text and images – computers, telex machines, telephones, photocopiers, printing machines – now all these distinct tasks might be undertaken by a desktop microcomputer, equipped with a scanner, a laser printer, and a link to a communications network or the Internet. Not only can the individual tasks be undertaken using the desktop machine, but data can be merged, linked and transferred among them.

This trend towards convergence has led organizations to attempt to devise new schemes for managing and utilizing their information and technical resources. This often represents not just a recognition of a better way of doing existing things but of a possibility of wholly new ways of doing wholly new things. The flexibility of the technology is seen as placing new emphasis on exploring innovative use of information for the benefit of organizations, and on understanding and managing the risk associated with unsuccessful or flawed information systems.

Organizational pressures

In the section above we have argued that the advent of new technologies has caused the information management agenda to alter, but the way information systems resources are organized and managed is not merely a consequence of the features of available technology. It is driven by organizational imperatives too. The main driving forces which have contributed to shaping information systems management throughout the recent history of information technology use by organizations are usually described in terms of some mix of *efficiency, effectiveness,* and *strategic business development.* Concern with efficiency leads to efforts to reduce the costs of information handling procedures, to increase the speed of data processing, or to increase the quantity of data handled by an organization. Concern with effectiveness leads to considerations of issues such as how to increase the use made of information resources, how to develop organizational structures to secure the survival and growth of the organization, and how to empower the various parts of the organizations with relevant and timely information and the decision-making tools they need. Concern with strategic business development leads to efforts to use information and new technologies to maintain or improve the organization's competitive positioning within its sector, or perhaps to diversify into new business sectors.

There are also external pressures and opportunities stemming from the structural changes occurring in the business, economic and social environment of organizations. For example, participation in the European marketplace has caused many firms in Europe to reassess themselves, identifying core businesses and divesting themselves of other parts. As part of this, many organization have come to reassess the balance of need for information systems expertise in-house, and to consider taking more from outside – contracting out a substantial part of systems development or even information processing itself to specialist software and systems management companies. Changes in demographics and skill requirements may also encourage an organization to explore the possibility of using a different mix of human resources, perhaps more part-timer workers or people working from home using communications technology – telecommuters. Organizations may also start to use more sub-contractors and consultants.

In order to understand these imperatives and the resulting mix of requirements for information systems management, it is useful to consider three distinct perspectives on managing computer-based information systems: processing data, serving organizational information needs and adjusting to the emerging possibility of buying services and skills in the market place. Each of these will suggest distinctive characteristics of the skills required, and the appropriate administrative and management framework, yet most organizations have to find ways to accommodate all three.

Processing data

Notwithstanding the productivity paradox issues discussed in the introduction to part 3, administrative efficiency and productivity gains have been associated with the deployment of computers within a central service department, particularly in the 1970s when this was the dominant mode. Historically, this has been achieved mainly with large mainframe computers running regular transaction processing tasks such as payrolls, order processing or stock control, and more recently a similar set of ambitions have accompanied the introduction of computer-aided manufacturing systems, as well as many microcomputer applications. Management information may derive from such systems, and may be seen as a valuable commodity for the organization, but nonetheless it is often seen as a by-product, and in practice may be ill exploited.

The focus of information systems management in this style is internal to the organization and based on improved task achievement. Management of information systems is bound up with a close understanding of the technology and how to match it to established organizational requirements. Information systems management is not called on to be particularly creative in how information systems are developed or deployed, and a data processing department can perform its function adequately in relative isolation from the rest of the organization. The department can also measure success with some confidence, in terms of timetables and budgets adhered to, new systems delivered and administrative overheads controlled. Since the target is primarily established organizational tasks, the structure generally adopted is that of a monopoly provider, offering computing services on a central basis across the whole organization.

Within this type of central service department there will in general be three functional sub-groups, associated respectively with systems analysis, programming and operations – figure 10.2. The systems analysis group undertakes the preparatory work for new systems including the detailed analysis and the development of specifications. This group will constitute the main liaison with the rest of the organization. The programming group undertakes the actual construction and maintenance of systems, while the operations group controls the computers and the applications that use them. The information systems department is thus organized on functional lines, with a centralized triumvirate in which the systems analysis group will generally take the higher profile, even if not constituting the largest number of staff. The overall emphasis of such a central service department will be on adequately managing the technology and the application that it supports.

The systems developed within such a structure will, to a greater degree, continue to 'belong' to the data processing department throughout their life and the ultimate decisions on which systems to build, and in what manner, will remain within that department. The result is that, within the organization, computing is seen as an administrative overhead with a centrally allocated budget that is under the control of the department.

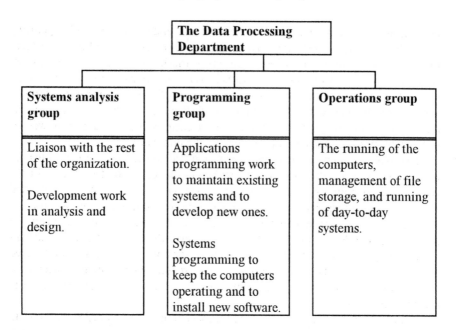

Figure 10.2 A centralized data processing department with three sub-groups

One important consequence of this form of management is that all requests for new applications, or changes to existing ones, go to the central service. They cannot all be immediately put in hand, and so a backlog of requested and even approved development work tends to be created. This backlog has been a perennial source of friction between the specialist department and the rest of the organization. When requested work is not done, and is seen to have a low probability of ever being done, relationships become strained. In the end people stop requesting new applications or changes, while for the managers of the centre there is a continuous problem is assessing and prioritizing the requested work.

Serving organizational information needs

The style of management just described has its limitations. It may serve some high volume information handling activities well, by providing efficient solutions to established needs, but it cannot cope with the variety of information technologies described earlier in this chapter, or the diverse clients for them. More importantly, as the focus turns from efficiency to effectiveness, and to supporting the particular needs of individuals and groups within the organization, the task of managing information systems also changes. It becomes less concerned with optimizing the use of technology and more with discovering and even promoting new ways for it to be deployed, and managing and supporting this diffusion throughout the organization. The balance of effort in systems management changes to include new responsibilities for a wider spread of 'customers' and a wider spread of technologies. Since computing is no longer tied to high volume transaction processing or automating existing procedures, it finds a ready audience across a far wider range of the activities of the organization, including office workers, middle and senior managers as well as on the factory floor and supporting other production workers.

As more and more data is committed to computers there is also an increasing concern with managing that data to exploit its best potential. In the jargon phrase, data or information comes to be seen as a *corporate resource,* and concern with the management of technology and individual applications is joined by a range of new concerns focusing on the management of information resources [King & Kraemer, 1988]. Who collects information, stores it, accesses it and audits it becomes as important as where or how it is processed and stored by computer. Thus there is a shift in focus for the department responsible for information systems often reflected in a name change, from data processing to information services.

It has become widely accepted that information systems need to 'belong' to those who will be most directly involved in their operation. This will generally mean those whose responsibilities or jobs are supported by the system. The root definitions discussed in chapter 2 express this clearly, for example, when they describe 'a system *owned and used* by the Maintenance Department of A.B. Smith...'. If a system is to belong to a group other than the computing professionals, then it is reasonable that these people will need to be involved in the establishment of requirements, controlling development and in day-to-day running. The SSM method presented in chapter 2 also highlights two other interested parties who will wish to be involved, the actors who carry out the main activities of the system, and the customers of the system, its beneficiaries or victims. Each of these players too might reasonably be expected to make some contribution to the management of a system.

Indeed, the upshot of much of the development in technology has been that people at work expect to and do take control of many of the computing components of their own information systems. They expect to be able to specify them, develop them and maintain them in use, what is known as *end-user computing* [Brancheau & Brown, 1993], and it is now quite common for organizations to find that over 50% of their computing activity and expenditure is made by employees *outside* the professional department. Small office systems such as a database, a spreadsheet model or a system for designing and producing mailshots are quite within the grasp of the informed amateur and even more substantial systems that require networking and shared databases can be within the grasp of a suitably motivated group who have access to some technical support from specialists.

When such systems have no impact beyond the individual concerned there is perhaps no management problem. The trouble is that a system with such limited impact is rare indeed. Systems may be built just to service a particular task, but the broader organization might reasonably be assumed to rely on that task being carried out correctly, and hence organizations need to maintain at least some control over individual initiatives. This area of information systems management, the management of end-user computing, has caused particular anxiety. The possibility of exercising a total ban or tight control on end-user computing has been seen to be impossible and counter productive – it just goes underground. On the other hand a totally *laissez-faire* approach can lead to expensive anarchy and islands of information. Rather, information systems management has had to be exercised through such activities as a careful budgeting processes, providing support in the form of awareness training, a menu of recommended software and hardware, help in systems analysis tasks and negotiating organization-wide purchasing and maintenance agreements [Gerrity & Rockart, 1986].

It is nonetheless the case that not all the information systems in an organization lend themselves to neat apportionment to particular owners. Some systems, such as a database of customers or a network, must be shared among many. This has given rise to the establishment of the concepts of *core* and *application* systems [Grindley, 1991]. Core are those that are central to the organization and widely shared. They will often comprise the basic, high volume data capture tasks that record transactions that a company has with its customers. Core systems will also generally include the main communications facilities that enable these information resources to be shared. They can also be characterized as the type of system for which clear economies of scale exist, or for which explicit or sophisticated control is vital. Core systems will tend to be managed by specialists on behalf of the organization as a whole.

If core systems are those that can only sensibly be established and managed on an organization-wide basis, or for which an overriding case for central management is established, there are many more systems that can sensibly be classified into the second category of application systems. These may be large systems or small, but the distinguishing feature is that they are most sensibly conceived of as belonging to a specific part of the organization, and as principally aiding that part to perform effectively. Examples might include decision support applications, personnel systems or marketing systems. These application systems may share core components, databases or communications, but the essence of their operations relates to a specific group within the organization. Such application systems can be more flexible, be changed with fewer implications, and be largely steered by those who make the most use of them.

To reconcile the needs for allowing freedom for the development and control of information systems resources by their users, and for securing overall control of the corporate resources, the central information services department often adopts a marketing approach, listening to their 'customers' needs, selling the technology throughout the organization and servicing their clients. When this happens the triumvirate organization of the old data processing department is no longer all that is required. At the very least a new role is apparent in liaising with other parts of the organization, helping them to develop their own (probably small) systems and providing advice, training and guidance. One popular solution to this is to set up a separate 'user-oriented' department with a title such as the *information centre* or *end-user support*. Through this channel micro-computer users can be helped in selecting their own equipment and developing their own systems. Training and education in the use of information technologies becomes more and more important, and a professional approach to this task is required as well. The role of such a department may be further extended to include working on decision support systems for middle managers, and may include responsibilities for executive information systems, those that serve the highest levels of management.

The exact scope of such a user-oriented department will vary and, while some organizations may try to support all end-user computing within a single service, others recognize pragmatically that particular areas such as computer aided design or office automation may require their own distinct service departments. Office automation in particular poses problems in that it might be seen as an appropriate responsibility for the computing department, or equally for the management services department which have historically had responsibility for other office technology such as photocopiers or telephones and which may have a better understanding of office procedures.

The outsourcing debate

Through the 1990s the growth of an information service industry offers possibilities for contracting out the function of information systems and the administration of data resources. This process is often referred to as *outsourcing* or *facilities management*. Outsourcing offers the promise of significant savings of information systems expenditures, often reported as high as 50%. Moreover, it seems to resolve many of the problems troubling information systems departments, such as securing the increasingly more demanding technical skills required for new applications. But what exactly is outsourcing, and what management requirements does it entail?

In a very general sense, outsourcing is the use of external agents to perform one or more organizational activities that were previously provided internally [Hirschheim & Lacity, 1993]. It is not a practice referring to information systems in particular. Typical examples of outsourced services are cleaning or catering; functions which, as many organizations find, can be provided by a specialized firm at a lower cost and better quality than their internal departments. Nor it is a new option in relation to information systems. Buying information systems services from a specialized vendor was a widespread practice at the early days of data processing, when few organizations could justify the purchase of a mainframe for basic applications and many used the services of computer bureaux to run their systems. The market for information systems services that started developing in the 1970s provided organizations with other options such as hiring staff including programmers and analysts on a short term basis for the development of applications under internal management – a practice more accurately described as in-sourcing. Other services that are available include training, user-support activities, as well as the handling of disaster recovery.

Today, however, outsourcing is a much more critical decision for information systems managers because of the increased scale and significance of activities that may be outsourced. Organizations still have the option of contracting out in a piecemeal way parts of their information systems projects and services, or to turn to the market in order to 'in-source' their projects and provide for fluctuating work load. But the question for many in the 1990s is whether they should take the more drastic step to give up the organization's information systems assets – people, computers, buildings and systems – and rely on obtaining the required services from a third party contractor, who will provide the services for a certain time period and for a fee. A number of deals such as this have been made by large corporations, passing all such assets to specialist service companies.

Although research suggests that such 'total outsourcing' – shifting 80% or more of the information technology budget to a service supplier – is not widespread yet, the debate on the potential benefits and risks is of great interest to managers who are obliged to consider possible options to provide and sustain increasingly sophisticated information systems infrastructure, often with diminishing budget increases.

There are two critical issues for managers to address: first how to weigh the benefits of outsourcing an information systems activity against the risks, and second how to manage the outsourcing relationship. But in order to tackle these issues we need to understand what is involved in an outsourcing venture.

Of particular significance for outsourcing is the contract between the service supplier and the client organization, which defines the legal and formal aspects of their relationship. The contract specifies in detail the services or products to be provided, the financial arrangements, the staff to be allocated or transferred, assessment criteria, and monitoring phases. Contracts are generally written to include a service level agreement (SLA), setting out what the customer should expect, and the financial and other penalties if this is not delivered. While the contract drives the relationship between the two organizations in a legalistic way, the delivery of the agreed services or products has to be based on co-operation which itself requires continuous communication, both formal and informal. The two parties will have to show commitment and share resources and knowledge. Thus, the fulfilment of the contractual agreement will need a relationship of trust, which can only partly be secured by legal means. Strict contracts which do not allow flexibility for adjustments following the evolution of the inter-organizational co-operation hardly serve the interests of either party. It is to the best benefit of both to maintain a flexible co-operation and avoid the legal enforcement of contractual arrangements.

One main risk for a client is dependency on the service provider. An organization which has transferred resources and control of information systems to a contractor may, over time, find itself dependent on the contractor's services. Such dependence, which implies unequal power between the partners, might have undesirable consequences and restrict freedom of action. Initial cost savings may be lost as additional services and upgrades are negotiated, or when contracts are renewed. Moreover, the client organization may lose control of systems which are critical for their business. Another risk is that the client organization might gradually find itself losing the in-house expertise it needs to decide upon and control its information systems; a situation of particular concern for those organizations which consider information systems to be of strategic importance for their business.

Thus, Willcocks and Kern [1997] suggest that the following factors should be considered when deciding outsourcing:

- Whether the activity or service is a *differentiator*, meaning that it provides the basis for competitive advantage, or of a *commodity* type, such as payroll, which needs be done competently but does not make a significant difference to the organization's position in its sector.

- Whether the activity or service is *critical* for the achievement of the organization's goals, or simply *useful*, making incremental contribution to its performance.

- The degree of *uncertainty* in the business environment of the organization, and, consequently, its longer term information technology needs.

- The degree of *technology maturity* of the information technology activity or service, which depends either on how new or unstable is a technology, or on how innovative an application is and how relevant technical expertise exists in the organization.

- The degree of *integration* of the information technology activity with the information systems of the organization.

- The relative *in-house capability* the organization has to undertake the information technology activity in-house in a cost-effective way.

Considering these factors, one can see that the risk is lower when an organization operating under conditions of low uncertainty outsources activities of a commodity type, which are not highly integrated, and which use technologies that can be provided more cost effectively by a supplier rather than in-house. The client organization will not run a high risk of jeopardisng their competitive position or the integrity of their total information systems infra-structure, and can feel confident about securing high quality technology services or products cost-effectively via the market.

However, the most significant benefits may be achieved if entering in a partnership with a supplier for the use of technology which is still new and unstable – and therefore relevant capability is still limited not only in-house but also in the market of information systems services – and for critical organiz-ational activities precisely aiming to address the threats or opportunities of a business environment with high uncertainty. This is why the most critical aspect of outsourcing is competent management capability, not only to make the correct judgement in weighing risk against benefit, but also in order to undertake control of the outsourcing venture. Even in cases of total outsourcing – or rather, particularly in such cases – an organization needs to retain the ability to decide about the kind of systems to acquire, to ensure that the information technology acquired can meet current and future business requirements, and to manage the contracting out and co-operation relationship with the supplier of services.

This critical role for information systems management when extensive outsourcing arrangements are in place has been described as the 'residual information systems organization'. It may be entrusted to a small group of people, but it makes all the difference between a successful inter-organizational relationship, or an irreversible condition of dependence and loss of control. Willcocks and Fitzgerald [1994] identified the following tasks that need to be fulfilled in the residual information systems organization:

- strategic IT thinking in relation to the business as a whole;
- business development in relation to the outsourced activities;
- ability to integrate systems, both in a business and a technical sense;
- contract management;
- acting as an informed buyer, capable to determine required services, place contracts and negotiate deals;
- managing the relationship between vendor and users of the technology;
- further exploiting the relation with a vendor by means such as sharing risk and rewards, and generally maintaining a mutually beneficial partnership.

Thus, it is important to understand that outsourcing does not relieve an organization of the burden of information systems management. On the contrary, information systems management becomes more demanding because it has to handle inter-organizational co-operation. Consideration of outsourcing also emphasizes the need for central strategic control over standards, information holding and the communications infrastructure of networks, even if these activities are actually undertaken by third parties. Information systems management thus becomes increasingly concerned with establishing strategy, plans and guidelines, and develops a role overseeing an organization-wide process as a planner, purchaser and regulator.

The context for information systems management

In the introduction to this chapter a contradiction was proposed between the need for specialist skills to manage and make use of information technologies, and the need for those directly concerned with information handling to take control of their own destinies and not put all their faith in technical experts. The efforts that organizations make to redefine the division of responsibilities for information systems management, between the participants in information systems and a central information systems department, are aimed mainly at resolving this contradiction. In the 1990s, most medium-sized or large organizations exhibit aspects of information management associated with each of the three perspectives outlined above, and will continue to do so well into the next century. But it should be clear from the discussion that, if information systems is to remain to any degree a centrally managed service, then it will be as a much larger and more diverse operation including end-user support activities, together with data administration and communications responsibilities. Some organizations do indeed run such large central service departments, but the pressure to divide them up is substantial. As suggested, this division may be achieved by retaining the data processing department with responsibility for a carefully defined core of organization-wide systems and applications, and establishing new services to support the various classes of more independent users. It also becomes the case that a single organization-wide budget for information systems and information technology can no longer be used as a basis for paying for and controlling information systems. It is therefore common today to see individual departments having their own budgets for information systems-related activities, even if they are largely spent with the service department. What was once considered as an administrative expense or overhead, accounted for centrally, has become, in part at least, a business expense accounted for within each distinct business activity. Some organizations go further and establish their information services department as a profit centre in its own right, possibly selling services outside the organization as well as within.

Alternatively, a broader policy of decentralization may be pursued, giving individual parts of the organization full responsibility for their own information systems, and in effect establishing a number of smaller full service departments closer to their client base. This latter approach is more common in very large corporations with a number of distinctive business units, each capable of managing their own information systems affairs. The centre may then be left without any operational responsibilities, but with a new mission for setting overall information systems policy and strategy, and ensuring that critically dysfunctional diversity does not come about. The existing specialist staff within central IT departments are often ill-adapted to take on these new responsibilities, and this can become a major problem in facing up to these new realities.

Exercises and discussion issues

1. Why, through most of the 1980s, did information systems departments tend to ignore the coming of the microcomputer?
2. What might be the advantages and disadvantages for a local authority in contracting out the computing associated with issuing parking tickets?
3. Office automation, broadly defined, now comprises the largest single component in most organizations' information systems expenditure. By what criteria would you set out to judge how well this investment is turning out?
4. What would you see as the ideal way to allocate and control expenditure on information technology and information systems? Consider the possibility of allocating a single sum to a central service department, allocating budgets to each user group to be spent with a central service, or allowing each user group to set and spend their budget as they please. Could you consider a policy that combined more than one approach?

    Consider answers to this question for the case of a multinational oil corporation, a medium-sized engineering firm with three factories and a head office, and a medium-sized city council.
5. It has been suggested in this chapter that information systems have come to challenge the established shape and structure of many organizations. Do you believe that this is a valid observation? Back up you answer with some evidence as to how information systems have changed or failed to change organizational structures.
6. A group of engineering companies with a number of factories and products established a central computer application for processing all orders. The system worked well and contributed considerably to the success of the group. Three years later it was decided to sell one of the factories and to withdraw from the market that it serviced. What problems would you envisage, what might have been done to avoid them?
7. Use the distinction of three domains for exploring information systems management – information technology, information systems and information management – as the basis for interviewing a practising information systems manager in an organization to which you have access. Does the distinction make sense to them?

References

Brancheau, J.C. & Brown, C.V. (1993) 'The management of end-user computing: status and directions', *ACM Computing Surveys*, Vol. 25, No.4, December. pp. 437-482

Ciborra, C.U. (ed.) (1996) *Groupware & Teamwork: Invisible Hand of Technical Hindrance?*, Wiley, Chichester.

Earl, M.J. (1989) *Management Strategies for Information Technology*, Prentice Hall, Hemel Hempstead.

Gerrity, T.P. & Rockart, J.F. (1986) 'End user computing: Are you a leader or a laggard?', *Sloan Management Review*, Summer, pp. 25-34.

Grindley, C.B.B. (1990) *The Price Waterhouse Information Technology Review*, Price Waterhouse, London.

Hirschheim, R.A.. (1985) *Office Automation: A Social and Organizational Perspective*, Wiley, Chichester.

Hirschheim, R.A. & Lacity, M.C. (1993) *Information Systems Outsourcing: Myths, Metaphors and Realities*, Wiley, Chichester.

Inmon, W.H. (1992) *Building the Data* Warehouse, QED, Boston.

Keen, P.G.W. & Scott Morton, M.S. (1978) *Decision Support Systems: An Organizational Perspective*, Addison-Wesley, Reading, Massachusetts.

King, J.L. & Kraemer, K.L. (1988) 'Information resource management: Is it sensible and can it work?', in *Information & Management*, Vol. 15, pp. 7-14.

Kremar, H., Bjørn-Andersen, N. & O'Callaghan, R.(eds.) (1995) *EDI in Europe: How it Works in Practice*, J. Wiley, Chichester.

Orlikowski, W.J. (1992) 'Learning from Notes: Organizational issues in Groupware'. Proceedings of the ACM 1992 Conference on Computer-Supported Cooperative Work. Reprinted in Kling, R. (1996) *Computers and Controversy: Value Conflicts and Social Choice*, Academic Press, San Diego, pp 173-189.

Willcocks, L. & Fitzgerald, G. (1994) 'Towards the residual IS organization?' in Baskerville, R., Smithson, S., Ngwenyama, O. & DeGross, J. (eds.) *Transforming Organizations with Information Technology*, Elsevier, Amsterdam, pp 129-152.

Willcocks, L. & Kern, T. (1997) 'IT outsourcing as strategic partnering: The case of the UK Inland Revenue'. Proceedings of the 5th European Conference on Information Systems, Vol. III, pp 1970-89.

Further reading

Sprague & McNurlin provide a useful overview of information systems management issues of the 1980s and 1990s. The Scott Morton book provides a research based review of how organizations have adapted to the new realities, and considers issues of the traditional core of information systems and the new empires. Earl's edited collection has a number of relevant contributions, including his own on 'Configuring the IS function in complex organizations'.

Some of the books referenced above also offer good further reading opportunities. The Hirschheim book on office automation, although over a decade old, provides a broad and comprehensive review of office automation and how it relates to issues of organizational productivity and effectiveness. It also includes a good discussion on questions of the appropriate methodology to be used in designing office information systems. The Gerrity and Rockart paper discusses the management frameworks within which end-user computing may be supported, while Brancheau & Brown provides a useful review of research into office and end-user technology. The Keen & Scott Morton book is a classic. It provided one of the first and certainly the most influential descriptions of how computers could be used in aiding individual managers in making better decisions by using the information that could be provided by a carefully constructed computer-based system.

Earl, M.J. (editor) (1996) *Information Management: The Organizational Dimension*, OUP, Oxford.

Sprague, R.H. & McNurlin, B.C. (1993) *Information Systems Management in Practice*, (3rd edition), Prentice Hall, Englewood Cliffs, New Jersey.

Scott Morton, M.S. (editor) (1991) *The Corporation of the 1990s: Information Technology and Organizational Transformation*, Oxford University Press, New York.

11 Information systems and organizational change

- *Organizational restructuring*
- *A new ideal organization?*
- *Working out organizational change*
- *Supporting business strategy*
- *Methodical practices*

Throughout the forty or more years of computer applications being introduced into organizations it has been maintained, at least by some information systems professionals and academics, that the development of new information systems should be accompanied by efforts to work out more effective organizational arrangements. Indeed, in the first part of this book we suggested that the launching of a systems development project should investigate broader requirements for change in the organization, and that systems analysis should involve also organizational analysis in order to decide what organizational change needs to be implemented in parallel with the implementation of the new technical means of information processing and communication. In part II we saw again this multiple concern with the technical, the organizational and the social as the fundamental principle of the socio-technical approach, and we outlined the way that one particular methodology, ETHICS, attempts to guide the redesign of work arrangements in order to improve work conditions for those participating in a new information system.

Nevertheless, it was not until the end of the 1980s that the most vocal calls were made for the need to associate the development of information systems with the design of organizational change in a systematic way. This new impetus came mainly from business organizations, where IT was increasingly recognized as a critical component in working out organizational changes required for survival in the emerging global economy. Thus, the efforts of information systems experts to 'release the potential' of IT in the work place were linked with other managers' ongoing concerns to reshape their organizations and make them fit for the changing competitive markets.

As we described in the previous chapter, the focus of information systems management has shifted beyond the question of how individual systems are developed and has now come to encompass the question of how the overall impetus of this massive expansion in activity can be directed towards and sustain overall organizational goals. More generally, there is a widespread notion that information technology, and the information systems that it enables, can be used, indeed should be used, by organizations to help them to succeed in their chosen field.

Against this background, this chapter explores two main questions; what kind of organizational effect are we trying to achieve with the introduction of new information systems in organizations; and how do we work out and work towards the implied organizational change?

Organizational restructuring

Henry Mintzberg, one of the most influential contemporary writers on organizations, defined the structure of an organization as 'the sum total of the ways in which it divides its labor into distinct tasks and then achieves co-ordination among them' [Mintzberg, 1979]. This involves perceiving an organization in terms of various parts, each performing a set of functions, which are joined together by flows of authority, work material, information and decision processes.

Throughout the 20th century the most prevalent organizational structure has been hierarchical. In its most schematic form it is seen as comprising a broad operating core at the bottom, where the basic work related directly to the production of products and services is done, a narrow strategic apex at the top, ensuring that the organization serves its mission and the needs of those who have power over the organization (such as owners, shareholders, government, trades unions), and a chain of middle line-managers, who have the formal authority to join the strategic apex to the operating core. This simple triangular structure has two more components supporting all levels of hierarchy: the so-called technostructure of 'analysts' who are charged with designing the work performed in the organization, and the support staff, whose work although vital is not seen as directly related with the mission of the organization, such as the 'payroll department', the legal department or the mailroom.

As discussed in chapter 6, many organizational theorists, including Max Weber, Frederick Taylor and Henri Fayol, have contributed to the elaboration of versions of the hierarchical organizational form. For example, in the most typical bureaucratic hierarchy work is broken down into distinct units of specialization; each of these units is in turn subdivided into smaller and smaller units until the job of each individual in the organization is specified in detail. In the 'professional bureaucracy', such as a university, which hires specialists – professionals – for the operational core, there is less direct formal control through middle management, and much more reliance on standardized work based on professional training and indoctrination.

Since the 1980s there has been increasing uneasiness with the hierarchical form, which has been criticized as inflexible and unsuitable for an economy which has to respond fast to varying and changing demand across the world. Economies of scale and uniformity of decision making are no longer considered to be the features of the business firm which can secure a competitive position. On the other extreme, entrepreneurial organizations which are less formally structured and depend on the charisma of a leader to sense the market and orchestrate an organization's resources to excel in a particular market may enjoy the advantage of flexibility to respond to changing demand. Even so, such organizations may not have adequate management capacity to cope with the complexity of new market conditions or to deal with adversity.

As a result of such anxiety some new forms of structure have been suggested, which invariably involve innovative uses of technology to provide an infra-structure. For example, 'the matrix organization' which allows for parallel decision making structures in order to manage the complexity of producing a range of diverse products, often in different geographic locations was considered to be suitable for large multinational firms. Another widely discussed form is the 'adhocracy' or team based organization, where work is organized in inter-disciplinary teams of experts allocated to projects and tasks as they arise; this is considered particularly appropriate for dynamic and complex environments which require innovation.

More recently, a plethora of new terms has been introduced into the organiz-ational and business literature since the 1980s, for example 'networked', 'know-ledge' or 'learning', 'adaptive', 'team-based, 'horizontal' or 'process based' organizations, even the 'virtual' organization. All these proposed types of organization seek to modify the hierarchical organizational structure and imply rich and complex information channels. A central message permeating all these ideas is that organizations must be reshaped to survive competition and deliver improved levels of service, and they should use IT and telecommunications to do so.

No other concept of new organizational form captures better these ideas than the 'virtual' organization. Although there is no common definition of what a 'virtual' organization is, it is usually understood to mean the formation of a temporary network or loose coalition of manufacturing and administrative services for a specific business purpose; the coalition is disassembled when the purpose has been met [Introna & Tiow, 1997].

Partners within the virtual organization can get rid of those activities they would not do efficiently and with good results, and concentrate only on those they are good at – their core competencies. They will then form partnership with other organizations capable of providing complementary activities in order to bring to the market products and services. In a context where customer demand is seen as changing, such coalitions should be seen as short-lived, only to be re-formed with other partners, for the delivery of another successful product or service. The formation of a virtual organization, and its operation, will usually rely heavily on the communication networks, perhaps the Internet. A virtual work team, scattered in various locations, will use the network to share inform-ation and carry out their tasks, co-ordinate and manage activities according to the targeted strategy.

The extent to which the virtual organization is a reality, or constitutes a form that can lead to survival and competitiveness is debatable. However, elements of this radically new perception of organization can be seen already in various industries where two apparently opposite trends take place simultaneously. One is outsourcing of particular activities. The other is partnering with customer organizations and sub-contractors to achieve mutual benefits which are not possible through the adversarial 'market' relations that traditional business practices create. Communication issues are of paramount importance in such inter-organizational partnering and the building of an appropriate information systems infrastructure can often make all the difference between an improved way of doing business or frustration.

Case study: the Metamorphosis of Oticon

An example of an organization which has used information technologies to transform its work and management structure is Oticon, a Danish manufacturer of hearing aids [Bjørn-Andersen and Turner,1994]. Oticon is one of the five largest producers of hearing aids in the world, with about 1,200 employees and annual sales of approximately $80 million. It is a truly international firm, exporting 90% of its production to over one hundred countries through subsidiaries and agents. However, in the 1980s, under fierce competition, Oticon was faced with decreas-ing market share, and in 1986 it suffered its first financial loss.

In 1988 the first efforts made by a new chief executive officer to restore the company's market position were drastic cost controls, but they proved insufficient. He then decided to launch a major restructuring effort, and turn Oticon from an industrial organization which produced high quality standard hearing aids to a service organization which crafted innovative products in response to customer demand. To that end, it was felt that Oticon should be metamorphosed to a flexible organization, capable of innovation and continuous learning.

Oticon abolished its divisions into traditional departments, it moved all head-office staff into one large open space location and abolished their specialized job roles, and eliminated managerial monitoring responsibilities. In its place it has organized work in the form of projects. Each project has a project leader, appointed by top management. Project leaders recruit teams of workers to work with them. They advertise their projects on the company's electronic bulletin board, and employees sign up for projects they wish to work in if they are free to leave the project they are currently working in or they can find a replacement for it. All work is considered and managed as a temporary task. New projects are set up as soon as a business need or opportunity arises, and resources are allocated in response.

Even tasks which are of a continuous nature benefit from the new arrangements. For example, in marketing work fluctuates throughout the year. There is a lot of work, requiring about thirty people, from August till November with preparations for exhibitions and trade shows, but a smaller team is required for the rest of the year. Thus marketing now has a small permanent team of a project leader and about five other people, and more people are recruited internally when needed to work in the marketing team.

To be able to switch so easily between projects – and since they often work on several projects at the same time – employees do not have fixed private desks. The open work space has a large number of identical desks, each with a work-station and a mobile phone/charger on. When a project is set up, the employees who sign up and get approval to work in the project move to desks next to each other, thus forming the location of the new project. In this way in a few hours a project group can be established and start working. This means, of course, that the company does not keep much paper. Whenever possible, information is stored in electronic form and can be retrieved from any workstation by anybody who has access authority. Oticon reduced paper by 95%. Employees also have personal calendars and tools for creating and transmitting documents in electronic form, again accessible from any desk. Even in such a 'paperless office', employees have a few personal items and documents that they need to take with them when they move. For this they have a small lockable 'caddie' with one drawer and a couple of shelves for storing up to ten files, which they wheel to any empty desk they move to for the purposes of a project.

Although Oticon has improved its competitive position since the implement-ation of this radical change in 1991, it is difficult to claim that this has been just the result of its organizational transformation. Nevertheless, Oticon has received much publicity and research, and commentators such as Bjørn-Andersen and Turner [1994] believe that the results of the transformation have been positive. It seems that in the new organization, and without traditional managerial control, employees work harder, but they find their work more challenging, and few want to go back to the old way of working.

A new ideal organizational type?

In the late 1990s, and as the debate on organizational forms and restructuring continues, we can draw some general features of the emerging picture of org-anizations competing in the global economy.

First, the hierarchical organizational form is still the most prevalent, but the number of levels of hierarchy has been decreased. The shortening of the height of the typical bureaucratic pyramid has resulted from the elimination of some of the middle management layers, and has been attributed in part to computerized information systems. A good example of this movement is found in the UK retail banks where substantial numbers of middle level managerial staff have been made redundant. Computer-based systems provide more direct links of super-vision and co-ordination of production and administration activities, and decreased the number of layers which were needed to provide effective control. Moreover, with innovation in production methods, such as 'just-in-time' production, many hierarchical organizations have developed a new capacity for flexibility and responsiveness to demand, without really abandoning the bureaucratic approach. Again, computer-based information systems have played a significant role in the survival of this most fundamental organizational form.

At the same time, a variety of alternative forms can be observed, which have been more accurately described as hybrids of the hierarchy, matrix and adhocracy forms, rather than pure new organizational types [Applegate, 1994]. These new schemes tend to put emphasis on a team-based organization of work. The qualities which are considered desirable are organizational learning, collaboration among individuals or teams, and empowerment of individuals or teams. More significant perhaps are changes occurring across the boundaries of individual organizations. First, many organizations sell off, or outsource, parts which do not contribute substantially to their 'value adding' ability, and concentrate on what they consider as their 'core competencies'. As a result, organizations today tend to rely significantly on a variety of other organizations, partners, who provide services ranging from cleaning to specialist management, legal services or R&D.

Second, there is increasing inter-organizational collaboration and new ways of partnership, even among business firms that have traditionally engaged in competitive struggles. For example, in retailing, suppliers and chains of super-market stores have traditionally been operating with strategies which aim at pushing costs and risks to each other. New ideas are now attempting to establish a context of collaboration, promising increased efficiency which can potentially benefit all 'partners' involved, and ultimately benefit the retailing industry as a whole. Although more often than not practice is less of an 'fairy tale ending', the attitudes seem to shift to favour collaboration rather than antagonism.

All these kinds of organizational change rely on the deployment of new information systems. Indeed, in many cases the technical capabilities to support new types of organizational or inter-organizational arrangements seem to drive the change, in the expectation that the organizational innovation will be better equipped to survive in the 'information age'. This suggests that there is increasing reliance on IT and telecommunication, but no single predetermined direction of change, no single ideal organizational form to be pursued by those who redesign an organization's information systems with the mandate to support more effective organizational structures.

Changing the organization of work

The discussion above has been in terms of macro organizational structures, but the potential of information technology to change the organization of work at a more micro level needs to be considered. We have already seen how the socio-technical approach has linked the development of new information systems with improving employees' job satisfaction. More recently, Zuboff's conceptualization of the distinction between 'automating' and 'informating' work has been particularly influential, as have recent debates on empowerment [Zuboff, 1988].

The starting point for most studies on the organization of work is the controversial issue of specialization. Work specialization was first studied systematically at the beginning of this century by Frederick Taylor. He suggested that the breaking down of complex jobs into simpler components increases the productivity of workers and could form the basis of a fair system of gaining high earnings from the job that each individual is best suited for. As mentioned in chapter 6, this theory of 'scientific management' proposes the systematic study of a particular task to discover the most efficient way to break it into simpler components, and a systematic study of management to find the most efficient methods of controlling the workers who undertake these components.

Breaking work down has often been seen as a solution to problems of scarcity of skills. Simpler task elements can be learned more quickly by less skilled and cheaper labour. This has provided a way of making savings through paying lower salaries to less skilled labour rather than an incentive for higher earnings for the employees. Because specialization requires detailed planning of the production process, to co-ordinate and control the fragmented tasks performed by the workers, control has in effect been removed from the shop floor or clerical office to the planning department. Job fragmentation in the work place then leads to alienation and deskilling, and Taylor's system has been connected with dehumanizing, machine-like work and a deterioration in working conditions.

However, it is not only humanitarian issues which have led to criticism of this method of organizing work. It was often realized that relying on the principle of punishment avoidance and of reward provides little motivation for productivity. It is a wasteful system, because it does not seek to use people's ability to exercise initiative. In a machine-based economy this is perhaps a debatable point, in an information based economy it is disastrous.

Other studies of organizational behaviour have shown that work structures which recognize the human needs for job satisfaction tend to be more effective in increasing productivity and organizational survival. In environments where the performance of routine tasks is the established work mode, more satisfactory work procedures can be achieved by engaging each employee in a wider variety of tasks. This is called horizontal *job enlargement* and requires employees to interchange their routine tasks with their colleagues. Although the work is still fragmented in routine task elements, each employee performs a number of them. A further step can be taken by vertical job enlargement, or *job enrichment*. An employee, or group, is given responsibility for performing a group of tasks; the group of employees can decide how a complete task, such as the production of a car, can be shared and carried out. In job enrichment it is not only variety that is introduced but also some control of the performed tasks as well.

Such knowledge is directly relevant to the utilization of new technology and the development of information systems. An analyst working on an information system needs to be aware that specialization, in the sense of Taylorism, is unlikely to lead to effective overall performance. Although efficiency gains from work fragmentation may appear to be significant, the potential losses in employees' motivation are too serious to risk if they can jeopardize overall effectiveness.

Caution against applying information technology in a way that fixes, 'automates', existing fragmented work tasks has been eloquently expressed by Zuboff. She studied how the use of computers affected the work performed by the employees in a number of organizations. She found that the most common approach was to automate the already fragmented tasks and to develop mechanisms of monitoring for management to keep control of employees' performance. She argued that such a use of technology limited employees' ability to deliver value through their work and produced poor results for the organizations concerned. She further suggested that more value would be produced if information technology was used to inform employees and empower them to release their potential at their work place. To express this she proposed the contrast between an approach that automates, and one that informates – augmenting human effort and providing an environment and information resources to allow individuals to take control of their work and exercise their intelligence in performing it.

Similar ideas are conveyed by the notion of empowerment [Psoinos & Smithson, 1996]. Empowerment, meaning the decentralization of responsibility and authority to the point of production, is viewed as a means of achieving high quality products or services. Empowering subordinates to make decisions independently requires not only redistributing authority but also providing them with resources such as information, budgets, knowledge and rewards. Empowerment is often thought of as involving self-managing teams of people with responsibility, authority and accountability for accomplishing a task with little or no supervision. The challenge is to develop information systems that will assist such groups to undertake responsibility for complete work tasks and see them through.

Promising as such ideas may sound, it should be noted that in the history of using information technology in organizations they have not been widely applied and, when applied, the results are not always as positive as expected. There are two obstacles towards applying such ideas effectively. The first concerns the intention of job-enrichment, informating, or empowerment. Under the pressures of competition, the dominant rationale driving such changes of work organization is efficiency, effectiveness and cost reduction, rather than the improvement of employees' work conditions. Such an instrumental attitude is often discredited and does not deliver the benefits expected in order to motivate people in order to work in the best of their capacity.

The second problem faced is that the notions themselves are not clear enough, and there is not adequate understanding of how to apply them in practice. It is not clear, for example, what is the difference between the ideas of participation, involvement, and empowerment, and in which context each is appropriate. We are still lacking theories and sound professional practices to determine the information systems requirements for changing a work organization from hierarchical to self-managing. The legacy of earlier generations of centralized technologies, which fit well in the hierarchical organizations of industrial economies, restricts our creativity in designing new styles of information system. However, as the new, more flexible information and communication technologies become widespread, and a more experimental attitude regarding management and organizational structures is encouraged by economic pressures, the debate and experience on empowerment continues. Interesting research into that effect has been done in the area of groupware technologies and computer-supported co-operative work [Ciborra, 1996].

Working out organizational change

The search for effective organizational forms in an evermore competitive business environment has presented information systems professionals with a new challenge: no longer can they just pay lip service to the changes in the structure and management of work that accompanies the development of information systems. Indeed, in many cases those responsible for developing information systems are expected to be protagonists in the performance of organizational transformation, and not merely supporting players. How can information systems professionals respond to these new expectations? Should they incorporate methods for planning and designing organizational structures in their systematic professional practices of constructing and implementing technology-based information systems?

Orlikowski [1996] searched the literature on technology-based organizational change for some answers to these questions and identified four perspectives:

The first perspective of the *technological imperative*, considers technology as a determinant of organizational characteristics. Technology is seen as an autono-mous driver of organizational change. Therefore, the implementation of new technology is expected to lead to predictable changes in an organization's structure, work routines, information communication and performance.

The second perspective of *planned* change suggests that managers perceive opportunities to improve organizational performance and have the foresight to initiate and implement changes accordingly. Such change is orchestrated as a major discrete event, separately from the ongoing process of managing the organization's activities.

The third perspective of *punctuated equilibrium* considers organizational change as a discontinuity which is triggered by environmental modifications or internal developments, such as new technology, process redesign or industry deregulation. According to this perspective change is rapid, episodic, and radical, rather than slow, incremental and cumulative. Both the punctuated equilibrium and the planned change perspectives assume that the 'normal' state of organizations is stability. Change is considered to be a short lasting disequilibrium event, which is then followed by a stable state of equilibrium.

The fourth perspective, proposed by Orlikowski as particularly appropriate for organizational change in relation to information technology, is *situated change*. Unlike the planned and disequilibrium types of change, situated change is ongoing, relatively slow and smooth. It occurs continuously as participants in organizations try to make sense of the world and improvise to cope with problems, to accommodate technological innovation in their work practices, or to adapt to modifications of the environment. In other words, change is seen as emergent from everyday practice and inseparable from the ongoing actions of the members of organizations.

Clearly, each of the perspectives identified by Orlikowski have implications for the actions of those responsible for orchestrating organizational change and pursuing information systems innovation.

Technological innovation

The technological imperative perspective hardly requires any effort other than the development of new technology-based information systems. The role of inform-ation systems professionals is to conceive and develop systems that can improve the organization's capacity to serve its mission. It is expected that the organization will inevitably adjust itself to the new information system. This, however, is a risky approach, uninformed by studies which show that the organizational and social aspects of information systems' environments are at least as significant as their technological potential.

As we have repeatedly argued in this book, information systems involve human actors who use technologies within an organizational and social context. Even perfectly designed powerful technologies can be marginalized and misused if people are not willing, or do not have the suitable work environment that will allow them to follow the logic of the designer. There are many systems which despite the initial objectives of their developers to drive organizational changes were adjusted to the features of their organizational context rather than changing them. For example, it is not enough to design a decentralized information system in order to get rid of the rigidities of a centralized bureaucracy. It is also necessary to take action to change the way work is organized, perhaps to abolish centralized decision making and control, to redistribute authority, and to make employees confident that they can work by taking initiative and shouldering the consequent responsibility. Unless such a major reform is pursued, the technical system will not be used as intended, or will be caricatured to conform to the dominant centralized mode of organizational operation. Many projects which were seen as drivers of modernization of government bureaucracies, but were not accompanied by the politically more costly organizational reform, have ended up having no effect; rather they just computerized the inefficiencies that they were supposed to eliminate.

Mastermind the reengineering

Both perspectives of planned change and punctuated equilibrium imply management interventions to initiate and work out desirable organizational change in conjunction with the development of new information systems. The best example of action compatible with this view of organizational change is Business Process Reengineering (BPR), [Hammer, 1990; Hammer and Champy, 1993; Davenport and Short, 1990..

In presenting BPR, Michael Hammer [1990] stated clearly the objectives to be pursued: 'use the power of modern information technology to radically redesign our business processes in order to achieve dramatic improvements in their performance'. Thus, BPR encourages 'discontinuous thinking', meaning the breaking away from the rules that an organization has established and follows to conduct its business, and the inventing of new ways to accomplish work by imaginative uses of information technology.

Fundamental to BPR is the focus on process. A business process is a collection of activities which takes some inputs and creates an output of value to customers. We are strongly advised to ignore the existing tasks that can be found in an organization, because they have usually been arrived at over time, are suboptimal and overly complicated. They are the result of a history of efforts to assign simple components of work to individual workers or groups. Current work allocation in fragmented individual tasks is not necessarily the best way to produce a service for a customer, which – BPR reminds us – is all that should matter for a business organization.

Hammer not only challenged us to break away from the inefficient work processes that can be found in most organizations, he suggested a way to do so. Being a consultant himself he sought to provide practitioners with 'principles' that should be followed in order to reengineer a business firm successfully:

- Organize around outcomes, not tasks; in other words, a person or small group should perform all steps of a process to deliver a particular service.

- Have those who use the output of the process perform the process. This suggests abolishing specialized departments, such as for purchasing materials; instead, everybody should do all the tasks that are required to perform the processes they are responsible for.

- Subsume information processing work into the work that produces information. This principle suggests that there should not be specialized departments, such as accounts payable, for processing information produced by others.

- Treat geographically dispersed resources as though they were centralized. The idea behind this principle is to use databases, telecommunications, and standardized information processing systems to get benefits of co-ordination and scale, while working in a decentralized and flexible fashion.

- Link parallel activities instead of integrating their results. Again, by using communication networks and shared databases, work processes done in parallel can be co-ordinated and thus avoiding the need to integrate their results retrospectively.

- Put the decision point where the work is performed, and build control into the process. This principle suggests abolishing the separation of doing the work from monitoring and controlling it, and to organize self-managing and self-controlling groups. Information technology can provide support for the decisions that need to be taken, and therefore to enable the organization of processes with built-in controls.

- Capture information once and at the source. Most organizations collect and store information as it is needed for their various tasks, and therefore repeat data capturing and duplicate data in fragmented data stores. Instead, they should develop integrated systems to create and use common data resources.

The above principles highlight two further aspects which are fundamental to BPR: that information technology has a central role in the reengineering effort, and that work is reorganized in a less overtly hierarchical way with elements of self-management.

BPR recognizes that new information technology offers many new possibilities. Rather than using it to automate or increase the efficiency of existing tasks, it can be used to enable completely new ways of working and doing business. From this observation, BPR boldly suggests basing reengineering on innovative ideas of technology use. Rather than identifying problems that could benefit from technology, identify opportunities that new technology offers and design new work arrangements accordingly. Shared databases, expert systems, decision support tools, telecommunication networks and multimedia systems, are some of the technologies which feature in the examples of successful stories of reengineering. Still, according to the major proponents of BPR, technology should not be considered to be a determinant of change, but a critical enabler of desirable business performance.

BPR aims at organizing work in process teams. In this way it bears two promises: to overcome the shortcomings of the bureaucratic hierarchical structure of work, and to enrich jobs and 'empower' people at their work place. Jobs are not fragmented in simple tasks anymore, they are multidimensional and substantive, and produce a result that customers care about. Moreover, people do not just follow rules, they have authority to make decisions and are responsible for the completion of the processes undertaken by the team. This means that employees in an ideal 'reengineered' business do not only need to have multiple skills, they must also be capable of exercising judgement and taking initiatives. In such a context performance should be measured on the basis of results achieved rather than time and effort spent at work.

In the early 1990s, BPR created a strong impression among managers and information systems professionals alike. As the business world was trying to resolve the pessimistic and rather counter-intuitive productivity paradox, mentioned in the introduction to part 3, BPR provided ground for new hope and, indeed, enthusiasm. Productivity gains from investment in information technology could be achieved by reengineering the firm to set it free from the inefficiencies accumulated through its history and the restrictions of old technologies.

Others have been more cautious. After all, none of the principles of BPR were completely new, and while they appeared sensible and were beneficial in some cases where they had been applied, they did not always have the dramatic impact promised. Perhaps the innovativeness of BPR lay in combining together all these principles, aiming at a holistic transformation through uprooting the organization's norms and traditions. This, however, made it a high risk endeavour, amounting to a transformation of culture. In particular, there was scepticism about the effectiveness of such top-down change, which paid no attention to the concerns of employees, and little sensitivity to the dynamics of power. Such an approach to change contradicted BPR's very idea of empowerment in the work place. Employees were not given much choice but to forget the specialized expertise they had developed over the years, to surrender the power they had gained within their work environment, and comply with a new work pattern. Moreover, they were at risk of losing their jobs, as one of the main benefits for the reengineered organization was 'downsizing': doing business with fewer people. A rather un-democratic forcing of the targeted democratic business team structure.

Seven years later BPR is familiar jargon among managers and business consultants. Empirical studies have provided evidence that BPR has been widely practised. In 1993/94 64% of companies were found to be planning or undertaking BPR, while in 1995 the percentage continued to be as high as 59% [Willcocks & Smith, 1995]. However, few organizations have radically changed their structure in this period. In practice, most BPR projects do not pursue radical but incremental change. Rather than reconfiguring new processes, they tend to seek improvements in existing ones. Rather than ignoring organizational politics to design rational effective processes, they accommodate people's interests and managers' power struggles; after all, they themselves have to put the reengineered processes into practice and make them work.

We might say that BPR has acted more as a challenge than as a method. Grint & Willcocks [1995] see BPR as a form of utopian thought which outlines a possible alternative to the *status quo* and thus constituted a proactive stimulus to change. The experience of BPR serves more as an example of an effort for systematic planning of radical organizational restructuring using informational technology, but which is often in practice altered to lead to feasible changes and improvements, even if this means the sacrificing of methodological purity – caricaturing the essence of BPR. Planning and implementation of structural change then proved to be more a case of 'satisficing' – to use Herbert Simon's concept for compromising and muddling through – rather than the rational design of the 'best'.

Management of emergent change

The situated change perspective implies a very different approach to steering organizational change and of the role of information systems. This perspective directs our attention to the ongoing changes which take place once a new system is implemented and employees gradually come to develop new ways of working with it.

Such a view of change is not contradictory to planned systems development and organizational change; rather it complements it. In most cases, the development and implementation of a new information system needs to be accompanied by pre-planned changes in the way work is structured and carried through. However, it is important to appreciate our limitations to foresee the possibilities that new powerful technologies provide. The newly designed organizational arrangements are necessarily incomplete. They are conceived with knowledge possessed within the old context, at best on an understanding of the generic potential of technologies and organizational behaviour. But, as argued above, such possibilities depend on the ability of the participants to realize them in their particular context. In other words, the initially planned change is followed by gradual change, as employees appropriate their new technology tools and discover how to work within the pre-designed work environment.

Such change occurs as people improvise their actions to cope with the various aspects of their work. Improvisation, according to Ciborra [1996] is situated performance where thinking and action seem to occur simultaneously and on the spur of the moment. This kind of change is embedded in every day practice, and inseparable from the ongoing activities of organizational participants. Gradual as such change may be, it can amount to radical trans-formation over time.

Orlikowski [1996] demonstrated how such change may occur with a case study in which subtle shifts in action by the people of an organization transformed over a two-year period their work practices, organizing structures and co-ordination mechanisms. The company implemented a new software package to support customer service staff. Gradually the members of this organization adjusted their practices to accommodate their new tools, re-distributed work from individual to shared responsibility, began proactive collaboration with others, expanded the use of the tools to create inter-departmental and cross-functional linkages, and developed ways to control access to their collective knowledge which was stored in the system's database.

Recognition of the significance of this kind of change has implications both for the type of information systems an organization chooses to develop, and their management after implementation. Clearly, the systems development and management practices which aim at getting the requirements right, delivering and maintaining technologies and work practices accordingly, with little provision for extra effort after implementation is not capable of supporting such continuously emerging changes. Instead, flexible technologies and a manage-ment style prepared to encourage and support a dynamic environment of continuous change are needed. In essence, the most crucial management effort shifts from planning to continuous decision making on the basis of the evolving information systems and the experience of using new technology tools.

Supporting business strategy

There is another perspective on organizational information systems which has been very influential in the past two decades. This is the linkage of what is done with information systems to an organization's general business strategy, and the development as part of this general strategy of an explicit information systems strategy. This approach can be seen as a part of the planned change perspective presented in the previous section. The issue is to find a direction in respect of information systems innovation, and ensure that it is compatible or aligned with the general direction of the organization. Developing some form of information systems strategy then needs to be undertaken at the highest level in the firm or organization and as a key part of the development of an overall business strategy.

The argument for involving information technology and information systems developments in business strategy has been extensively explored [Earl, 1996; Earl, 1989; Angell & Smithson, 1990]. The problem of alignment of information systems to business needs has regularly been cited among the most important issues for senior information systems managers [Grindley, 1990]. Indeed, this is often taken one step further, and posed as the question, 'Can information systems provide the organization with a competitive advantage?'

When addressed in these terms, information systems issues are injected directly into the most senior management decision making.

The value chain

Among the plethora of frameworks, models and taxonomies presented in the literature to assist information systems planning, the idea of the five competitive forces and the value chain, as set out by Michael Porter, stands out as one of the most fully developed and widely discussed [Porter, 1980; Porter and Millar, 1985]. This provides a clear and attractive set of concepts, broadly applicable and directly expressible in information systems terms. In particular Porter's view of the firm as made up of primary activities linked in a value chain, and sustained by support activities, has helped the information systems discipline to shift and re-orientate its thinking.

Porter's analysis is based around a simple model of the route to the achievement of superior performance in a business environment. This model can be expressed through two interlinked concepts. The first concept is that of the five competitive forces that act upon an organization, and which define the context for its business policy and strategic decision making. The second concept, the route by which one may thwart these often hostile forces, is that of the value chain, the sequence of key activities passing throughout a business and linking it to its environment, both *upstream* to suppliers of materials and services and *downstream* to buyers of products or services.

The five types of competitive forces that Porter describes are as follows:

- the existing competitors in an industry;
- the potential new entrants into an industry;
- substitute products or services that customers might use;
- suppliers of raw material and inputs – up the value chain;
- consumers of product or services – down the value chain.

Porter argues that only by careful study of these five forces can an organization develop a competitive business strategy. In particular, this demands that the organization be aware of the rules of competition that determine their industry's attractiveness, and monitor the potential impact on profitability (return on capital) of developments originating from any of these five directions. Such an analysis, as one would expect for a model of strategy, develops a perspective that draws attention away from the organization itself, and develops first a focus on an understanding of the industry structure, the environment within which an organization operates. Thus, issues of the appropriate direction for the individual organization, firm or business unit are seen as relative to the forces that act upon it. This emphasizes such issues as the developing economic and technical characteristics of an industry, changes in its principal distribution systems and markets, or changes in the regulatory regime under which it operates. The aim is to consider the potential for securing advantageous positions, defensive or attacking, with regard to any or all of these significant forces. Beyond this, and of increasing importance to information systems, Porter advocates that organizations, in developing strategy, must take a proactive stance in shaping their industry structure in ways that are to their, and crucially their industry's, advantage.

Porter's second key concept is that of the value chain. This is a model that attempts to offer a systematic way of examining all the activities that a firm performs, and how they interact together to deliver a product or service that is valued by the customer or consumer. In this model creating value for customers that exceeds the cost of production is a primary aim of strategy. Value delivered, Porter argues, must be the key metric for competitive analysis. It is on the basis of value delivered that costs can be understood in absolute or relative terms, market potential analyzed, and that prices can be set. Innovations that do not in some way deliver value need to be looked at in a very harsh light. In particular, understanding value often means understanding the way customers or clients operate, their own problems and their respective value chains.

The value chain model is intended to disaggregate a firm into the strategically relevant activities that contribute to producing value. The generic value chain that Porter proposes is made up of five primary activities and four support activities to be found in an organization serving a distinct competitive environment. The primary value activities are those that most directly contribute to producing a product or service for a customer or client. These activities are:

- *inbound logistics* on the up stream margin, bringing materials and services into the organization;
- *operations*, undertaking some transformations to produce products or services;
- *outbound logistics*, moving products or services out of the organization and delivering them to a customer or client;
- *marketing and sales*, locating and attracting customers and securing their custom;
- *service*, supporting customers or clients in their use of a product or service.

The support activities that contribute to these primary activities are:

- *firm infrastructure*, maintaining the organization as an organization;
- *human resource management*, managing the people within the organization;
- *technology development*, finding new ways of undertaking the organization's activities, and new products and services;

- *procurement*, finding and securing the sources of the materials and services needed by the organization.

The individual value chain and value activities of the firm must also be seen within a larger value system, including the value chains of suppliers, buyers, and from an information systems perspective, the information channels that link them together.

This model, if taken too literally, might be used simply as a recommend-ation to target the primary value activities for particular attention, in particular down stream and close to customers, and to de-emphasize the support activities. Such an analysis may support a simple view of information systems helping organizations to become more competitive but this temptation needs to be resisted. The value chain concept is crucially about *all* the value activities and their *linkage*. The cost and effectiveness of any one activity will be crucially affected by what is done elsewhere. What is required is appropriate linkage and trade-off. Furthermore, such linkage is not about the simple linear first-order interconnection of the individual primary activities, but about a creative understanding of the key set of interconnections across the whole value activity space as well as beyond the margin of the organization. It may be the linkage of human resource management, technology development and service in a high-technology industry; it may be procurement and inbound logistics in a manu-facturing operation using just-in-time techniques; it may be firm infrastructure (finance) and procurement in a capital intensive industry.

The task of the information technologist and business strategist is to understand not only their own value chain, but also the value system within which it is embedded. This analysis then leads back to consideration of the competitive forces that are working to alter this value system. Porter proposes that it is on this basis of the competitive forces, the value chain, and the value system that competitive advantage and long-term superior performance can be achieved.

Implications for information systems planning

Porter's work has helped to shift thinking away from simply targeting computers at helping to run the internal operations of a business, to push paper and keep accounts, or even at improving the performance of individuals or groups. Attention is turned rather towards how the whole value chain can be supported or possibly reorganized in a manner that improves the ability to deliver value. This focus on the possibility of major reorganization of activities may suggest a link to the ideas of BPR.

Porter's ideas also allow us to see some of the changes that have occurred in thinking about information systems purpose within organizations. While once the management information system was thought of as the highest ambition of organizational information systems, and the ideal to aspire to, now there is a rather different model. In simple terms we could describe the distinction in the following way. A management information system is a system that delivers to managers accurate, timely and relevant information on the state of affairs within the business. The information comes from a common pool of corporate data, and hence the corollary of the management information system ambition is information management in the form of databases – information *stores*. A value chain model is different in that it sets out to provide and manage the information *flows* that support and co-ordinate the vital concrete activities of the business, rather than the information stores.

Making this distinction is not intended to suggest that the management information system ambition is itself foolish. What the value chain approach emphasizes is that information systems need to be established *for a reason*, and that these reasons need to be well founded in the principal and key activities of the organization *and their linkages*. It is not then enough to assert that more or better information will allow better management decisions. This may or may not be true, but two or three isolated 'better decisions' can add up to a result that is certainly worse. Rather, what is suggested is careful attention to getting information systems to operate up and down the value chain, both within and beyond the organization. These systems should serve clearly understood organizational requirements, such as minimizing inventory, customizing products, improving service quality, supporting flexibility and reactiveness, reducing time to market or supporting a marketing strategy.

This idea – that business success, organizational excellence and superior corporate performance are to be found in the careful analysis of fundamental business activities, and in their linkage – is attractive to those who work with information systems for two specific reasons. The first is that it is possible to see a direct connection between a value chain of raw materials converted through the production process within an organization into products delivered to satisfied customers, and the organizational information systems that directly or indirectly support this chain. In this way the value chain concept may be seen as providing the vital link between an information systems strategy and an overall business strategy, if the business strategy is built principally around the delivery of such value.

Another reason why Porter's analysis has been seen as particularly valuable is that it looks beyond the organization and into its business environment. It considers the forces that operate in that environment, and seeks to provide an analysis that allows organizations to make more rational and better focused decisions about how they operate within that environment. Such an analysis suggests that the way that an organization interacts with its environment should be carefully considered in developing and managing information systems. Perhaps it is put more powerfully the other way round; it allows those in the organization who deal directly with the environment to express and explore *their* concerns and ambitions in terms of a particularly relevant and potent type of technology that can support identified information and communication needs.

The ambition of business strategists who consider information technology has tended to be to find a route to sustainable strategic advantage for the firm or business unit in its own market. If superior systems based on information technologies can be developed that link value activities together within a firm's value chain, then this may present a very much harder target for competitors or new entrants to copy or emulate. Systems built around a notion of the value chain may tend to be embedded closer into the organization, or the organization may come to be wrapped around the value chain, fostering a useful synergy between business and organizational goals.

The competitive analysis also helps us to understand how information technology-based innovation can enhance or detract from the relative power of different partners in the value system. For example, a network-based initiative to develop a central computerized catalogue of products, suppliers and prices may seem a very sensible and rational use of information technology. It will however have an effect. Within a price-competitive industry it might be expected to deliver power to buyers and increase price competition. In an industry where competition is based on the specification of a product it may do the reverse, helping the buyer to find the best source of supply on the basis of specification, and reducing price as a discriminant.

One example of an industry that has travelled down this route is the airline industry with huge global reservation systems that provide customers with choice of airline and choice of fares. The medical and surgical products market in the United Kingdom offers another example. A number of major companies that manufacture and sell medical and surgical products to hospitals and health authorities already use EDI to support their trade, exchanging such information as orders, invoices and delivery notes. The benefits of this technology in improving efficiency and reducing transaction costs are appreciated by all parties, as they all derive some benefit. Indeed this could be cited as an example of a case of information technology providing *collaborative* rather than competitive advantage. The extension of this collaborative venture to the establishment of an electronic catalogue of medical and surgical supplies, however, received a more critical assessment from some of the parties involved. Some have argued that such a catalogue would increase price as a determinant when orders were being placed, and that other qualities of products or of their suppliers would be downgraded. The development of such an electronic catalogue might also offer an attractive route for new entrants into the business, providing a simple and low cost marketing tool. Existing organizations in this market have to consider all these issues before committing themselves to the catalogue development. It is also the case that the business of maintaining and operating the catalogue itself may be an attractive information business in its own right, and one that a 'new entrant' into the industry may seek out.

The range of issues that the catalogue proposal raises is not primarily concerned with technology as such. They relate rather to exploring the effects and consequences of a proposed technical system, effects and consequences that span a number of organizations. The value chain and value system model can provide a useful framework within which this exploration can be undertaken.

Overall, the lessons from Porter's analysis for innovation based around information systems can be summarized in the following five points:

- at the highest level using information technology and developing the right information systems is as much about shaping industry structure as it is about organization level innovation;

- success with information systems is not principally about cost displacement, and information systems must be developed in the context of valued and differentiated service;

- exploiting innovative use of information systems poses some real problems in permitting an organization to select a route to unique superior perform-ance, and it may at times be more about keeping up with the competition rather than unique advantage;

- the information technology underlying an organization's information systems raises many questions on the appropriate alliances and coalitions that an organization should enter, yet such alliances are essential;

- the development of information systems must be seen as part of a process of the establishment of an effective organization, not as a substitute.

Methodological practices

From the 1970s to the 1990s a great deal of effort has been expended to create models and frameworks that enable information systems managers to think about how to harness information systems to overall organizational goals. A bewildering number of methods and models have been developed, including some with a focus on Porter's analysis of the competitive forces that surround a business, some on ideas of reengineering [Hammer & Champy, 1993], some on the analysis of the strategic direction that a firm is taking [McFarlan & McKenny, 1983], while others concentrate more closely on charting the route by which organizations develop their information management resources [Nolan, 1979] or offer detailed advice on how to elaborate and enumerate the required systems [IBM, 1975]. An outline of some of the most influential methods and ideas can give an idea of the various orientations that such efforts have taken over time.

Business Systems Planning (BSP) [IBM, 1975] was developed by IBM in the 1970s. It prescribes the steps of a top-down analysis of the overall information requirements of an organization. The analysis begins by describing an organization's business mission, objectives and functions, and by identifying the business processes required for their attainment. Each of the identified processes is then analyzed for data requirements. This produces a detailed mapping of the organization's data and provides an analysis for a database and an overall architecture of information systems to support the business processes. Thus, the method leads to a schedule for future information systems development projects. A broadly similar approach from the 1980s is Information Engineering, discussed in chapter 9 and based more closely on data oriented analysis [Finkelstein, 1989].

Another method which is used to align information systems plans with business priorities is the *critical success factor* (CSF) analysis [Rockart, 1979]. This method begins by identifying those small number of factors that business executives consider as the most vital for the success of their organizations. In this way, it guides information systems planners to determine information systems areas that will be most of significant for the business.

A very different method is suggested by Nolan [1979]. It is based on a model which describes computer information systems growth in organizations. In its simplest form the stages of growth model suggests that organizations go through a number of stages in the use and management of information technology:

- *initiation* – during which efforts focus on making some first applications succeed;
- *contagion* – during which information technology applications proliferate and responsibility for their management is scattered in various parts of the organization;
- *control* – during which a central grip on information technology resources is tightened, and the development of corporate databases secures central data resources;
- *maturity* – when a balance between central control and user autonomy is achieved.

This stage model was initially presented as a descriptive tool, but soon it started to be used as a theory which could sustain predictions and guide decisions on information systems planning and management. It has been widely applied to that end, despite criticisms that such a use is inappropriate [Benbasat *et al.*, 1984; King & Kraemer, 1984].

Another frequently used model is the 'strategic grid' developed by McFarlan & McKenney [1983] – figure 11.3. This is intended to assist managers to understand whether, why, and how information technology is critical to their organization. The idea is that information technology is not equally significant in all organizations or all parts of an organization. Helping managers to appreciate how crucial information technology is in their business area is expected to lead them to better decisions on further information systems investments.

Strategic impact of
applications development portfolio

	LOW	HIGH
LOW	Support	Turnaround
HIGH	Factory	Strategic

Strategic impact of existing information systems

Figure 11.3 The strategic grid [McFarlan & McKenney, 1983]

The above brief samples of information systems planning models, to which we should add business process reengineering, demonstrate how different the approaches can be. Clearly, no single method covers all relevant aspects for the successful development of an information systems infrastructure to provide for future organizational needs. Earl [1989] provides further details and suggests a scheme of information systems planning that he calls the 'multiple methodology', and which combines three routes for planning:

- Alignment of business objectives with information systems objectives. The planning process begins with the determination of significant business concerns and proceeds to specify appropriate information systems to meet them. Methods such as CSF or the competitive forces can be used for this purpose.

- Evaluation of the organization's current information systems capacity, its technological infrastructure and managerial structures. The planning process aims at understanding the strengths and weaknesses of existing information systems, in order to determine feasible future developments that can yield significant added value. Suitable methods for this purpose include the application of Nolan's model or the strategic grid.

- Identification of opportunities afforded by information technology which can yield significant benefits for the organization, namely competitive advantage or new strategic options. Such planning recognizes the need to be creative and innovative and favours methods such as brainstorming. However, as we will discuss below, this is the most difficult objective to achieve through methodical planning.

The strategic character of information systems

Overall, information systems planning has proved not to be amenable to methodical practices. Despite the great emphasis put into working out appropriate models and detailed planning procedures, surveys indicate that methodical information systems planning is not a widespread practice [Galliers, 1988], and that managers have not appreciated the value of methodical planning and fail to commit themselves to using such methods [Lederer & Sethi, 1988].

Despite this apparent lack of commitment on the part of organizations to information systems planning practices, the work of last decade on information systems strategy has been very influential. It has contributed to the shifting of thinking about the character of information systems and, correspondingly, the restructuring of the of management of information systems as outlined in the previous chapter. The significance of this contribution to broadening the information systems perspective cannot be denied, but there are two major shortcomings in the resulting perceptions and practices.

The first criticism concerns the emphasis on methodical information systems planning practices. Much effort has been directed towards developing information systems planning methods, although, as mentioned above, there is little evidence that methodological planning at a strategic level is often done, or that it can lead the organization to strategic gains. It has been argued that, at best, methods linking information systems plans with specific business objectives tend to be reactive and to miss the presumed potential for information technology to open new and unforeseen business opportunities. As Ciborra argues [1991], designed top-down action for information systems development is defensive and can, at best, only imitate already known information systems areas. Therefore, it cannot achieve the much discussed strategic advantage. Ciborra suggests that tinkering and prototyping by people who are close to the operational level, and can combine and apply known tools and techniques to solve new problems, is a much more effective innovation approach than top-down methodical planning. Instead of adopting methodological practices for the systematic alignment of information systems and business objectives, the promotion of an organizational culture encouraging initiative in information systems-based change, and an outward orientation, may be more effective. In this attention needs to turn to the ideas of emergent or situated change outlined in the earlier part of this chapter.

Nevertheless, one is in danger of substituting one myth (that excellence and competitive success can be methodologically planned) with another (that pioneering and experimenting with information systems innovations results in competitive advantage). Experimentation with ambitious information systems-led change can equally result in expensive and demoralizing failure – competitive disadvantage. Even in sectors where information technology has proved to be a significant factor in shaping business, empirical studies have shown that investment in information technology does not correlate with business success.

The second, and more serious criticism is that current perception of the nature of information systems is dangerously limited. The predominant perspective on the strategic character of information systems is as a significant factor contributing to profitability when making transactions within and among organizations, or among organizations and individuals. Knowledge of the field reflects research within large commercial corporations, predominantly undertaken in the United States. It pays little attention to the concerns of other types of organization – small businesses, non-profit organizations or public administration – nor to the context of other cultures. Yet information systems are vital to these types of organization and are built and used in all parts of the world.

As the boundaries of designed information technology-based systems expand across and dissolve organizational, economic and national boundaries, such a focus becomes more and more inadequate to explain and guide information systems change. More actors come into the domain where information systems are shaped: government and regulatory bodies; financial institutions; telecommunications and value-added service providers; educational systems; customer organizations or citizens all contribute to the evolution of ever more complex information and communication systems. The participants in such systems are not any more one organization's employees or even their customers. Development in such cases can only be partly traced to rational planning decisions of an organization's managers; to a significant extent it results from such factors as pressures of customers' and employees' expectations, incentives or restrictions of national and regional government, and structural changes to the economic and political environment.

It is now widely recognized that the processes of information systems development and management are primarily political, driven by the concerns of the social actors that participate in them. It seems therefore odd to insist that further developments should be considered on the basis of a single dimensional perspective – organizational profit. We need to adopt broader perspectives capable of accounting for the multiple concerns that shape the information systems development process.

Exercises and discussion issues

1. A small local newspaper, under the threat of competition from bigger national papers, undertakes to install new technology to allow journalists and the advertising department to generate, edit and layout material and print on colour presses. The new system, which took 2 years to select, develop and install, replaces old fashioned and highly structured working methods. The first few weeks of use are chaotic, but in time the new system is working according to plan and some staff come to love its advanced

features. Even so, other staff leave unable to cope with the change, including the old data processing manager and a long-serving senior editor. The fame of the project causes new people to be attracted to work in the new environment. As the age profile of the staff changes, so too does the editorial content.

Consider the situation and express what is happening using the four perspectives of change proposed by Orlikowski: technological imperatives; planned change; punctuated equilibrium; situated change. Which view would be of most interest to the paper's managing director or to the new information systems director?

2. Describe the value chain and the value activities of a baker's shop and a motor insurance company. Does it help you to discover areas that might be served by information systems innovation?

3. In the late 1980s, in Britain it was common for large financial institutions such as banks and insurance companies to enter into the residential estate agency (realtor) business. For the most part they did this by purchasing existing estate agency businesses. The rationale for this is usually stated as their need to secure an important route through which they could sell their products – in this case life insurance and mortgages. Analyze this situation in terms of the competitive forces that operated around these organizations.

   Most of the estate agency businesses that were purchased were small or medium-sized, often with owner managers. The new owners clearly had to establish a new basis for the way these businesses worked, including setting up new information systems. What criteria would you expect to be applied by the senior managers in exploring and evaluating alternative approaches to this problem?

4. What are the implications of BPR for the professional systems analyst? Does it alter his or her job profile? Does it suggest the need for new methods?

References

Applegate, L.M. (1994) 'Managing in an information age: transforming the organization for the 1990s' in Baskerville, R. Smithson, S. Ngwenyama, O. & DeGross J.I. *Transforming Organizations with information Technology*, North-Holland, Amsterdam.

Angell, I.O. & Smithson, S. (1991) *Information Systems Management: Opportunities and Risks*, Macmillan Press, London.

Benbasat, I., Dexter, A.S., Drury, D. & Golstein, R.C. (1984) 'A critique of the stage hypothesis: Theory and empirical evidence', *Communications of the ACM*, Vol. 27, No. 5, May, pp 467-485.

Bjørn-Andersen, N & Turner, J. (1994) 'Creating the twenty-first century organization: The metamorphosis of Oticon' in Baskerville, R. Smithson, S.

Ngwenyama, O. & DeGross J.I. *Transforming Organizations with information Technology*, North-Holland, Amsterdam.

Ciborra, C.U. (1991) 'From thinking to tinkering: The grassroots of strategic information systems', in the *Proceedings of the 12th International Conference on Information Systems*, New York, pp. 283-292.

Ciborra, C.U. (1996) 'Improvisation and information technology in organizations', in the *Proceedings of the 17th International Conference on Information Systems*, Cleveland, pp 369-380.

Davenport, T.H. & Short, J.E. (1990) 'The new industrial engineering: information technology and business process redesign' in *Sloan Management Review*, Summer, pp 11-27.

Earl, M.J. (1996) (editor) *Information Management: The Organizational Dimension*, OUP, Oxford.

Earl, M.J. (1989) *Management Strategies for Information Technology*, Prentice Hall, Hemel Hempstead.

Finkelstein, C. (1989) *An Introduction to Information Engineering: From Strategic Planning to Information Systems*, Addison Wesley, Sydney.

Galliers, R.D. (1987) 'Information Systems planning in the United Kingdom and Australia – a comparison of current practice', in *Oxford Surveys in Information Technology*, Vol. 4, pp. 257-310.

Grindley, C.B.B. (1990) *The Price Waterhouse Information Technology Review*, Price Waterhouse, London.

Grint, K. & Willcocks, L. (1995) 'Business process re-engineering in theory and practice: business paradise regained?' in *New Technology. Work and Employment*, Vol. 10, No. 2, September, pp 99-109.

Hammer, M. (1990) 'Reengineering work: Don't automate, obliterate' in *Harvard Business Review*, July-August, pp 104-112.

Hammer, M. & Champy, J. (1993) *Reengineering the Corporation: A Manifesto for Business Revolution*, Nicholas Brealey, London.

IBM (1975) Business Systems Planning- Information Systems Planning Guide, Publication No. GE20 0527-4.

Introna, L. & Tiow, B.L. (1997) 'Thinking about virtual organizations and the future', in the Proceedings of the 5th European Conference on Information Systems, Vol. III, pp 995-1009.

King, J.L.& Kraemer, K.L. (1984) 'Evolution and organizational information systems: An assessment of Nolan's stage model', in *Communications of the ACM*, Vol. 27, No. 5, May, pp. 466-475.

Lederer, A.L. & Sethi, V. (1988) 'The implementation of strategic information systems planning methodologies', in *MIS Quarterly*, Vol. 12 No. 3, pp. 445-461.

McFarlan, F.W. & McKenny, J.L. (1983) *Corporate Information Systems Management: The Issues Facing Senior Management*, Dow-Jones-Irwin, Homewood, Illinois.

Mintzberg, H. (1979) *The Structuring of Organizations*, Prentice-Hall, Englewood Cliffs, N.J.

Nolan, R.L. (1979) 'Managing the crises in data processing', in *Harvard Business Review*, Vol. 57, No. 2, March-April , pp. 115-126.

Orlikowski, W.J. (1996) 'Improvising organizational transformation over time: A situated change perspective', in *Information Systems Research*, Vol. 7, No. 1, March, pp 63-91.

Porter, M.E. (1980) *Competitive Strategy*, Free Press, New York.

Porter, M.E. & Millar, V.E. (1985) 'How information gives you competitive advantage', in *Harvard Business Review*, Vol. 63, No. 4, July-August, pp 149-160.

Psoinos, A. & Smithson, S. (1996) 'Exploring the relationship between empowerment and information systems'. Proceedings of the 4th European Conference on Information Systems, Vol. II, pp 367-384.

Rockart, J.F. (1979) 'Chief executives define their own data needs', in *Harvard Business Review*, March April, pp. 215-229.

Willcocks, L. & Smith, G.. (1995) 'IT-enabled Business Process Reengineering: organizational and human resource dimensions' in *Journal of Strategic Information Systems*, Vol 4, No. 2.

Zuboff, S. (1988) *In the Age of the Smart Machine: The Future of Work and Power*, Heinemann, Oxford.

Further reading

Sprague and McNurlin provide a good summary of the most common information systems planning methods. Ives and Learmonth's article is now a classic and states clearly the main arguments for the perceived significance of information systems for business competitiveness and includes their own contribution, the customer-resource life cycle. Galliers and Baker provides a useful reader with a number of seminal papers reprinted, as does Earl [1996] cited above.

Galliers, R.D. & Baker, B.S.H. (1994) (editors) *Strategic Information Management: Challenges and Strategies in Managing Information Systems*, Butterworth, Oxford.

Ives, B. & Learmonth, G.P. (1984) 'The information system as a competitive weapon', in *Communications of the ACM*, Vol. 27, No. 12, December, pp. 1193-1201.

Sprague, R.H. . & McNurlin, B.C (1993) *Information Systems Management in Practice*, (3rd edition), Prentice Hall, Englewood Cliffs, New Jersey.

12 Conclusions

This book started by attempting to answer the simple question, 'What is an information system?'. It then offered a loose description highlighting concepts such as information, data and human organizations, and aligning them with the technology of computers. Having read on to this final chapter a reader should have managed to flesh out these ideas in a number of ways. The book has investigated how an information system is developed, and explored various underlying theories and models that are used to establish the validity of particular approaches to the activity of information systems development. It has then gone on to consider the wider organizational context within which information systems are conceived and managed, and the character of the organizational goals that they serve and shape. There is no need to argue at this point that these activities of information systems development and management are important. In so far as readers will work within the mainstream of the computing industry, or in a business environment, the subject matter of this book is appropriate knowledge to acquire. Even so, it would be surprising if a reader did not have some questions and doubts about the scope and relevance of such a study of 'information systems'.

The themes that the book has covered are those of the main 'problems' that the study of information systems has come to address in its short history [Friedman & Cornford, 1989]:

- how to systematize the process of applying information technology in organizations;
- how to organize information resources and to support decision making to the benefit of the organization, understood as improvement of its efficiency and effectiveness;
- how to create opportunities for an organization, or to change various aspects of its character, by developing its information resources and by utilizing new information technology.

This character of the study of information systems emerged out of practical efforts to utilize a powerful technology in 'modern' organizations, and this book has developed its argument along these same, rather conventional, lines. Though the previous chapter has indicated some of the limitations of this perspective, in this concluding chapter we wish to argue for the need to expand the study of information systems to address a wider range of issues.

The context of the emerging discipline of information systems – that is, the context within which the problems listed above occur and solutions are sought –

has been predominantly that of business organizations in advanced industrializ-ed regions of the world. Although the discipline has addressed itself to some social dimensions of information systems, such as job satisfaction of employees, or legal rights of citizens, there is a clear bias towards the primacy of meeting organiz-ational needs. The dominant preoccupation of the discipline has been releasing the potential of a powerful cluster of new technologies to achieve business success. Even in the public sector, where many of the largest information technology applications are developed, most effort has been aimed at adopting perceived best *business* practices, and the information systems discipline has devoted precious little attention to the particular character of such public institutions.

It would be pointless to criticize either the fact that the process of inform-ation systems development and management is driven by business imperatives, or the efforts made to establish sound professional practices to that end. It is, however, shortsighted to gear the study of information systems to following solely such concerns. Many broader changes are taking place in our societies with the use of new information technologies. These are significant and deserve to be studied in their own right. New modes of distribution of productive activities, new modes of work, transformation of the traditional social welfare services, internationalization of economic activities, and new schemes for education and life-long learning are but a few social changes enabled or driven by the spreading of new information technologies. Business-centred studies of information systems often touch upon such changes in various ways; for example, if broader social change makes the adjustment of business strategy necessary. Such studies provide, however, a limited perspective, leaving many aspects of social change unexplored.

In all the social sciences the relation between serving immediate practical needs and studying the fundamental characteristics of human societies is an uneasy one. A useful parallel can be drawn with the subjects of *management* and *organizational theory*. Management, a subject concerned primarily with running organizations as businesses, has a practical orientation, responding to the perceived needs of enterprises. Organizational theory is a field of sociology which explores the phenomena of human organizations generally. It can there-fore assume a longer-term perspective than that which immediate practical problems impose on managers, and a broader problem space than that of business concerns. Organizational theory concerns itself with many diverse forms of organizations and interest groups including state institutions and voluntary organizations. The findings of organizational theory have proved useful to a varied set of professional roles, including policy makers in government and international institutions, managers and officials of labour organizations, although these findings rarely take the form of a direct pre-scription of appropriate actions. Rather, organizational theory provides an analytical framework, a way of thinking about organizational issues.

Undoubtedly, there is a great deal of overlap between the two disciplines of management and organizational theory. Organizational theory has devoted most of its effort to the study of the changes taking place in business organizations. After all, this is the basic unit for the organization of the capitalist socio-economic system, a system that has prevailed worldwide. At the same time, management has drawn many lessons from research in organizational theory, which have provided it with an understanding of the dynamics of leadership and decision making in organizations, and of the context within which such management takes place.

What is lacking from the study of information systems is the equivalent to the sociological discipline of organizational theory. As mentioned above, the study of information systems so far has evolved mainly as an intersection between the study of information technology (engineering) and the management of business organizations. The analytical study of the changes of information systems in broader domains, such as a country, a community, a region, or the world is as yet in its infancy.

It would be misleading to say that no work has been done at all in this direction. From the very early days of the development of information technology, a few researchers, drawn from many different disciplines, have addressed themselves to the broader significance of the technology and not just to its business implications. There have been several efforts to monitor the changes that are happening and relevant new concepts and theoretical hypotheses have been proposed to explain the observed patterns.

In economics, the term 'information economy' has been suggested to convey the prevailing perception that nations follow a trend of devoting increasing proportions of their effort to information handling. The information economy is often measured in terms of occupations concerned with the creation and handling of information. The pioneering work of Fritz Machlup [1962] identi-fied the production of knowledge as an economic activity and observed an increase in the ratio of knowledge-producing labour to physical labour in the United States. Since then, statistics from other countries have shown similar trends [OECD, 1986]. Beyond such measures, economists have developed models to assess the contribution of the information sector of an economy in terms of such variables as employment, final demand and income.

Efforts to estimate changes in the significance of information activities within countries are linked with efforts of sociologists to explain the growth of inform-ation activities as a general feature of advanced societies. The most influential view is that the trend of growing information activities observed in the industrialized economies in the post-war period signifies the arrival of a post-industrial economic stage. According to Daniel Bell [1973], the best known proponent of this thesis, in the post-industrial economies human and information services, such as health, education, recreation, research and development, hold a dominant position in society.

Many aspects of Bell's view of the evolution of advanced economies have been challenged by researchers, such as Gershuny and Miles [1983], Mandel [1975], Morris-Suzuki [1988] and Webster [1995]. Even among those who do not dispute the validity of this post-industrial economy thesis, many have been sceptical about the consequences of such changes for the structure of our economies. Perhaps the most widely read and the most influential text on such concerns is the report by Nora and Minc [1980] to the President of France at the end of the 1970s. The two authors show vividly how the new information technologies and the increasing emphasis on information activities affect many more aspects of a society than its economic structure. Among other issues, they expressed concern about the ability of their country to retain its sovereignty, about the threat of unemployment, and about the survival of France's culture.

Other research since then has shown that the changes taking place in our societies have indeed many such dimensions. Geographers, such as Hall and Preston [1988] and Castells [1989,1996,1997] have examined the changes in the distribution of economic activities among regions and social groups. Public policy experts have examined the pattern of decline of certain industries and the growth of emerging new industries in relation to unemployment and the creation of new skills in a country's work-force [Freeman, Clark & Soete, 1982]. There has been concern that the benefits of new technology are unevenly spread in societies, leaving some large social groups, such as women or the disabled, particularly vulnerable [Webster & Robins, 1986]. Others examined the disparities in inform-ation and information technologies around the world and criticized the 'international information order' [MacBride Commission, 1980; Sauvant 1986, Hamelink, 1984]. Many studies on information systems applications in developing countries have shown how inadequate information resources are in many parts of the world, and how difficult it has been to utilize information technology as part of a development strategy for poor countries [Bhatnagar & Bjørn-Andersen, 1990; Odedra-Straub, 1996].

Research has also addressed the social impact of the diffusion of new technology-based information systems. Indicative studies include the pioneering work of Ida Hoos [1973], who criticized the validity, the moral basis and the consequences of computer-based information systems in public services in the United States. Continuing research at the University of Irvine in California has monitored the changes occurring in government with the implementation of new generations of information systems [Kraemer *et al.*, 1987]. Another example is the work of Shirin Madon who examined the impact of a microcomputer-based system on the administration of a rural development programme in India [1992].

Most of the research mentioned above is at the margins of established disciplines such as economics, geography, public policy, sociology. Information systems, the study of information flow and use, although it very often touches upon such issues, has not examined them systematically. Yet without understanding the changes which take place in the society within which individual organizations are embedded, any effort to intervene and introduce change in the organizational microcosm runs severe risks.

Our society is now deeply enmeshed with information technology. In business, in public administration and in daily life, the fundamental enablers are information and the use of information and communications technology. It is also certain to become more important, not less, in the decades ahead. This reliance demands that it be understood, directed and managed not just as electronics and software, or even as discrete information handling activities, but as part of the very texture of the lives that we live. When this book is finally put down, and the fairly conventional matters it has covered are well enough understood, it is to the broader canvas that we would urge our readers to address themselves.

References

Bell, D. (1973) *The Coming of the Post-industrial Society*, Heinemann, London.

Bhatnagar, S.C. & Bjørn-Andersen, N. (1990) *Information Technology in Developing Countries*, North-Holland, Amsterdam.

Castells, M. (1989) *The Informational City, Information Technology, Economic Restructuring and the Urban-Regional Process*, Blackwell, Oxford.

Castells, M. (1996) *The rise of the Network Society*, Blackwell, Oxford.

Castells, M. (1997) *The Power of Identity*, Blackwell, Oxford.

Freeman, C., Clark, J. & Soete, L. (1982) *Unemployment and Technical Innovation: A study of Long Waves and Economic Development*, Frances Pinter, London.

Friedman, A.L. & Cornford, D.S. (1989) *Computer Systems Development: History, Organization and Implementation*, Wiley, Chichester.

Gershuny, J.I. & Miles, I.D. (1983) *The New Service Economy: the Transformation of Employment in Industrial Societies.* Frances Pinter, London.

Hall, P. & Preston, P. (1988) *The Carrier Wave - New Information Technology and the Geography of Innovation 1846-2003*, Unwin Hyman.

Hamelink, C.J. (1984) *Transnational Data Flows in the Information Age* Chartwell-Bratt, Sweden.

Hoos, I. (1983) *Systems analysis in public policy: A critique*, (revised edition), University of California Press, Berkeley, California.

Kraemer, K.L., Dickhoven, S., Tierney, S.F. & King, J.L. (1987) *Datawars - the politics of modeling in federal policymaking*, Columbia University Press, New York.

MacBride, S. (1980) *Many voices, one world: communications and society, today and tomorrow*, Unipub, New York.

Machlup, F. (1962) *The production and distribution of knowledge in the United States*, Princeton University Press.

Madon, S. (1992) 'The impact of computer-based information systems on rural development: a case study in India', unpublished PhD thesis, Imperial College of Science, Technology and Medicine, London.

Mandel, E. (1975) *Late Capitalism*, New Left Books, London.

Morris-Suzuki, T. (1988) *Beyond Computopia - Information, Automation and Democracy in Japan*, Kegan Paul International, London.

Nora, S., & Minc, A. (1980) *The Computerization of Society*, MIT Press, Cambridge, Massachussetts.

Odedra-Straub, M. (ed*.) Information Technology and Socio-Economic Development*, Ivy League, New York.

OECD, (1986) *Trends in the Information Economy*. Information Computer Communication Policy, No. 11, OECD, Paris.

Sauvant, K.P. (1986) *International Transactions in Services: The Politics of Transborder Data Flows*, Westview Press, Boulder, Colorado.

Webster, F. & Robins, K. (1986) *Information Technology: a Luddite Analysis*, Ablex Publishers, London.

Webster, F. (1995) *Theories of the Information Society*, Routledge, London.

Further reading

A number of writers have voiced serious concerns and stated opinions radically different from those generally assumed about the consequences of the diffusion of information technology based information systems in our societies. Among the most influential are:

Wiener, N. (1954) *The Human Use of Human Beings: Cybernetics and Society*, Doubleday Anchor Books, USA.

Ellul, J. (1980) 'Technique and Non-power', in Woodward, K. (editor) *The Myths of Information: Technology and Post-industrial Culture*, Routledge and Kegan Paul, London.

Roszak, T. (1986) *The Cult of Information*, Lutterworth Press, Cambridge.

Weizenbaum, J. (1984) *Computer Power and Human Reason: From Judgement to Calculation*, Penguin, Harmondsworth.

Two books containing collection of papers which provide an introduction to various social issues related with information systems are:

Forester, T. (ed) (1989) *Computers in the Human Context*, Basil Blackwell, Oxford.

Kling, R. (ed.) (1996*) Computerization and Controversy: Value Conflicts and Social Choices*, Academic Press, San Diego.